P9-DCM-033

A *fabulous* KINGDOM

Bergi
regio
Indię noue pars
Asię pars orien
talis extrema
Oceanus Scy
thicus
Hęc insula
optima est & salu
berrima totius
septentrionis.
Grocland

A *Fabulous* Kingdom

The Exploration *of the* Arctic

Charles Officer
Jake Page

OXFORD
UNIVERSITY PRESS
2001

OXFORD
UNIVERSITY PRESS

Oxford New York
Athens Auckland Bangkok Bogotá Buenos Aires Calcutta
Cape Town Chennai Dar es Salaam Delhi Florence Hong Kong Istanbul
Karachi Kuala Lumpur Madrid Melbourne Mexico City Mumbai
Nairobi Paris São Paulo Shanghai Singapore Taipei Tokyo Toronto Warsaw

and associated companies in
Berlin Ibadan

Published by Oxford University Press, Inc.
198 Madison Avenue, New York, New York 10016

Library of Congress Cataloging-in-Publication Data
Officer, Charles B.
A fabulous kingdom: the exploration of the Arctic/Charles Officer, Jake Page
p. cm.
Includes bibliographical references (p. 197) and index
ISBN 0-19-512382-4
1. Arctic regions—Discovery and exploration. I. Page, Jake. II. Title.
G608.O33 2001
919.8—dc21 00-038538

Book design by Adam B. Bohannon

9 7 5 3 2 4 6 8
Printed in the United States of America
on acid-free paper

This book is dedicated to the memory
of the unsung heroes of Arctic exploration
—John Rea, Matthew Henson, Lincoln Ellsworth, and Hubert Wilkins—
and to the Inuit people who taught the explorers
how to survive in their land.

On our tenth day at sea we expected to see land. There was a message from the Captain after breakfast to say that we were approaching some large icebergs. I felt very excited. There is something magical about those floating crystal jewels. I rushed on deck. . . . Ahead of us two giant bergs, aquamarine streaked with deep turquoise, rose majestically, like two pillars at the entrance of some fabulous kingdom. Emerald-green waves splashed against their bases, sending up showers of tiny sparkling gems. Irregular in shape, the bergs towered high above us. A curving spine surrounded gaping mouths which seemed to call us to them. There was something sinister about their beauty. As we glided tremulously between them, I held my breath, expecting any moment that they would draw together and crush our tiny ship.

Marie Herbert, 1973

Contents

Preface

THIS IS A BOOK ABOUT THE BRAVE, sometimes foolhardy, sometimes deluded, and sometimes mendacious individuals who have explored the Arctic on behalf of the nations of Europe and North America. It is a story of heroes and in some cases fools; both sorts of men have perished in their attempts to learn what lay to the North, to find the idyllic land of the Hyperboreans that existed beyond the frigid zone, to learn where Ultima Thule was, to find gold or fame, to navigate an open passage through the sea ice from one continent to another, or to stand on the northernmost point on the planet, the North Pole. For centuries it was widely believed that there existed an open polar sea, an ice-free Arctic Ocean, and men sought this out, often with tragic results. The Arctic has always been layered with myths, and this book is also a look at how such myths arise and how they are—sometimes—dispelled.

Some of the names of the Arctic explorers are familiar—John Cabot, Henry Hudson, Robert Peary, Admiral Richard Byrd, and a submarine called *Nautilus*. Other names are more obscure, such as Himlico, a Carthaginian who sailed north in about 500 B.C.; the Zeno brothers, sixteenth-century scam artists of Venice; and Roald Amundsen, perhaps the greatest of all polar explorers.

Besides the quest for straightforward geographical knowledge—what is the lay of the land?—there has been also a quest to understand the nature of this strange place, a quest that in our time we call science. A great deal of science has been done in the

Arctic, but perhaps less than in most other places. A great deal more science needs to be done, because the Arctic, for all its ferocious winds, its ice, its cold, and its rawness, is a highly sensitive region. But this is less a book about science than an extended tale of the exploration of the Arctic by Europeans since before the time of Christ. In recent years numerous books have become available about one or another aspect of Arctic (and Antarctic) exploration. Why, then, another? Without mentioning every expedition, we have sought to put all the major exploratory attempts into a single story, to put them into perspective vis-à-vis each other and some of the non-Arctic historical events—and scientific understandings—that influenced these attempts.

In the long interval during which Europeans have probed the North and speculated about it, there have been three main goals. One, the search for a northeast passage from the North Sea through to the Pacific, was carried out chiefly by the British, the Russians, and the Scandinavians. The second was the search by British and Scandinavians (for the most part) for a northwest passage from the North Atlantic to the waters off Asia. And third was the quest to reach farther and farther north, finally to stand on, fly over, and pass below the ice at the North Pole. This last quest continued up until nearly the end of the twentieth century. Now tourists can—and do—cavort there, on the very top of the Earth. Today, for the most part, we seek instead data about ice packs, frozen seas, melting glaciers, the currents of the oceans, and how the Arctic influences the changing climate of the rest of the world. What we have learned in a half century are, among other things, the answers to many of the questions explorers have been posing for more than two millennia. And so this book begins with our present knowledge about the nature of the place. We will have the luxury of seeing where miscues were made and understanding how they were made. Also, we will be all the more aware of how stunningly unknown this region was for so long a time, what a cipher it presented to men of temperate climates, and perhaps we will gain an even greater respect for their courage, ingenuity, and sacrifices.

A *fabulous* KINGDOM

ONE

The Nature *of the* Place

In the Arctic your sense of location and time are likely to go haywire. In our familiar temperate and equatorial latitudes we speak of north, south, east, and west, the familiar cardinal directions. At the North Pole, all directions are south. The meaning of time as the notion is used in our temperate latitudes diminishes the farther north one goes, until it is virtually irrelevant: Because the meridians (longitude circles) converge at the Pole, so do the time zones. What time of day is it at the Pole, where you could place your foot in all the world's time zones at the same instant? At the Pole the Sun rises once a year and sets once a year, the Moon rising and setting once a month.

The long periods of darkness during winter and long periods of sunlight in summer in the polar regions—and to a lesser extent in the temperate regions—are caused by the fact that the plane on which the Earth rotates, the equatorial plane, is at an angle to the plane on which the Earth revolves around the Sun, the plane of the ecliptic. The angle of tilt between the two planes is 23.5 degrees. The moment when the Sun is farthest south is on December 22, known as the winter solstice. On this day the entire region north of latitude 66° 30' N is in total darkness. Conversely, on June 21 each year, the summer solstice, the same region has twenty-four hours of daylight. The North Pole itself has six months of daylight from about March 21, the vernal equinox, to September 21, the autumnal equinox, and six months of darkness for the rest of the year. The

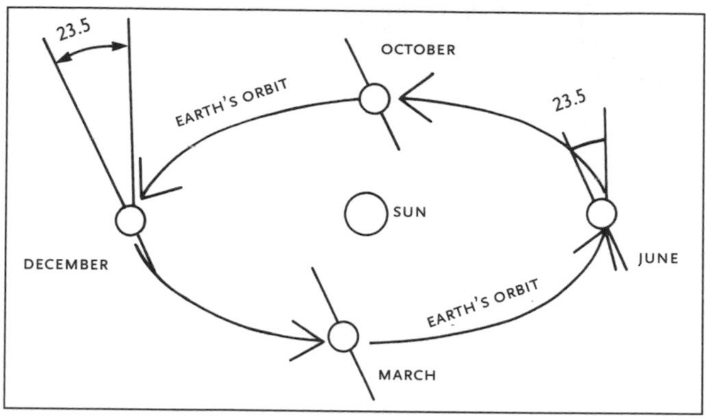

The annual revolution of the Earth around the Sun (From Maloney 1978)

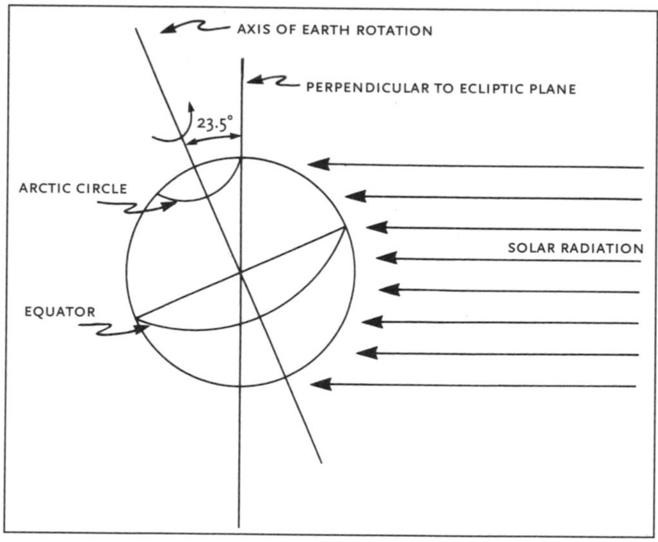

Earth and Sun orientations at the winter solstice

Arctic Circle is defined as the latitude 66° 30' N, a convenient division between the Arctic and the North Temperate Region south of it.

A different kind of map is needed in the Arctic. The conventional map we are most familiar with is called a Mercator, or modified Mercator, projection (after the sixteenth-century cartographer). The trouble with any map is that it has to represent a three-dimensional object, the planet, on a two-dimensional surface. and so it must distort part of the world. The simplest of Mercator projections arises, figuratively, from the exercise of placing a cylinder around the world, touching it at the equator, with its axis in a north-south direction. If you project out from the center of the Earth through every point on the Earth's surface and onto the cylinder, then unwrap the cylinder, you have a Mercator projection. It gives a pretty good representation of things at tropical and temperate latitudes, but it is of little use at the higher latitudes. There everything is out of proportion, much too large, with Greenland, for example, being larger than all of North America, and in the extreme, the North Pole is off the map altogether—out at infinity.

For polar regions, most maps in use today are centered at the North Pole, and all the directions (called azimuths) and distances are true from the Pole. These maps are called azimuthal equidistant projections. The latitudes are circles around the

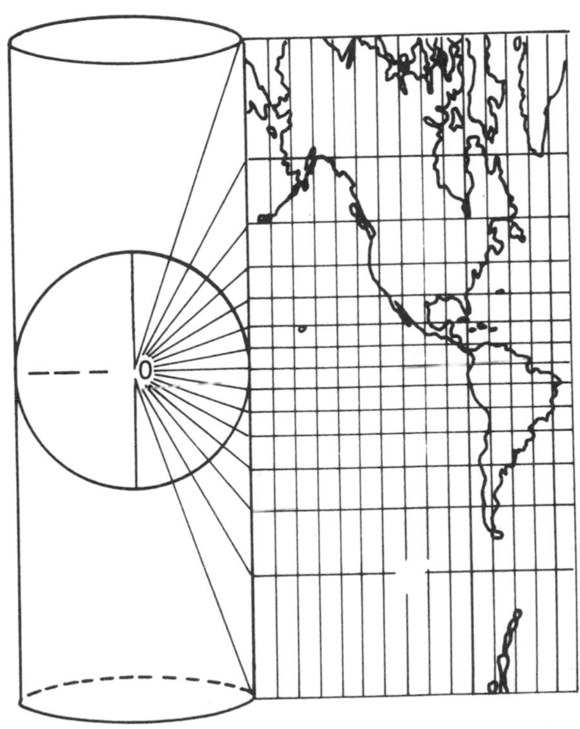

Mercator central projection upon a cylinder (From Maloney 1978)

Pole, and the longitudes radiate out from the Pole. Such maps are made arithmetically, unlike Mercator maps, which are geometric projections. But, of course, an azimuthal equidistant projection is perfectly accurate only at the pole; elsewhere it produces its own distortions, which are larger the farther you get from the pole. To get a true idea of the sizes of the Earth's landforms and oceans, and a real sense of their directional relationship to each other, there is nothing like a globe.

The Arctic Ocean is roughly circular in form, with its center slightly offset from the North Pole. It is relatively isolated from the deep waters of the world and surrounded by a sequence of landmasses. Starting from the northern shores of Greenland and proceeding clockwise are Ellesmere Island, with Devon and Baffin Islands to the south; the Canadian Archipelago; the shores of northwestern Canada; Alaska; then around to the vast extent of Siberia, with the islands of Novosibirskye, Novaya Zemlya, Franz Josef Land, and Svalbard (formerly Spitzbergen) offshore; and ending with northern Europe (specifically Finland and Norway).

These Arctic lands—most of them, at least—are underlain by what is called permafrost. Except for a thin layer that melts in the summer, called the active layer, the extreme cold of the Arctic has permanently frozen the ground to depths of 800 to 1,500 feet, and even deeper in Siberia. To the south, in what is called the subarctic, the permafrost can be up to 400 feet deep, and farther south it underlies great layers of peat and boggy areas. Since continuous permafrost totally cuts off drainage underground, shallow lakes are common throughout the Arctic landmasses, and in warmer months standing water is home to legendary swarms of blackflies and mosquitoes. During the summer, waterlogged soil flows downhill over frozen ground, creating long, smooth slopes in areas where mountains do not rise from the land. Much of the exposed rock of the northern parts of the Arctic is broken up by frost into angular boulders.

To return to the ocean, the major bathymetric (deepwater) feature of the central Arctic is the Lomonosov Ridge, which

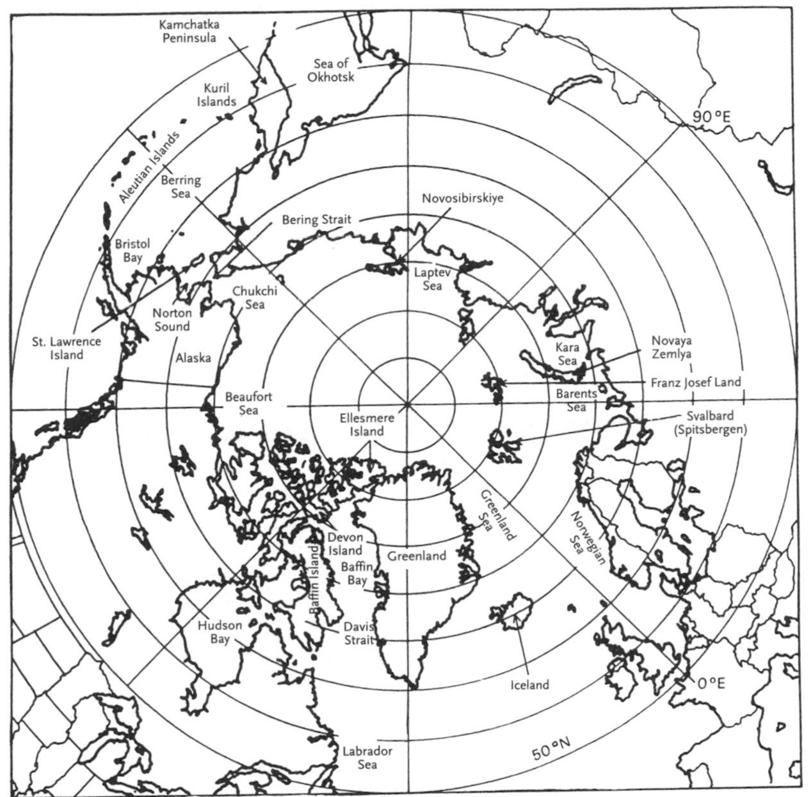

Location map for the north pole region (From Parkinson et al. 1987)

divides the deepwater basin of the Arctic into two parts, the European Basin, in the Eastern Hemisphere, and the Canadian Basin in the western hemisphere. Surrounding the Arctic Ocean are several seas, considered separate mainly because their ice cover is seasonal, unlike the permanent ice pack of the central Arctic.

The lands bordering the Arctic Ocean are sparsely populated by nomadic peoples. Until very recently, hunting was the only way to make a living in such a northerly climate. Plant life is nonexistent in areas of permanent ice, and the tundra and other exposed surfaces are not friendly to the kind of plants that normally sustain humans. Agriculture is, of course, virtually impossible. About a million people live in the Arctic, more than half of them in Siberia. The Inuit (formerly called Eski-

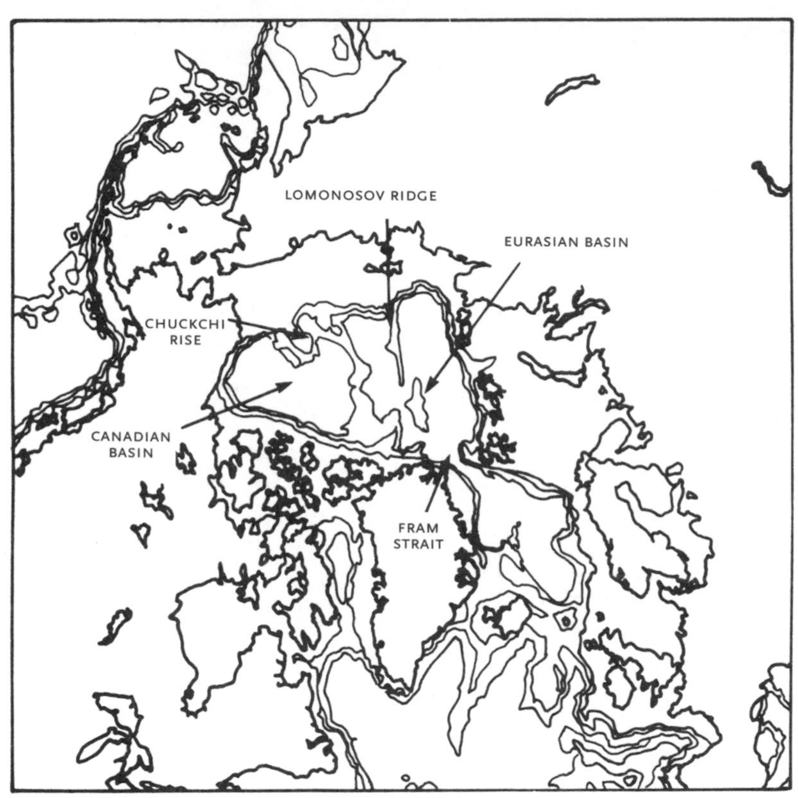

Bathymetry of the Arctic Ocean (From Parkinson et al. 1987)

mos, a name given them by others) number about a hundred thousand, inhabiting a broad expanse from Greenland through northern Canada to Alaska. That nearly a million people do inhabit the Arctic year round is astonishing, what with the extreme harshness of the climate and the desertlike bleakness of the landscape. Indeed, the Arctic is a desert—a cold desert—because virtually all its fresh water is locked up as ice and annual precipitation measures only 6 to 9 inches, making it a place of practical aridity.

The polar climate is a result, in great part, of the heat imbalance of the spheroidal Earth. Given the angle at which the Sun's rays strike the Earth, more radiant energy is received near the equator than at the poles. Furthermore, much of the radiant energy that does reach the polar regions is reflected back into the atmosphere and beyond by polar snow and ice. The global tendency is to redress the heat imbalance, to redistribute the heat dynamically by means of the general circulation of the atmosphere. Generally, warmer and less dense air at the equator rises and moves toward the poles, while colder and denser air at the poles sinks and moves toward the equator. This would create two separate cells of circulating air—as if a wide sleeve were wrapped around the earth north and south of the equator. But the Earth rotates, spinning on its axis, and this causes each pole-to-equator system to break up into three separate circulation cells: one is polar, the next is at midlatitude (called the Ferrel cell), and one is equatorial (called the Hadley cell).

The Earth's rotation creates what is called the Coriolis force, which dictates that air in the Northern Hemisphere, which

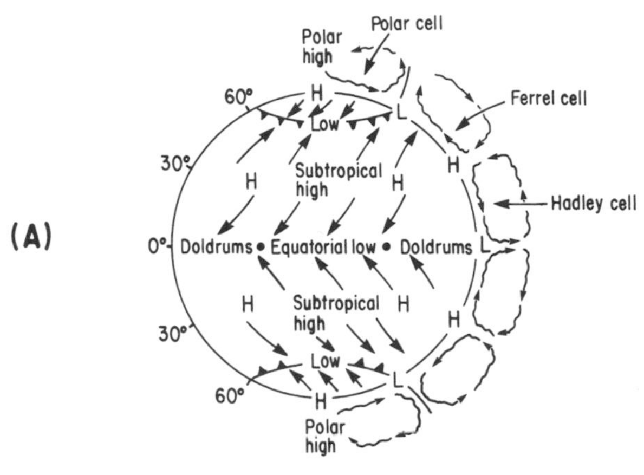

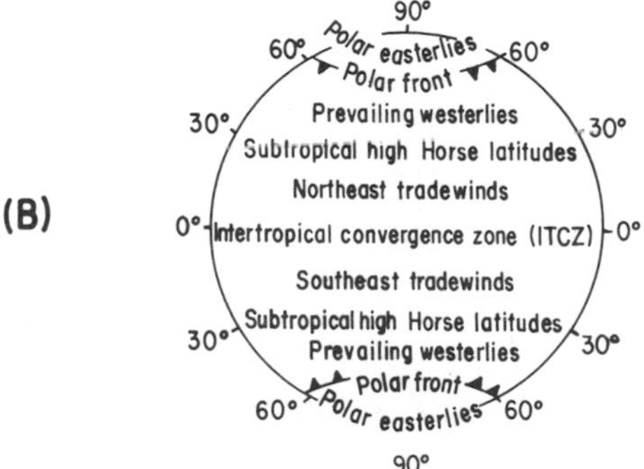

Diagram A shows the wind and surface pressure distribution over a uniformly water-covered rotating Earth. Diagram B gives the names of the surface winds and pressures for the same system. (From Ahrens 1988)

moves north if it is warm or south if it is cold, is also deflected to the right of its north-south motion. In the Southern Hemisphere, the effect is opposite; air is deflected to the left. So when cold, dense air at the North Pole sinks and moves south, it is deflected to its right, or in a westerly direction, creating winds that are called polar easterlies. (Winds are designated by the direction they flow *from* rather than *to*.)

In the Hadley cell in the Northern Hemisphere—the cell nearest the equator—warm, less dense air rises and flows northward as it is replaced by colder air from the north, so here too the north-moving air is deflected to the west by the Coriolis force, creating the northeast trade winds.

What happens in the cell in the middle, the Ferrel cell? Air is rising at the southern boundary of the polar cell and descending at the northern boundary of the Hadley cell. At the Earth's

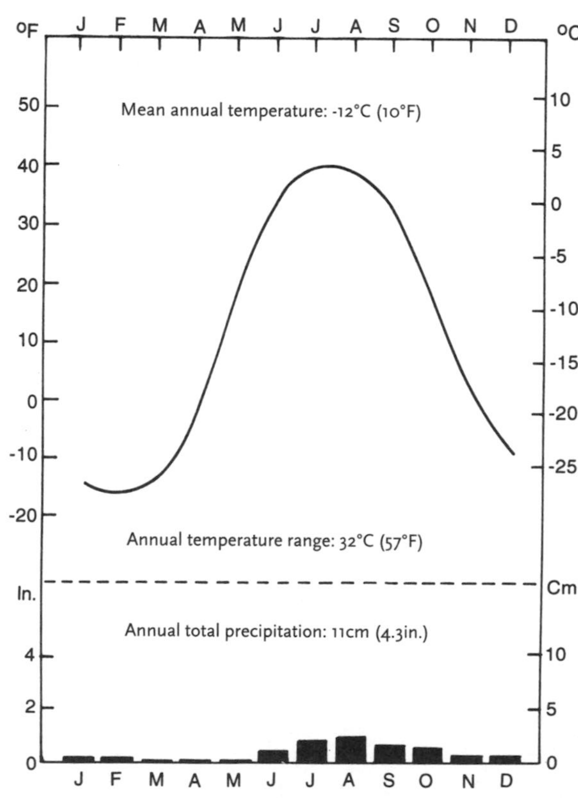

Climatic data for Barrow, Alaska, latitude 71° N (From Ahrens 1988)

TABLE 1

FREQUENCY DISTRIBUTION OF WIND SPEED OVER THE CENTRAL ARCTIC OCEAN

Month	Wind speed (m/sec) 0	1	2	3	4	5	6	7	8	9	10–14	15–19	>20	Total of observations
Jan.	11	7	8	10	13	12	8	8	6	4	10	2	1	564
Feb.	10	6	11	15	17	15	9	5	5	1	6	0	0	548
Mar.	6	6	8	18	22	15	7	6	4	2	5	1	0	585
Apr.	6	5	15	15	17	15	8	7	5	4	3	0	0	479
May	7	5	11	16	16	15	11	7	6	3	3	0	0	744
June	5	5	9	15	13	15	11	9	6	4	7	1	0	669
July	4	3	9	12	13	16	10	9	9	6	8	1	0	609
Aug.	4	4	7	11	11	15	11	11	8	5	11	2	0	570
Sep.	8	4	9	13	15	15	8	10	5	4	7	2	0	545
Oct.	7	5	9	12	12	12	10	9	7	4	11	2	0	586
Nov.	9	7	10	13	16	15	7	6	6	4	6	1	0	607
Dec.	11	10	14	14	17	12	6	5	4	3	4	0	0	607

1m/s=22 mph

(From Vowinckel and Orvig 1970)

surface here, the air is moving north and is deflected to its right (the east), creating what are called the prevailing westerlies. Much of the United States lies under the midlatitude Ferrel cell with its prevailing westerlies, which is why weather tends to come from the west. In the Southern Hemisphere the cold air comes from the south instead of the north, but direction of the Coriolis force is flopped as well, the results being polar easterlies, prevailing westerlies, and southeast trade winds—much the same as in the north.

The value of these circular patterns for the Atlantic Ocean in the days of sailing vessels is obvious: Ships sailed from Europe with the northeast trade winds blowing from astern, propelling the square-riggers across the water steadily. They could then head north on the Gulf Stream and back to Europe on the prevailing westerlies. But there were traps for the unwary. At the equator, as we have noted, warm air rises. Some flows north, some south, creating the two trade winds. In between, the air flows weakly and horizontally at the Earth's surface; this is called the intertropical convergence zone or, to sailors of wind-driven vessels, the doldrums. Similarly, the winds are also weak between the equatorial and midlatitude cells—a zone called the horse latitudes. As in the doldrums, ships were often becalmed there, and the crews jettisoned any expendable cargo, presumably including horses, to lighten the load they had to tow behind rowboats.

At the North Pole the winds are generally calm, increasing in magnitude away from it. Table 1 shows the frequency distribution of wind speeds over the central Arctic Ocean. They are not high as a rule, averaging 9 to 11 miles per hour. They are highest in April and May, but never more than 33 miles per hour.

During the Arctic's sunless winters the skies are typically clear and it is extremely cold; January temperatures over the pack ice average -22° to -33°F. In summer, when with the return of

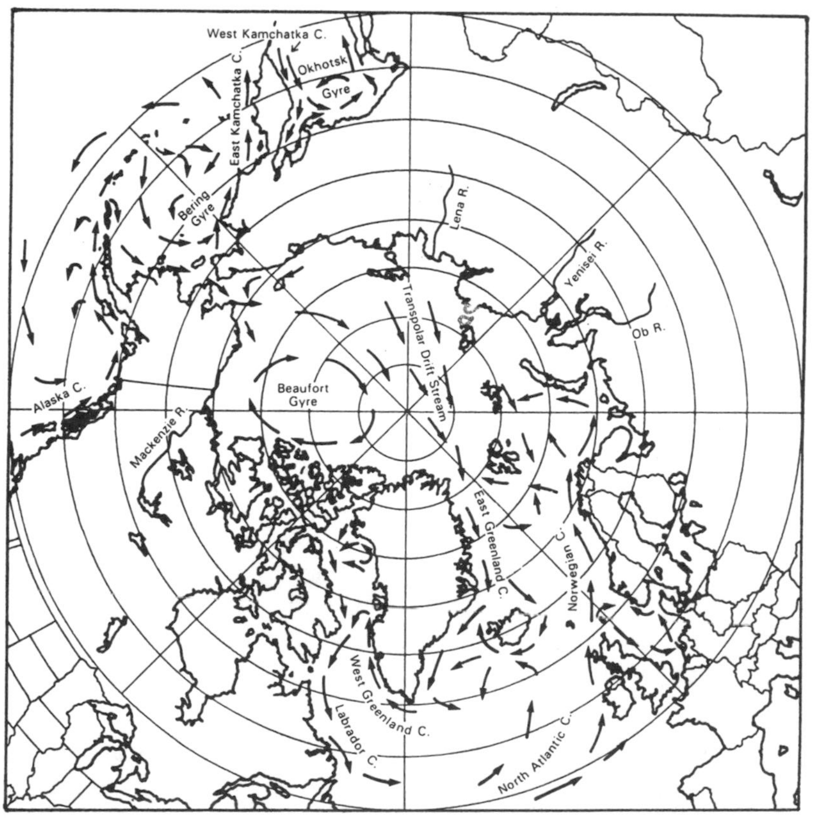

Schematic of the large-scale horizontal circulation patterns in the surface waters of the north polar region. The four major rivers providing the major river inflows to the Arctic Ocean are also shown (From Parkinson et al. 1987)

solar radiation come melting snow and ice and the resultant open water, temperatures are held near the freezing point for water (32° F), and it is likely to be damp and foggy. Annual precipitation, as noted, is about 6 to 9 inches, falling mostly in summer and early fall. Typically the landmasses lying around the Arctic Ocean are somewhat warmer than this in both summer and winter.

Just as Arctic winds rarely achieve high speeds, the ocean currents tend to be stately. The vertical structure of the ocean currents is determined, as one would expect, by the density of the masses of water, with denser water flowing in under less dense water. Density is determined by the water's temperature and its salinity, with salinity being more important than temperature. The colder and saltier the water, the denser it will be. Much of the water flowing into the Arctic Ocean is a warm and saline undercurrent, flowing along the coast of Norway and referred to as the Norwegian Current. The major outflow is the surface transport of the East Greenland Current south through the Fram Strait.

Within the Arctic Ocean water circulation is governed, in part, by the Lomonosov Ridge; in the Western Hemisphere the clockwise gyre of water north of the Canadian Archipelago is called the Beaufort Gyre. In the eastern hemisphere, the Transpolar Drift System flows across from Siberia to the Fram Strait. Off Siberia, the flow averages about 1 to 1.5 miles a day, increasing to about 4 to 5.5 miles a day in the narrower causeway of the Fram Strait.

The Arctic sea ice is always on the move. It follows the drift of the underlying ocean currents and the changes in the direction and speed of the wind. For polar explorers and Pole seekers, the most important feature of the Arctic—the single feature that needed most to be understood—was the structure and drift of this shifting, ever-changing ice pack. The ice never completely covers the Arctic Ocean, because differential motion, fracturing, and melting all lead to open waters. Some of these are narrow, roughly linear leads, ranging in width from yards to a

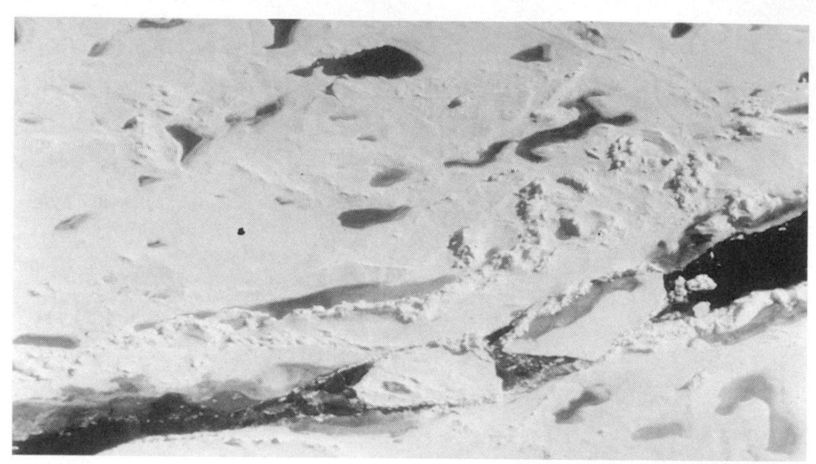

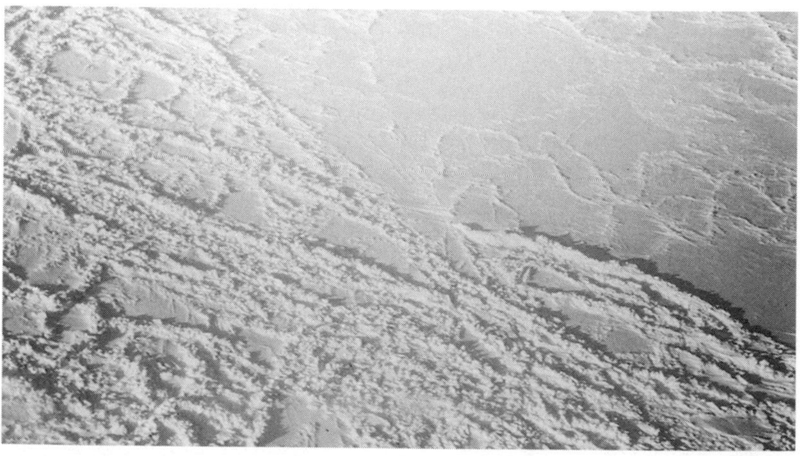

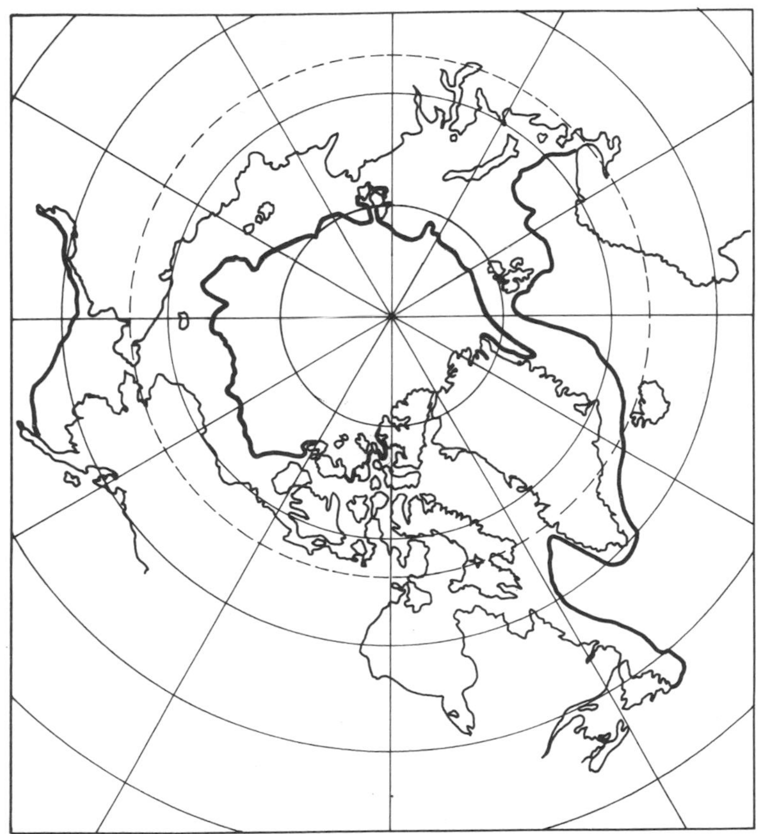

Average summer ice extent (minimum) and average winter ice extent (maximum) are both shown as heavy lines. (From Central Intelligence Agency 1978)

OPPOSITE, TOP: A lead, approximately 20 meters across, partially covered with thin ice in the Beaufort Sea ice pack, August 1975. The dark blue-black coloring of the lead contrasts with the turquoise blue of the melt ponds. Ponds that have melted through the ice appear darker. Note also the snow cover, (From Parkinson et al. 1987)

MIDDLE: End of a small pressure ridge near the north pole (Walter Tucker, Cold Regions Research and Engineering Laboratory, Hanover)

BOTTOM: Multiyear ice in the Beaufort Sea, showing weathered hummocks and pressure ridges (Walter Tucker, Cold Regions Research and Engineering Laboratory, Hanover)

mile, and some are broader polynyas, which can be thousands of square miles in diameter. The frequent deformation of the pack ice breaks up the otherwise uniform expanse into irregular shapes called floes, which are separate platforms of ice. Other important features are pressure ridges, formed when ice is compressed with enough force to crumble it into rows of elevated ice several yards in height and also extending some distance down into the water below. Pressure ridges are ubiquitous, and on average there are four ridges some thirty yards in height to climb over or detour around for every mile one treks across. The pack ice, then, is extremely difficult terrain, and it extends all the way to the Pole. The native populations never

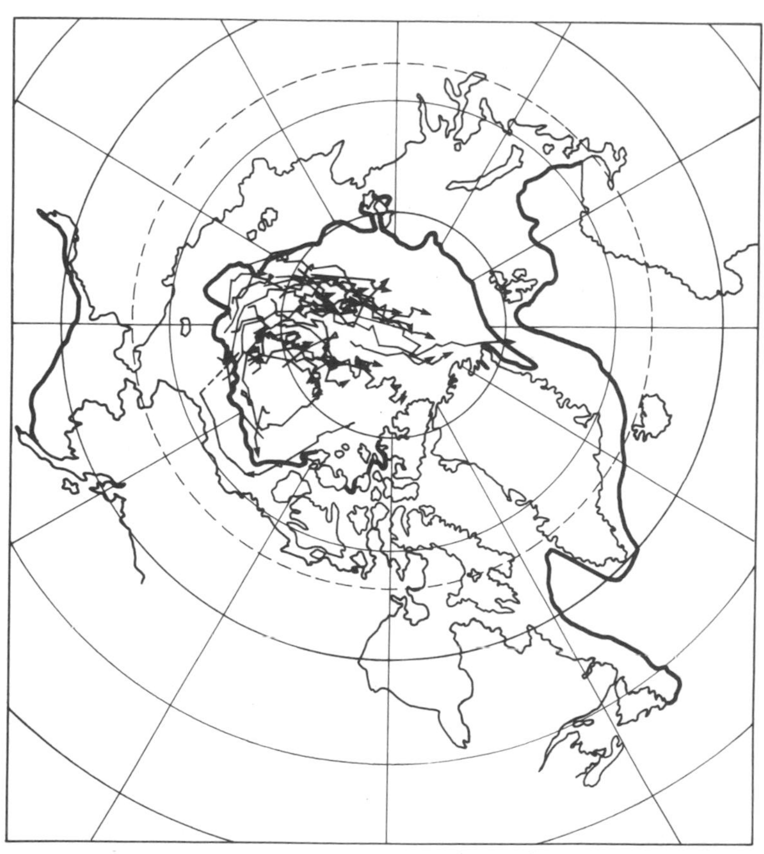

Tracks of manned drift stations, 1958–1975, for both the Soviet Union and the United States (From Central Intelligence Agency 1978)

had any interest in going into the polar region until paid by European explorers to do so.

At its southern boundaries the ice has a seasonal growth-and-decay cycle, nearly doubling in extent from the summer to the winter. During the summer melt period water percolates through the ice, and when winter approaches, the ice is left with a rolling, hummocky surface that adds to the difficulty in crossing it. The only relatively smooth and undeformed ice one encounters in the Arctic is first-year ice, formed at the edges of the ice pack and about two yards thick. Multiyear ice tends to be about three yards thick and may be tens of years old. In September, when the ice is at its minimum extent, the ice pack is confined mostly to the Arctic Ocean, with only a small amount reaching into the Greenland, Kara, and Barents Seas and the Canadian Archipelago. At this time virtually no ice is to be seen in the Bering Sea, Hudson Bay, the Sea of Okhotsk, and Baffin Bay. On the other hand, in March, when the ice is at its maximum, it covers the Arctic Ocean, the waters around the Canadian Archipelago, and large portions of other peripheral seas and bays. Through the eons, this schedule has varied as the Northern Hemisphere has experienced long periods of unusual warmth or unusual cold.

For polar explorers a century ago, the movement of the pack ice was as important to know as the location, height, and extent of pressure ridges. In simple terms, you can't know what direction you need to go to reach, say, the North Pole, if you don't know which way the ice you're going to cross is drifting. Today, thanks to the placement of drifting manned stations on the ice pack by Russians, Canadians, and Americans over the past sixty-odd years, we have a fairly good picture of these motions. The ice generally follows the direction of the Beaufort Gyre and the Transpolar Drift System, but it can be quite erratic, sometimes doubling back on itself. It travels about four miles a day, sometimes less, sometimes as much as two miles more per day.

Finally there is the matter of navigation and bearings out on the Arctic ice pack. The early explorers did not have the advantage of satellite navigation. They couldn't even avail themselves of then-conventional celestial navigation, in which one measures the angle from the horizon to a star at a given moment in time. From the intersection of two or more such lines from two or more star sightings, and with the aid of the *Nautical Almanac*, a catalogue of star positions, your location is given. To use this technique both the horizon and the stars (or planets) have to be visible simultaneously, limiting celestial navigation to early evening and early morning. On the polar ice pack in summer, however, the horizon is visible but no stars are; in winter the stars twinkle but there is no horizon to be seen in the dark.

In this situation you have to rely on a less accurate system, determining the height of the Sun above the horizon at local apparent noon, which calls for a series of Sun sights until the maximum elevation has passed. Through appropriate tables, the Sun's elevation can be translated into your latitude, and the time of the local *apparent* noon (the Sun's maximum height in the sky) translates directly into one's longitude. (Until the invention of the chronometer at about the time of the Renaissance, there was no way to determine longitude, and explorers setting out in earlier times simply couldn't know where they were.)

These Sun sights are all very well in much of the world, but as you approach the Pole there is little change in the Sun's elevation, and the concept of local apparent noon loses its meaning. Magnetic compasses are of minimal value in the polar latitudes, since the magnetic pole undergoes large and somewhat unpredictable variations. It is currently in the vicinity of latitude 76° N and longitude 100° W, but these locations not only are indefinite but change irregularly over a period of years. It is preferable to get an estimate of geographic *south* from the Sun's position at its maximum elevation.

With the unpredictable vagaries in the drift of the ice pack, it is essential to take daily readings at noon. Dead reckoning—deducing position from your direction and speed—without considering the drift of the ice can lead only to huge but unrealized errors, and it often did in the long history of Arctic exploration.

Imagine, then, being an explorer four hundred or even a thousand years ago, not knowing any of this as you proceed northward past the waters and landforms of your known world in a small, seaworthy craft into a world inhabited (but only sparsely) by strange creatures in the sea—seals, walruses, narwhals with their unicornlike single horns, the occasional seabird arrowing off through the mist, strange ice forms floating in the fog like cosmic rubble and rising steeply above you, distant black-and-white shores soon lost to sight in the gathering frozen night. . . .

The Arctic has been described as bleak, beautiful, terrifying, depressing. It has driven Europeans into madness; worse, it has claimed lives with a carelessness that denies, for some, the presence of a loving God. One of its most eloquent troubadours, Barry Lopez, has trekked its length and breadth and found a wisdom "that lies in the richness and sanctity of a wild landscape, what it can mean in the unfolding of a human life, the staying of a troubled human spirit." He speaks of the North and its exploration as a continuing movement through uncharted waters, "an expression of fear and accomplishment, the cusp on which human life finds its richest human expression."

A magical kingdom, one might say.

TWO

Sea Lungs, Godly Commerce, *and* Projections

PYTHEAS, ONE OF THE FIRST MEN from the classical world of the Mediterranean to explore the ocean and lands of the far north, came upon a region where the Earth, the sea, and all the elements were held in some kind of suspension "which you can neither walk nor sail upon." He described this phenomenon as resembling the "sea-lungs," which was a name for certain jellyfish. What he might have had in mind is anyone's guess; perhaps it was a sea fog so dense it made him claustrophobic, as if, Jonah-like, he were trapped inside a giant jellyfish. Far-fetched? Yes, but would an astronomer of the fourth century B.C. have looked at the rough pack ice in the Arctic and been reminded, say, of the air sacs (the alveoli) of the mammalian lung? Not likely.

Pytheas was a citizen of the Greek colonial city of Massilia, present-day Marseilles, and an accomplished scientist and astronomer. Among his accomplishments was to associate the phenomenon of the tides with the motion of the Moon, something no one had noticed until then. The ocean tides are practically nonexistent in the Mediterranean, with its narrow neck opening to the Atlantic at the Straits of Gibraltar, called in those days the Pillars of Hercules. So Pytheas must have ventured through those pillars. He was also the first, or at least among the first, to use celestial navigation to locate himself at sea. With these nautical accomplishments, it is not surprising that in about 325 B.C. the merchants of Massilia selected him to see if he could open a trade route by sea to such northerly places as Cornwall in England, the south coast of Brittany, and the Baltic Sea. Massilia's merchants were already plying an arduous river and overland trade route to those places, involving a long trek up the Rhône, among others. A sea route would be easier, they reasoned, just as it had been for the Phoenicians, who had sailed there for almost a thousand years, starting in about 2000 B.C., for the same reasons: alluvial deposits of tin from Cornwall and Brittany, and amber that washed up from the ocean on the shores of Denmark and near Lithuania. And when the Phoenician city-states declined and were overrun by Assyrians around 1000 B.C., Carthage emerged as the major sea power of the time and took over the tin and amber routes.

The first actual mention in the literature that has come down to us of a northern sea voyage mentions that of a Carthaginian named Himlico, whose voyage evidently took place around 500 B.C. Described is a projecting ridge, "a high mass of rocky ridge [that] turns mostly toward the warm south wind." Called Oestrymnis, it is probably the chalk cliffs of Dover. The account also mentions islands that are probably those off Brittany, rich in tin and lead. It speaks as well of a place called Hierne (Ireland), not far from Albion (England again), and of people who didn't make keels but, "strange to say, they make their ships of hides sewn together" and "plough in skillful fashion far and wide the foaming sea, and the currents of monster-bearing Ocean in these small boats."

Yet the account of Himlico's voyage comes to us secondhand. His own account, if such there ever was, does not exist. Instead, we are told of Himlico and his sightings by a Roman author, Rufus Festus Avienus, writing almost a thousand years later, in the fourth century A.D. Better, then, to trust in Pytheas as the first of the classical explorers of the northern seas. He set out, we are told, at the same time that Aristotle was holding classes and Alexander the Great and his army were marching on India.

In all, it seems, Pytheas and his crew were gone for some six years, spending a fair amount of time in present-day England and Scotland, noting that people there grew wheat and corn; mined tin; had tools of iron, domestic animals, and chariots of wood; and made a "wine" from fermented grain. He sailed on northward, finally reaching a place he called Thule, where evidently the "sea-lungs" stopped him. Not much farther north, he reported, the summer sun didn't set and the winter sun was never seen. He evidently believed that Thule was six days' sail north of Britain and one day south of a "congealed" or frozen sea, meaning the pack ice. Upon his return he wrote a treatise, *On the Ocean,* which unfortunately, like Himlico's own account, was lost. We know of Pytheas' treatise and his trip north only from subsequent writers, chiefly two Roman geographers who thought he was a liar.

The better known of the two was the geographer Strabo who wrote of Pytheas about three hundred years after the fact and apparently from secondhand sources. Strabo read about Pytheas in the works of a shadowy explorer named Polybius, who was motivated to downplay Pytheas' accomplishments lest they outshine his own. Strabo also referred to the works of the mathematician and poet Eratosthenes, who believed there was such a place as Thule but didn't know how much more of Pytheas' account was reliable. Strabo concluded that Pytheas was a fraud, an arch-falsifier of information, saying that other people who had since gone to Britain and Ireland never mentioned Thule and, anyway, people couldn't live as far north as he said they did. Strabo, of course, was wrong, and Pytheas was right.

Another major classical writer to discuss Pytheas' version of events was Pliny the Elder, author of *Natural History*, in the latter years of the first century A.D. He evidently had heard of Pytheas through yet other writers, but unlike the virulent Strabo, he simply reported what he had read without taking much of a stand one way or the other. For example, he wrote:

> [T]he light nights in summer substantiate what theory compels us to believe, that, as on summer days the sun approached nearer to the top of the world, owing to a natural circuit of light the underlying parts of the earth have continuous days for six months at a time, and continuous nights when the sun has withdrawn in the opposite direction

towards winter. Pytheas of Marseilles writes that this occurs in the island of Thule, six days' voyage north of Britain.

No educated person in classical times, it should be pointed out, questioned the notion of the midnight sun and the long nights of winter. They were well aware that the earth was a globe and that the changing angle of the sun would bring about such day lengths at the "top" of the globe. They just had no idea what lay toward the top (or the bottom) of the globe. Speculation was rife: Was there a frigid sea beyond which a halcyon land existed, inhabited by blessed people called the Hyperboreans? Or was it a frozen mountain, or an open sea, or some kind of unimaginable and precipitous end of the earth?

Today most historians seem to be satisfied that Pytheas was probably the first classical explorer to venture into the near Arctic, but there remains a good deal of disagreement about where Pytheas was when he came upon Thule. The main candidates are the Shetland Islands (north of Scotland), Iceland, and Norway. But the Shetlands, given the length of the day there at midwinter, and the fact that they are far more than a day south of the pack ice and less than six from Scotland, have been largely ruled out. An Icelandic explorer of the twentieth century favors Iceland; a Norwegian explorer, not surprisingly, favors Norway. One problem with Norway is that it doesn't have much sea ice near its coast. On the other hand, most Icelandic historians say Thule wasn't Iceland. Thule thus has eluded us and probably always will; indeed, our phrase "Ultima Thule," derived from Pytheas' island, means the farthest place or, in essence, an ultimate, perhaps impossible-to-attain goal.

In any event, Pytheas had refound the sea route to the tin mines of Britain. It is likely that Massilian and other merchants followed in his wake, and it is perfectly possible that others approached or even entered Arctic waters over the centuries that ensued; we just have no record of such anonymous and unheralded doings. We know far more, in fact, about the people who at that time had already lived throughout the Arctic for five millennia or more, because they left signs of their presence throughout the region, later to be scratched out of the ground by archeologists.

By the time Pytheas reached Thule, wherever that was, people living on most of the landforms that surround the Arctic Ocean were hunting whales and other sea mammals such as seals with harpoons. They were also following the migrations of caribou, herding reindeer, and burying their dead with exquisitely carved representations of the local fauna. These various Arctic peoples all had evolved much the same anatomical adaptations to living in so cold a place, tending to have thick, short bodies, relatively short limbs, and small hands and feet, plus an increased flow of blood to body parts exposed to extreme cold. In addition, the Lapps, those renowned reindeer herders of the north, tend to shunt blood from one artery to a paired one, which warms venous blood returning from the extremities to the heart. This in turn means that their hands and feet can become relatively cold without affecting organs such as the brain.

These well-adapted people were essentially the sole inhabitants of the Arctic for some twelve thousand years. But while they all remained utterly anonymous in the course of history until some two hundred years ago, it was not until well into the twentieth century that any European learned much of anything about the Arctic that these indigenous people didn't already know. And as we shall see, until the airplane was capable of long-distance flight, no European (or American) explorer got very far in the Arctic or lasted very long there without the help or the carefully observed example of the indigenous peoples, chiefly the various Inuit peoples that Europeans came to call Eskimos.

If the earliest ventures into the Arctic arose as a result of commercial interests such as lead and tin and amber, the next recorded penetration of the Arctic by Europeans came about as the quest for a different sort of commerce altogether—commerce with God. By A.D. 800 the European world had changed radically from Pliny the Elder's times. Among other things, Huns, Vandals, Visigoths, and a host of other northerly groups had pressured the overextended Roman Empire, shoved it back, and finally defeated it. During the centuries that followed, much of classical culture and civilization was lost except in more easterly realms, where Arabs would preserve a great deal and expand on it. And in Europe, the refuge of culture, the place where learning, intellectual enterprise, and spiritual thought survived like a small ember, was the remote and windswept monasteries of Ireland. Under pressure from both Rome (to conform to its doctrinal pronouncements) and the roving Vikings, many Irish monks left in the 700s and 800s for the Faeroe Islands and even Iceland, establishing new monasteries on remote promontories overlooking the cold ocean. There are plenty of stories about how some of these monks, sailing the high seas in their carraughs, boats made of ox hides, reached as far west as North America, but there is, disappointingly for the romantic of spirit, absolutely no evidence that this ever happened. In the 1970s an adventurer named Tim Severin constructed a carraugh of the kind that the Celts used, made of hides over a wicker basketlike structure, and in it he sailed from Ireland to Iceland and from there to Newfoundland, proving that it could have been done by the monks of old (but not, of course, proving that they did any such thing).

Indeed, there are grand legends of the Celtic monks searching for the Land of the Blessed, the untroubled and graceful place where vines bore fruit twelve times a year and people lived in peace. These legends became unified in an eighth-century narrative called *Navigatio Brendani*. The man known as Brendan the Navigator did indeed exist, but he almost surely never went to Iceland. Saint Brendan was born on the west coast of Ireland in the fifth century, sailed to Scotland, where he founded a monastery, and later became abbot of a monastery in Wales, dying in the sixth century back home in Ireland. Before long he was a folk hero as well as a saint, with the great narrative being committed to paper several centuries after his death and going through more than a hundred versions in virtually all the languages of Europe. The narrative is a rousing seagoing epic of wondrous stories and amazing meetings, most of which surely didn't happen, particularly to the good abbot, including a landing on North American shores where the monks were greeted by a very old man who wore no clothes but was covered by his hair and beard, which were pure white.

Three hundred years after the real Brendan had been laid in his grave in western Ireland the Vikings, those land-hungry, loot-hungry seafaring warriors from Scandinavia, were in full attack mode. Much of Europe would fall to these marauders, the terrifying prows of their ships suddenly appearing in coastal and river communities, of which few survived intact. Danish Vikings, for example, destroyed Paris twice in the mid-800s and sailed through the Pillars of Hercules to terrorize both Italy and Morocco. Their takeover of all of England was blocked only by a young Welsh lord named Alfred, who rallied the various English groups into a single force in 878 and held the Vikings to only partial control of the British Isles. Alfred, a man of many parts—soldier, administrator, scholar—became known as the first true king of England: Alfred the Great.

Earlier, Danish Norsemen had "discovered" Iceland, but these were mostly fishermen and farmers, colonizing the island (and evidently driving out the remaining Celtic monks from their meditations). At about the same time, around A.D. 870, a Viking named Ottar ventured north into the polar sea, most likely to hunt for creatures such as walruses, thus becoming the first European known to have reached the Arctic, though others must have reached it before him. In his account, which Ottar made to King Alfred (and he, the good scholar, took it down), Ottar sailed north along the coast of Scandinavia to North Cape, then east for five days through the Barents Sea to the Kola Peninsula, and then south into the White Sea. He evidently found the southern shores of the White Sea to be inhabited. Hearing of this, later Vikings would follow his route, bent on plunder.

It was probably a Norwegian, Gunnbjörn Ulfsson, who discovered Greenland in the next century, but it comes down through most histories as an exploit of Eirik Raude or Erik the Red, a Norwegian and apparently a major landowner in Iceland, where he had settled after being banished from Norway for murder. In 982 his serfs in Iceland set an avalanche tumbling down onto

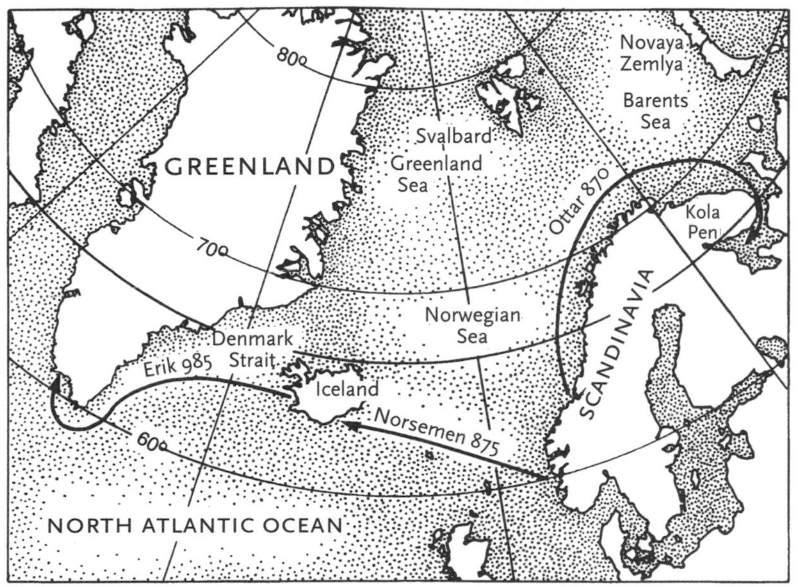

Early northern voyages by the Vikings (From Central Intelligence Agency 1978)

another man's home (or so it is written in Finn Gad's 1970 *History of Greenland*). The man's kinsmen exacted revenge by killing Erik's serfs, which led Erik to exact his revenge in turn, killing the slayers and a few others to boot. The penalty in Norse communities for unjustifiable homicide was loss of personal property and banishment from the community for three years, so Erik sailed off to the west, reaching the great landmass that Ulfsson most likely had already come upon. For three years he poked around the southern coastal areas and up into the fjords of this unwelcoming place, returning to Iceland in 985 with glowing accounts of the place, which he dubbed, in an early example of boosterism, Greenland.

The sales job worked, and in 986 twenty-five ships set out for this new land. Fourteen of those ships, bearing some five hundred people, arrived safely, and the settlers created a colony on the (subarctic) south shore, building houses of stone and turf and raising some diminutive breeds of livestock, hunting seals and walruses, and fishing. Soon another colony was established farther to the southwest, and the Greenland communities would thrive for about three centuries, trading their raw goods for iron, grain, and manufactured implements.

About the time Erik led the colonists off to Greenland, a merchant named Bjarni Herjulfsson, whose normal route was between Norway and Iceland, decided to follow his father (one of the colonists) to Greenland. He missed the coast and came to a land "well wooded with low hills," then north to another that was "flat and wooded," and north yet again to a land that was "high and mountainous and topped by a glacier." He didn't land at any of these places but headed east, eventually heaving to at the second, western settlement of Greenland, where he remained. Evidently he had seen Newfoundland, Labrador, and Baffin Island, in that order. And then, in the year 1001, Erik's son, Leif, bought Bjarni's ship and set out for the lands the merchant had sighted, evidently with a view to collecting some timber. Coming first to Baffin Island, Leif headed south to Labrador and then to Newfoundland, where he, or subsequent Norse explorers, established a temporary settlement on the shore at a place we call L'Anse aux Meadows. There in the 1960s Helge Ingstad, a former governor of East Greenland and Spitzbergen, and his archeologist wife, Anne Stinne Ingstad, uncovered the remains of the settlement—eight dwelling places, a forge, and artifacts, mainly slag and carpentry debris. It was evidently a base camp for further exploration, as there was little sign of garbage and no burials. The settlement apparently was abandoned in 1014, though other Norsemen probably plied the coastline for a few years thereafter, perhaps as far south as

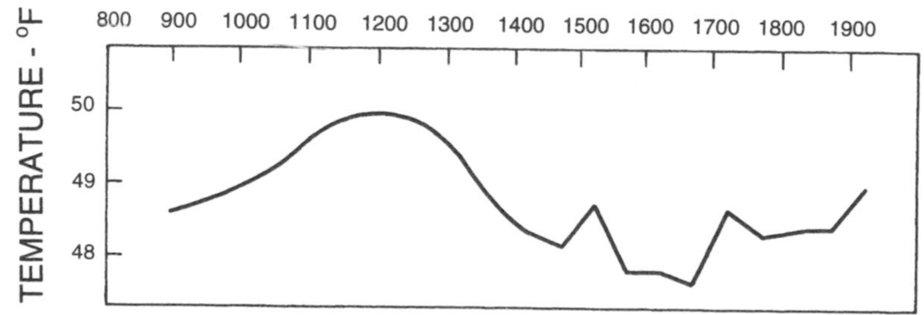

Estimated variation in yearly temperature for central England during the Medieval Warm Period and the Little Ice Age (From Lamb 1982)

Maine. But eventually difficulties with the local Indians, a group we know as the Beothuks, were too much for the overextended Norsemen at Newfoundland, and they left.

It is well known now that Leif referred to the place he settled on as Vinland. But wild grapes are not indigenous to Newfoundland, and this has caused plenty of scholarly and unscholarly speculation: Until the discovery of the site at L'Anse aux Meadows and its careful dating, one could insist that Leif had to have meant Maine, where wild grapes do grow. But Leif was exploring during what is called the Medieval Warm Period—an era during which a warm and moist climate graced both Europe and North America. Maybe there were grapes then in New-

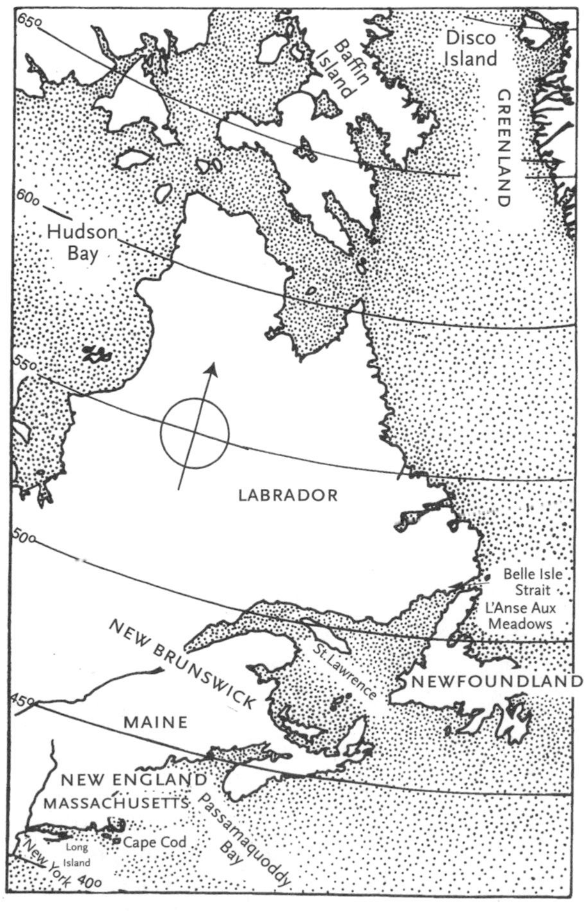

Newfoundland, Labrador, Baffin Island, Greenland, and the L'Anse aux Meadows site (From Magnusson and Pálsson 1965)

foundland. Or maybe he had learned a thing or two about boosterism from his father.

In any event, the Vikings came and went—unlike later Europeans, without even infecting any of the native population with smallpox or adding anything to Indian culture or oral history. Meanwhile, the Medieval Warm Period ended and was soon replaced in about 1300 by the Little Ice Age, when the climate turned colder by some 2°F. This interval lasted for about half a millennium: In the sixteenth century Pieter Breughel could paint his countrymen skating on frozen canals, the Thames froze over, and the dwellers in the small southern town that would become the capital of the United States could skate across the Potomac. Alpine glaciers ground over Swiss towns and, early on, along the southern coasts of Greenland, sea ice began to encroach, cutting off communication from Iceland and Scandinavia for much of the year. By 1350 the western settlements on Greenland were abandoned; a few stragglers hung on along the eastern coast until about 1500, when the last ones left, some of the others having married into the native Inuit population.

All these Norse settlements in Iceland and Greenland were, of course, south of the actual Arctic Circle. The Hyperborean region continued to elude European aggrandizement. The native polar peoples—Inuit, Lapps, and others—had another five hundred years to live in relative peace in their grand, lonely world among the fish and the great mammals of the sea and ice. For them it was home, the center of their universe. For the European mind the North continued to be, mythologically, the place from where dangerous people and noisy gods swept south and, at the same time and equally mythologically, a kind of promised land, a place where fortunes were to be made and national destinies resolved. In the sixteenth century an explorer could present to the Virgin Queen of England the horn of a narwhal, and Elizabeth and all in the royal court would be happy in the belief that it had come from a unicorn.

One can imagine the eagerness with which geographically minded scholars a half millennium later welcomed new accounts of far-off places, or of places poorly delineated before. During this era the art and industry of mapmaking began again after a long hiatus. It was during the classical age of Greece, Rome, and Alexandria when scholars had begun to map the known world and the regions that might lie beyond, bringing mathematical tools to the task as well as skill and imagination. For a long time major feats of knowledge, scholarship, and archive keeping had taken place in Alexandria's library, but the library was sacked by a Christian mob in about A.D. 300, and this period of knowledge came to an end. In the ensuing centuries after the fall of Rome, such enterprises as cartography took a backseat to matters of faith and Church politics. For a time, the Church for doctrinal reasons insisted that maps show the world as flat. But this began to change, as did so much else, in the period we call the Renaissance—which was also the beginning of the Europeans' Age of Exploration.

The year 1492 was not just Columbus': it saw the first attempt at rendering the earth on a spherical map, a globe. This was a time also when there was a good deal of dead reckoning in spite of the fact that the magnetic compass existed as early as the twelfth century (in China) and Europeans had begun to make rudimentary sea charts of nearby waters. Even so, for a long time, reckoned in centuries, a navigator would plot a course on such a chart (called a portolano) from his harbor to another point across an expanse of water, set forth and often miss his target just as had poor Bjarni Herjulffsson who, though lost, may have been the first European to lay eyes on the New World. Even in Columbus' era longitude and latitude were still only minimally understood, particularly longitude, which meant that a sailor was essentially lost whenever he sailed east or west any major distance beyond sight of familiar land. What actually lay beyond well-known waters was still a mystery, colored by guesswork, wrapped in fantasy and myth. Nor was this inconvenient lack of detail much diminished when the first Mercator projection appeared on a map.

Gerardus Mercator was the Latinate name taken by Gerhard Kremer, a German born in 1512 and raised in Flanders. In his studies to become a priest, Gerhard took seriously the problem of the contradiction between the teachings of Aristotle and those of the Bible. He eventually decided in favor of mathematics and astronomy and became the pupil of Gemma Frisius, a doctor, mathematician, and geographer from whom he learned, among other things, the making of scientific instruments of the era, including the astrolabe, a device for reckoning latitude. Before long Mercator began producing maps and introduced not only the word *atlas* for a collection of maps, but also a flowing, calligraphic style of labeling that became the standard. And, of course, he introduced the Mercator projection for maps, chiefly to simplify the lives of mariners, allowing them to steer courses over long distances merely by plotting straight lines. By the time he was about fifty years old, he was the century's leading cartographer and geographer, and in 1569 he published an atlas of the world that would profoundly affect Arctic exploration for another three hundred years.

To produce such an atlas was no small undertaking, particularly because so much of the world remained unknown to Europeans, or known only through reports from a handful of explorers and maps based on such incomplete reports, some of which we now know to have been made almost entirely from whole cloth. By this time European cod fishermen and whalers had long been plying the eastern coast of North America and, arriving from the south into Florida, the Spanish had been a major presence in the southeastern part. But this was an era of mostly private, for-profit ventures in the New World, and the adventurers (such as de Soto, who plowed through the American southeast all the way to the Mississippi River and beyond in the 1540s, but who kept his route to himself) were not about to share their hard-won geographical knowledge with others even of their own nationality, much less other European competitors. So mapmakers of the time were forced to employ a great deal of what we would today call hearsay, and this pertained in the extreme to Mercator's rendering of the Arctic.

To begin with, Mercator was aware of the problem we still face when looking at a Mercator projection of the world: Greenland, for example, appears to be larger than North America, when in fact it is one-tenth the size. He knew that were he to extend his projection to the North Pole, the top of the map would need to stretch away into infinity, so he provided an additional map, showing the pole as if seen from above it. Writing of the basis for his rendering, he explained that much of it came from *The Travels of Jacobus Cnoyen of Bois le Duc,* an account whose best information in turn came from a priest who had served the king of Norway in 1364. This priest had explained that in 1360

> an English minor friar of Oxford [Nicholas of Lynn], who was a mathematician, reached those isles [the Hebrides and Iceland] and then, having departed therefrom and pushed on further by the magical arts, he had described all and measured all by means of an astrolabe . . . He averred that the waters of these 4 arms of the sea were drawn toward the abyss with such violence that no wind is strong enough to bring vessels back again once they have entered.

We know something of Nicholas of Lynn, a Carmelite theologian at Oxford in the fourteenth century who Geoffrey Chaucer says (in a scientific treatise he wrote as well as *The Canterbury Tales*) determined Oxford's latitude with an astrolabe. He also carried out such measurements for the king of Norway, but there is no evidence that he proceeded any farther toward the North Pole.

In 1360 a manuscript entitled *De Inventio Fortunata* appeared, attributed by many—though not all—to Nicholas. No copy now exists, but it was passed on to Mercator by the Jacobus Cnoyan he cited, a Flemish adventurer. Mercator took the manuscript's description of what existed at the Pole as true and incorporated it into his map.

Yet another source Mercator used was the existing maps and description of the exploration of Nicolò and Antonio Zeno, brothers from a prominent Venetian family who in 1380 sailed northward and came across an island they called Frisland, which was "much larger than Ireland" and lay somewhere between Iceland and Greenland. Frislanders, they reported, carried on a lucrative trade with "Flanders, Brittany, England, Scotland, Norway and Denmark." The brothers Zeno had met the prince of a nearby island whose name was Zichmini and who had just defeated the king of Norway. The narrative continues with the discovery of Estotiland, which on the Zenos' map appears to be the Labrador coast of North America. The map also shows a large land mass extending north from Greenland into the Arctic Ocean.

It appears that the Zeno brothers' report and map were lost among the family letters, and it was not until 1558 that one of their descendants, also named Nicolò, published their account. Of course, there was no such place as Frisland, no Frislanders, no trade with Europe, no Zichmini, and no such defeat of Norway's ruler. It was in fact a total fraud, but one intended to make it appear that Venetians had discovered North America a century before Columbus, who hailed from the competitor city-state of Genoa.

This information was incorporated into Mercator's and subsequent maps, along with the existence of Lodestone Mountain, a vast landform with a magnetic field so strong that it was said to draw the nails out of any approaching ship and cause erratic behavior in magnetic compasses thousands of miles to the south. Mercator was using logic and the best sorting of available accounts that he could accomplish. And some of what he incorporated was not only plausible, but partly true. In fact, the magnetic pole is offset from the geographic North Pole, as was Lodestone Mountain, but the magnetic pole is not a magnetite mountain but instead the surface expression of a magnetic field generated in the liquid core of the Earth by magnetohydrodynamic currents. Mercator also noted a phenomenon occurring north of the Hebrides—"a monstrous gulf in the sea towards which from all sides the billows of the sea coming from remote parts converge and run together as though brought there by a conduit, pouring into these mysterious abysses of nature, they are as though devoured thereby and, should it happen that a vessel pass there, it is seized and drawn away with such powerful violence of the waves that this hungry force immediately swallows it up never to appear again." This was the Maelstrom, and there is such a place, an oceanic whirlpool off the northwest coast of Norway, near the Lofoten Islands. When it is active, it does capture small ships in its vortex, but it is not, as Mercator had it, at the North Pole.

Subsequent maps by others would vary in details, some keeping Mercator's four landmasses ranged around the Pole, others retaining the four rivers but having them flow outward from the Pole. But a major feature remained in almost all subsequent maps, and it was this that would profoundly affect the future of Arctic exploration: the open polar ocean. For this meant that there should be an easy trade route through the Arctic Ocean to the riches of India and China, northeast around the Asian continent, northwest past North America, or both. If such a passage were found, English and Russian ships would not have to make the

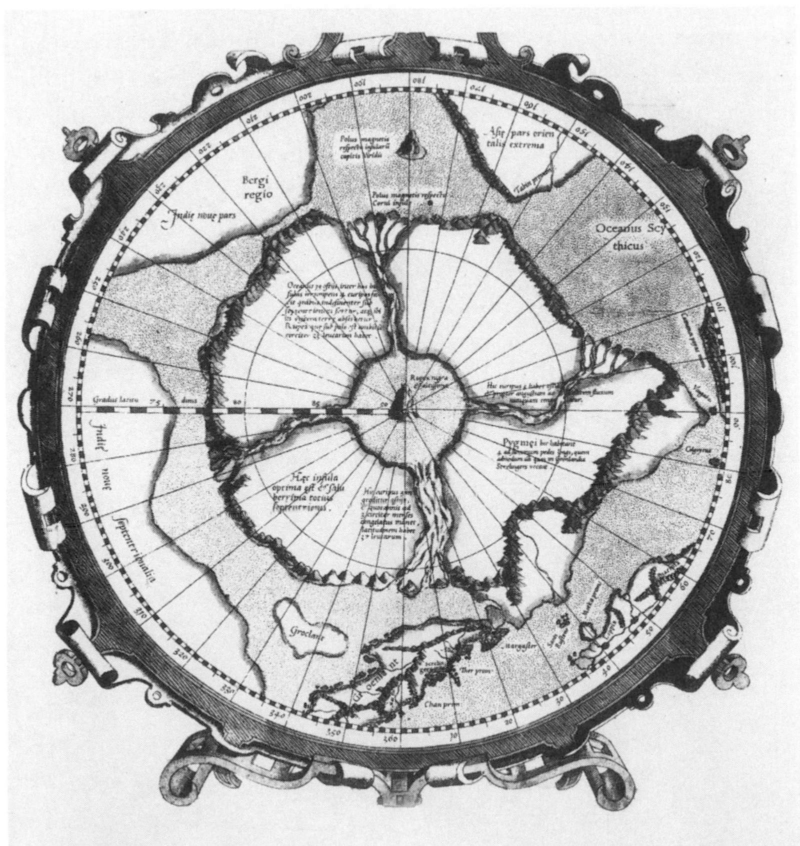

Map of the polar regions (Mercator 1569)

long and arduous passages around the southern tip of Africa or South America, routes that were already in the hands of jealous and protective Spaniards and Portuguese. Spaniards, ensconced for a half century already in Florida, had probed the eastern coast at least as far north as Chesapeake Bay, hoping to find sea passage through the continent to Cathay, a passage they believed had to be there. The French, ensconced along the Saint Lawrence River, were marrying into Algonquin Indian families and plying the waterways in canoes. To be sure, they were collecting beaver pelts, just as the Spanish further to the south were collecting souls, but the French also hoped to find the network of rivers and tributaries that led across the continent to the riches of the Orient.

Indeed, the search for both the Northeast and Northwest Passages was well under way before Mercator's enticing map appeared. In 1497, five years after Columbus' first voyage, another Genoese mariner set out from Bristol, England. John Cabot, born Giovanni Caboto, had taken up Venetian citizenship and failed to persuade Spanish or other backers to send him west to China, so he came to England, where he persuaded King Henry VII and some Bristol merchants to finance him. He sailed in May 1497, fetched up on what he called New Found Land

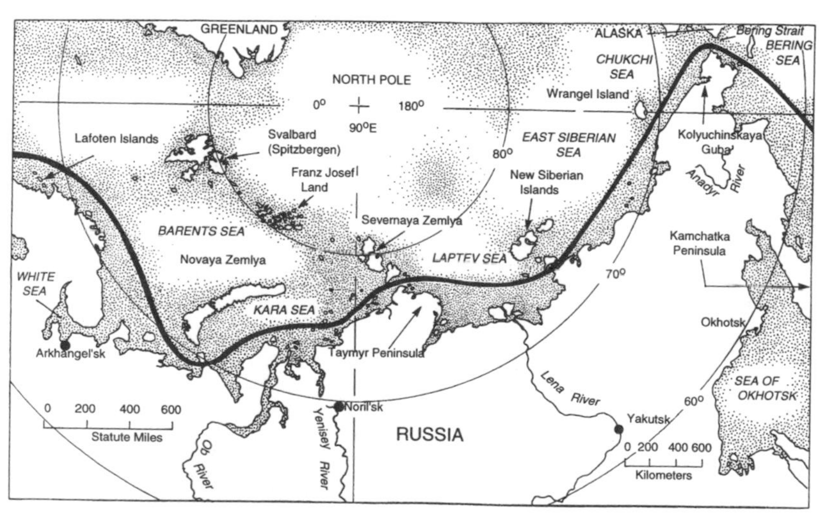

Northeast Passage and adjacent geography (From Central Intelligence Agency 1978)

(quite surely Newfoundland), saw no inhabitants but picked up a few traps and other artifacts, and was convinced that he had made a successful crossing to a remote and fairly primitive shore of Cathay. He returned to England, arriving in August, whereupon the king awarded him ten pounds for his effort.

Cabot left again the following year, this time with more significant backing and five ships laden with trade goods. His plan apparently was to find his way back to his New Found Land and sail southwest along its coast until he came to the wealthy lands so aptly and tantalizingly described earlier by Marco Polo. But nothing was ever heard from him or his five ships again. While he was almost certainly the European discoverer of North America, he left no account of his earlier voyage and, in one of the more bizarre oedipal confusions in history, had a son who ran off with his prize.

Sebastian Cabot is reckoned to have been thirteen years old when his father made his successful journey to Newfoundland, and there is every reason to believe that he was not a member of the expedition. But he later managed to persuade people that he had been on board, explaining at least once that his father had died a few years before the actual voyage, and for nearly four

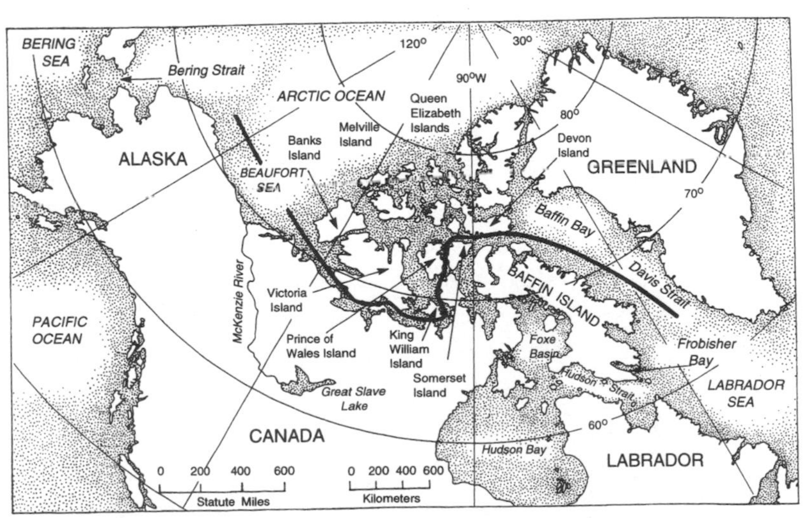

Northwest Passage and adjacent geography (From Central Intelligence Agency 1978)

centuries he got credit from most historians for John's voyage of discovery. (As late as 1897, the government of the province of Newfoundland issued a commemorative stamp honoring John Cabot and bearing a portrait of him. But no portrait of John survived, if one was ever made. Instead the stamp showed a rendering of the one portrait that survived of Sebastian, as an old man, which of course his father never got to be.)

Sebastian Cabot was evidently a man of many other talents as well as self-promotion. Later he recounted to a friend that he had outfitted two ships at his own expense in Britain in 1508 and led a crew of three hundred men due north until, in July, they encountered continuous daylight and so much ice in the sea that he was obliged to turn west and south, penetrating as far west as the entry to what was surely the passage to Cathay (likely the island of Cuba), or—according to another report to a different friend—sailing into a great opening to the west from the Arctic Ocean (what could have been Hudson Bay), surely the entrance of the Northwest Passage. This voyage was, it turned out, a complete fabrication.

Subsequently Sebastian went to work for Charles V of Spain, serving as pilot-major for the crown, a job that entailed training and testing all pilots as well as performing other nautical duties. He became adept at making nautical instruments and produced a map of the world based on "his" explorations, among others. He did make a transatlantic voyage for the Spanish king, this to South America, seeking a better passage than that of the successful Magellan. But his experience turned out to be such a disaster that, rather than face banishment to Africa, Sebastian returned to England and soon enough became the head of a company established to fund an attempt to find the Northeast Passage. By now he was seventy or more years old, but as this brave expedition sat at anchor in harbor, about to set forth, the old man tottered on board and performed a bit of a jig. And as the three ships set sail the true era of seeking a northerly passage began. It would become a long-term goal of several northern European nations, a bright and compelling dream—what might indeed be called one of European civilization's Ultima Thules.

THREE

Frizadores *for* Cathayo, *and the* Open Polar Sea

MAY 10, 1553, WAS A GRAND DAY for the Merchant Adventurers and for the ailing King Edward VI of England. For that day three ships, having been carefully prepared for their journey by shipwrights and victualers, and laden with cargo for trade, proceeded under tow down the Thames from the town of Radcliffe. Along the riverbanks people cheered, and when the little fleet reached Greenwich, where the king was waiting, cannons saluted the monarch and the people roared their approval. The Merchant Adventurers, a company formed "for the discoverie of Regions, Dominions, Islands and places unknowen," was led by Sebastian Cabot.

Thirty years earlier, returning to England from a few years in Spain after his alleged 1508 voyage, Sebastian had tried to seek financial backing for another voyage but ran into an obstacle erected by the British merchants. They wrote to King Henry VIII that it would be unwise to finance a trip to the New World "upon the singuler trust of one man, callyed as we understand, Sebastyn, whiche Sebastyn, as we here say, was never in that land hym self, all if he makes reporte of many thinges as he hath hard his Father and other men speke in tymes past."

It must be taken as a credit to Sebastian Cabot's persuasiveness that he had talked his way back into the graces of the London merchant circles, but he did by now know a thing or two about sea voyaging, however limited his own actual experience. It might have been his idea to sheath the three ships with lead against the burrowing worms that were said to infest the waters off Cathay. In any event, geographers (and no doubt Sebastian) had persuaded the merchants that the passage to Cathay could most easily be accomplished by sailing east through the wide swath of open sea along the Arctic coasts of Scandinavia, Russia, and beyond.

To lead the expedition, the Merchant Adventurers had selected a nonsailor as captain-general. This was Sir Hugh Willoughby, a "valiant" soldier who had seen duty in the Scottish border wars and was "well-borne" and tall of stature to boot. The three ships under his command were the *Bona Esperanza* (120 tons and the flagship), the *Bona Confidentia* (90 tons), and the *Edward Bonaventure* (160 tons). Progress north to the Norwegian coast was hampered by uncooperative winds, and when the little fleet reached the northern end of the Lofoten Islands at the end of July, they encountered a violent storm that separated Willoughby's *Esperanza* and the *Confidentia* from the other, larger ship, the *Edward*, which was under the command of a seasoned mariner, Richard Chancellor. Chancellor took himself to an island off the Danish coast, now called Vardo, which had been chosen as a rendezvous point against just such a contingency.

The other two ships, however, sailed aimlessly to the northeast and then the southeast; finally, on September 18, finding themselves utterly lost, they anchored in a harbor in the mouth of a river on what they took to be the mainland and was in fact Lapland. Around them, Sir Hugh noted in his journal, were riches of "seale fish & other great fishes . . . beares, greate deer, foxes . . . and such other which were to us unknowen and also wonderful." Sir Hugh, a landlubber, nevertheless made a wise nautical decision: Given the richness of the wildlife, the fact that his ships had been provisioned for six months, and the additional fact that the weather was turning "evile," he decided that the two ships and their crew of sixty-three, including himself, would overwinter in the river harbor. Sir Hugh ceased writing in his journal once a few parties had gone forth and found no inhabitants in the area; they evidently settled down to the nerve-racking and probably boring job of waiting out the winter.

By January the Arctic winter may have been getting to Sir Hugh, for he wrote a will in that month. The will was found by Russian fishermen the following summer, when they came upon the two ships and the corpses of all sixty-three men.

Meanwhile, Richard Chancellor, on the *Edward,* had waited at the rendezvous for seven days and then pressed on to the White Sea and Arkhangel'sk, trekking from there overland to Moscow and a cordial reception from Tsar Ivan IV (also known as Ivan the Terrible), who granted the Merchant Adventurers a license to trade with Russia via this northern route. A more conventional route at the time was through the Baltic Sea, which was firmly under the control of the Hanseatic League, a confederation of merchants from various German cities—what might perhaps be thought of loosely as the first multinational corporation. The League acted as intermediary between east and west and controlled such enterprises as the Russian fur trade. The opening in this closed system made by Chancellor in Moscow broke the Hanseatic League's hold, and the Merchant Adventurers were soon replaced by the Muscovy Company, with the aged but still hustling Sebastian Cabot in a leadership position until he died a few years later.

Meanwhile, it had become apparent that Willoughby and his crew had not died of starvation. The rescuers found plenty of food stores on board, and while most of the wildlife would have migrated south for the winter soon after the ships set anchor in the river harbor, foxes would have remained as a plentiful supply of live meat. It was long assumed that they had died either of the cold or from scurvy, a disease that was ubiquitous on sailing ships during extended trips where the food stores consisted conventionally of "fleshe, fishe, bisket, meat or bread . . . beere, wine, oyl or vineger." But a letter, uncovered long afterward, has shed a different light on these events. On November 4, 1555, Giovanni Michiel, the Venetian ambassador to London, wrote the doge of Venice:

> The vessels which departed some months ago, bound for Cathayo, either from inability or lack of daring, not hav-

ing got beyond Muscovy and Russia, whither the others went in like manner last year, have returned safe, bringing with them the two vessels of the first voyage, having found them on the Muscovite coast, with the men on board all frozen, and the mariners now returned from the second voyage narrate strange things about the mode in which they were frozen, having found some of them seated in the act of writing, pen still in hand, and the paper before them; others at table, platters in hand and spoon in mouth; others opening a locker, and others in various postures, like statues, as if they had been adjusted and placed in these attitudes. They say that some of the dogs on board the ships displayed the same phenomena. They found the effects and merchandise all intact in the hands of the natives, and brought them back thither with the vessels.

Looking at this account four hundred years later, a British medical historian, Eleanora C. Gordon, realized what had probably happened to Willoughby and his crew. The crew might well have run out of firewood, which would have been sparse at best on these shores. So they would have turned to burning sea coal and probably, in all innocence, sealed up the chimneys and portholes against the cold. Carbon monoxide, the silent, odorless, and tasteless gas that is produced by burning coal, would have killed them all virtually simultaneously, accounting for the bizarre sight that confronted the Russian fishermen who found them.

In 1556 the Muscovy Company sent another trading expedition off to the White Sea: two ships, the *Edward Bonaventure* and the *Philip and Mary* (named for England's king and queen), under the command of John Buckland. Among other tasks, they picked up Richard Chancellor at Arkhangel'sk and recovered the two ships in which Willoughby and his company of merchants and seamen had perished. But the return voyage turned into a catastrophe. The *Confidentia* was wrecked off the coast of Norway, the *Esperanza* was lost at sea, and the *Edward Bonaventure* was wrecked off the coast of Scotland in November, Richard

Chancellor dying in the wreck. The *Philip and Mary* alone made it back to London, (though not until the following spring) bringing with it Russia's first ambassador to the English court; in spite of the loss of the three other ships, the Muscovy Company sent trading vessels to the White Sea almost annually for several years, bringing about an attractive trade with Moscow and the Russians. One of the traders, a man named Jenkinson, retained an interest in the sea route to Cathay, stimulated by discussions with people from Siberia about tides and currents, and a story about a strange skull found on Novaya Zemlya that had only one horn. Unicorns were known to live in Cathay, so this one must have been brought to the archipelago north of European Russia by the currents of the sea.

The Northeast Passage still beckoned. Privateers (which is to say buccaneers licensed by the crown, now Elizabeth I) such as Francis Drake and Martin Frobisher were bringing back plentiful booty taken from the Spaniards and to a lesser extent from the Portuguese, who were deriving fabulous wealth from their control of the southern sea routes. So the merchants of the Muscovy Company launched another attempt in 1580. They were egged on, we can be fairly sure, by Gerardus Mercator, who had stated that "the voyage to Cathayo by the east is doubtless very easie and short, and I have oftentimes marveiled, that being so happily begun, it hath bene left of." It is not clear what happy beginnings Mercator referred to, but it certainly wasn't the first two expeditions of the Muscovy Company, which perhaps should have maintained its original and limited goal of Russian trade via the White Sea. But the company granted commissions to two experienced sea captains, Arthur Pet and Charles Jackman, both of Middlesex, "for a voyage to be made by them for the discoverie of Cathaye."

That the merchants had become cautious over the years is suggested by the fact that the two "good barkes," the *George* (40 tons) and the *William* (20 tons), had crews of ten and six, respectively. Pet, in command of the *George,* was also named admiral of this modest fleet, with Jackman as vice admiral. They set out in May 1580, each ship carrying a two-year supply of food and trade goods of such variety that it took two pages to list them. The cargo included frizadores (plush silk), motleys (cloths of many colors), "Jerzie yarne," hinges, "hullocke" (sailcloth), parchment, glue, soap, saffron, antimony, and the biggest map of England they could find. The admiral and vice admiral were enjoined also to push the sale of aqua vitae, which the English had found they could make very cheaply.

Taking advantage of favorable winds, the two ships set off on May 5, 1580, and soon lost sight of each other, coming back together at Willoughby's rendezvous point, the island of Vardo, in late June, with the *William* suffering from leaks and damaged steering. Unfavorable winds held them there until July. Thereafter they encountered ice, "a great fogge," and further miserable weather, while the *William* had to contend with a broken stern post, leaving the rudder hanging loose. In late August, sailing along the shoreline to avoid the ice, they ran aground on a hidden shoal, finally got off, and lost sight of each other, the people on the *George* never again laying eyes on the *William*. Admiral Pet labored on for a few more days, fighting ice and weather, but the ship was damaged and leaking and there was nothing to do but return to England, which he did through continuing foul and perilous weather. Pet learned later that the *William* had overwintered in Norway but was lost at sea the following year, trying to get home in the company of a Danish ship. The only notable accomplishment of the expedition was that they managed to pass south of Novaya Zemlya and become the first such voyagers to enter the Kara Sea. Given such a disappointing result, the merchants did nothing further about the Northeast Passage for almost another twenty years.

Meanwhile, however, Dutch merchants had the same hunger for trade with Russia via the White Sea–overland route as well as for a sea route to Cathay. In this regard, a group of Antwerp merchants came together to finance an experienced Dutch navigator, Willem Barents, then in his forties, to find the Northeast Passage. Barents made three journeys altogether, the first in 1594 with three ships, two of which went south around the Novaya Zemlya archipelago and into the Kara Sea while Barents himself went north around it. All three ships were forced to turn back by the ice in the Kara Sea. A year later, with seven ships, Barents again found the strait between Novaya Zemlya and the mainland full of ice, forcing his return. The voyages were not total failures, however, in that Barents was an indefatigable record keeper, and his charts and meteorological observations—helpful for long afterward—can be thought of as the beginnings of modern science in the Arctic.

Undaunted, and bankrolled yet again, Barents left Holland once more in May 1596 with two ships and headed straight north, eventually coming within sight of Spitzbergen (now called Svalbard). He left one ship in those waters to explore this new archipelago and was evidently forced east by what he could not have known at the time was the Arctic ice cap. At one point, on September 6, the crew encountered one of the unspeakable horrors that must have haunted the thoughts and dreams of most men arriving in the Arctic. Some of Barents' men were ashore when a "great leane white bear" stole out and grabbed one of the men by the neck. As another sailor nearby fled, the bear fell upon the hapless crew member and

> bit his head in sunder, and suckt out his blood, wherewith the rest of the men that were on land, being about 20 in number, ran presently thither, either to saue the man, or else to driue the beare from the dead body; and hauing charged their peeces and bent their pikes, set vpon her, that still was deuouring the man, but perceiuing them to come towards her, fiecely and cruelly ran at them, and get another of them out from the companie, which she tare in peeces, wherewith all the rest ran away.

Polar bears, also called ice bears and sea bears, spend as much time in the water as on land and are quite rightly known to scientists as *Ursus maritimus.* Weighing in at up to 2,000 pounds (which is larger than most horses) and rearing up to 12 feet on their hind legs, they are not the largest of bears; that honor falls to the Kodiak bear, which is half again as large, and to various extinct cave bears. But polar bears are probably the most dangerous to any hapless human. While they are capable of deftly plucking a shellfish loose from its bed with a claw, they can also, it is said, knock a small whale unconscious with a single swipe of a front paw. They have largely white coats, as do so many other Arctic mammals, such as the Arctic fox, hare, and others, and white fur on the bottom of their feet, which helps their feet to function variously as snowshoes or paddles. They can swim immense distances, their wool-like undercoat keeping them from getting wet to the skin, which in turn is underlain by a layer of blubber that is their main insulation against the cold. They surface almost silently. On land—or, more to the point, on ice floes, which they inhabit all summer, rarely coming to actual land—they can run in spurts at 25 miles an hour, plenty fast enough to intercept seals, which are the major portion of their diet. The bears are considered great wanderers, but recent research has shown that there are several more or less distinct populations, each with its preferred regions.

Females den in winter, usually well to the south of the ice floes, arranging the snow and ice cover with the same care, and along the same lines, as the Inuit arrange their iglus—to maximize the flow of fresh air while maintaining a constant temperature of about 32°F freezing. The cubs, usually two or three, are born deaf, blind, and helpless and rely on the mother's bodily warmth and her milk, which is as thick as cream, to survive their early weeks. Equally rich is the milk produced by many of the seal species that frequent the Arctic seas. While these include walruses and narwhals, those "sea unicorns" whose single horn is in fact a protruding tooth unique to the males, hooded seals may have the record for richness of mother's milk—and the shortest lactation period of any mammal. Hooded seals give birth to pups on the Arctic ice just as it is about to break up with the onset of spring— the time when the pack ice is at its weakest, meaning that predation from polar bears is least likely and the vulnerable pups have the greatest chance of survival. The pups weigh about 45 pounds at birth, and four days later they are weaned—now weighing 90 pounds.

This astounding rate of growth is possible because the hooded seal's milk is 60 percent fat (whipping cream is 40 percent fat), and the mother produces some 60,000 calories daily, enough to feed twenty-five humans.

None of this, of course, was known to the early European explorers, to whom the polar bear became a terrifying threat when out on the ice—and a possible source of food if one was lucky enough to get in a good shot or two before a nearby bear either attacked or vanished into the seemingly endless expanse of white.

Barents continued east past the northern tip of Novaya Zemlya until his ship was captured in the ice of the Kara Sea. Rather than hole up on the ship itself, the crew had the good sense to build shelters on the shore from driftwood and ship timbers, and there they waited. On November 4, almost three months after Barents' crew became trapped, the Sun disappeared from the sky and did not reappear until January 24: two and a half months in the dark. One of the ship's officers, Gerrit De Veer, kept a diary of this long, cold wait, and his entry for December 7 is a telling reminder of an earlier expedition:

> The 7 of December it was still foule weather, and we had a great storme with a northeast wind, which brought an extreame cold with it; at which time we knew not what to do, and while we sate consulting together what were beste for vs to do, one of our companions gave vs counseill to burne some of the sea-coles [soft coal] that we had brought out of the ship, which wuld cast a great heat and continue long; and so at evening we made a great fire thereof, which cast a great heat. At which time we were very careful to keepe it in, for that heat being so great a comfort vnto vs, we tooke care how to make it continue long; wherevpon wee agreed to stop vp all the doores and the chimney, thereby to keep in the heate, and so went into our cabans [cots] to sleepe well commforted with the heat, and so lay a great while talking together; but at last we were

taken with a great swounding and daseling in our heads, yet some more than other some, which we first perceived by a sick man and therefore the least able to beare it, and found ourseules to be very ill at ease, so that some of vs that were strongest start out of their cabans, and first opened the chimney and then the doores, but he that opened the doore fell down in a swound (with much groaning) vpon the snow; which I hearing, as lying in my caban next to the doore, start vp (and there saw him lying in a swoon), and casting vinegar in his face recoured him againe, and so he rose vp. And when the doores were open, we all recovered our healthes againe by reason of the cold aire; and so the cold which before had beene so great an enemy vnto vs, was then the only reliefe that we had, otherwise without doubt we had [all] died in a sodaine swound. After yt, the master, when we were come to our selues again, gave euery one of vs a little wine to comfort our hearts.

The shelter constructed by Willem Barents and crew in which they spent the winter of 1596–1597 (From De Veer 1609)

Thus they escaped being suffocated by carbon monoxide—the fate that almost surely met Willloughby and his crew.

Once the ice broke up in June, Barents' ship was far too damaged to be of use, so on June 13 the survivors embarked in two open boats, making a heroic passage home. But Barents himself was not long among them, dying about a week after they set out for home. The rest sailed north around the tip of Novaya Zemlya, down its northwest coast, and west along the Russian shore to Scandinavia, where on August 30 they were rescued by the second ship of the expedition, on its way home from Spitzbergen, where it had overwintered. Of the original seventeen crew members of the expedition, twelve made it back to Holland—the first time Europeans had overwintered in the Arctic. But there was nothing straightforward about the return trip. The men, without their trusted master navigator, encountered foul weather, dangerous ice, and terrible mists and fogs, and De Veer's journal provides a mournful insight into how difficult the effort was. At one point, laboring from morning into the afternoon to bring their frail craft out of harm's way, he wrote,

> [I]n al that time we rested not, which made vs extreame weary and wholly out of comfort, for that it troubled vs sore, and was much more fearfull vunto vs then at that time when Willem Barents dyed.

A few more attempts by Dutch and British would be made to find the Northeast Passage. Finally the British would hire Henry Hudson to have a look on their behalf. He would make two trips, in 1607 and 1608. In the first expedition he sought a passage via the North Pole and succeeded in mapping much of east Greenland as well as reaching a farthest north for that time of 80° 23' N. But, of course, he found no Northeast Passage. The second voyage took him to Novaya Zemlya, where ice prevented him from entering the Kara Sea. And thus would end any remaining enthusiasm among northern Europeans for slipping through a convenient waterway east to Cathay.

* * *

Both Barents and, later, Henry Hudson were tempted to sail straight north to the North Pole and thence to Cathay. If ever a siren dwelled in the Arctic Ocean, beckoning to intelligent and well-traveled navigators and intrepid explorers, it was the notion of an open Arctic sea. Mercator's map of the world, and most other such maps, clearly showed such a sea. But the thought was present in the European mind long before the maps.

As early as 1527 Richard Thorne, an English merchant living in Seville, took note of the great advantages accruing to the Portuguese, who were opening up an eastward route to the Spice Islands, and to the Spanish, who were opening a westward one in the wake of Magellan's circumglobal effort. Thorne set forth a proposal that the English explore a third route that would be much shorter and relatively safe. Of course, nothing was known in Europe about what lay north of the Arctic Circle, but Thorne probably had in mind some memory of the Greek notion of an ocean that encircled the world, leading him to assume that a polar sea connected the Atlantic with the ocean that Magellan had so recently crossed. Also, he may have been influenced by Spanish chartmakers of the time, who had the astonishing habit of not putting on their maps anything that they had not actually visited. Hence, Spanish maps of the Arctic were free of landforms.

Thorne was evidently well aware that, for all the ignorance that existed about the Arctic, it was generally considered an extremely dangerous place, and so he affirmed in his proposal that the polar seas were safe, because they had "in them a perpetuall cleerenessse of the day without any darknesse of the night: which thing is a great commoditie for the navigants to see at all times rounde them, as well the safegardes as daungers." Of course, in proposing this third route across the North Pole, Thorne was guilty of wishful thinking, arising from a nationalistic sense of commercial competitiveness, but he would not be the only one to be guilty of that. As late as the end of the nineteenth century, respected explorers, oceanographers, and other scientists would adduce a great variety of theories and guessed-at phenomena to assure themselves of the existence of the open polar sea—now more for glory than for commerce. Even the putative habits of whales and the instincts of migratory birds would be summoned up in its favor. And not even the discouraging results of Barents' and Hudson's early attempts—and the failures of others who came later—would diminish the passage's siren call in the following centuries, when it would inspire many seeking the Northwest Passage, and those who would seek the plum of being first to stand on the North Pole.

Indeed, the search for the Northwest Passage had been under way for more than twenty years before Barents' last voyage. A British expedition led to the first English attempt to start a colony in the New World—nine years before English colonists tried and failed to colonize North America at Roanoke, Virginia, twenty years before conquistadors established a permanent Spanish presence in New Mexico, and twenty-nine years before John Smith and company arrived at Jamestown. The result of a buccaneer's dream, it constituted the first gold rush in North America and wound up creating an embarrassing scandal in the commercial circles of Elizabeth's England.

FOUR

Fool's Gold, Hooch, *and* Mutiny

MARTIN FROBISHER, A CONTEMPORARY of Sir Francis Drake, was a stolid and occasionally short-tempered Welshman of great size and formidable strength. Evidently he was a man of few words, perhaps even a bit awkward in social situations. But Frobisher was the first Englishman to seek the Northwest Passage. During a career in the England's African trade (he was sent away from the Yorkshire home where he grew up, a problem child) and as a successful patriot sailor, or buccaneer à la Drake, he harbored a dream that he would find the northern route to Cathay that had to lie somewhere past Greenland. Finally, after fifteen years of effort, he persuaded one London merchant, Michael Lok, that such a voyage was "not onely possible by the north-west, but also, as he could prove, easie to be performed." (We are fortunate that for much of this period in his life Frobisher, who wrote little, was followed about by his own Boswell, a friend and shipmate, George Best, who chronicled Frobisher's thoughts and deeds.)

Lok managed to raise 875 pounds, enough for Frobisher to set sail on June 15, 1576, with two barks, the *Gabriel* and the *Michael* (25 and 20 tons, respectively), along with a pinnace (a smaller, unarmed ship of a mere 10 tons) and a total complement of thirty-two men. (By comparison, Columbus' *Santa Maria* was a ship of 100 tons, and the *Mayflower,* which would sail forty-five years later, was 180 tons. A bark is a ship with two main masts and a shorter foremast. A pinnace is a much smaller two- or three-masted light sailing craft.) As he sailed by the royal party standing onshore to see them off, Frobisher received a frail wave from Queen Elizabeth.

Off the coast of Greenland, which Frobisher assumed was the Zeno brothers' Frisland, a ferocious storm sank the pinnace and persuaded the officer of the *Michael* to turn tail and return to England. The *Gabriel* sailed on, arriving on July 28 in sight of a body of water that led northwest, between 62° and 63° N latitudes. Frobisher sailed into this presumed "strait," which he also assumed was the Northwest Passage, believing that he had North America to port and Asia to starboard. Emerging from the fog, he saw that the shoreline of the strait was barren and ice-bordered, an unpromising rocky land in a gray world. For days they explored what they called Frobisher's Strait, looking for signs of life, and on August 19 some of his men, poking about in a skiff, were approached by five Inuit in kayaks. This meeting led to another the following day, which saw the exchange of such things as bells and looking-glasses for sealskins. On August 21 five crew members rowed ashore for yet more trading and were never seen again. They had taken the only skiff, and the snow was beginning to fall. A search was impossible.

Frobisher, a decisive leader, prepared to leave, but then some kayaks approached through the

Martin Frobisher (Bodleian Library, Oxford)

falling snow. Dangling a trinket over the side, Frobisher tempted one Inuit to come close enough to snatch him (and his boat) out of the water by main strength and plop the no doubt terrified man on the deck. With that, they headed back to England, arriving with little to show but the Inuit (who died shortly afterward of a bad cold), some wildflowers, and a piece of black rock someone had thought to bring along.

According to George Best, the wife of one of the adventurers received a piece of the rock, "which by chance she threw and burned in the fires, so long, that at the length being taken forth and quenched in a little vinegre, it glistened with a bright Marquesset of golde." Whether that actually occurred, the merchant Lok was inspired to have the rock assayed. Three assayers said it showed no sign of "golde," but a fourth, an Italian alchemist

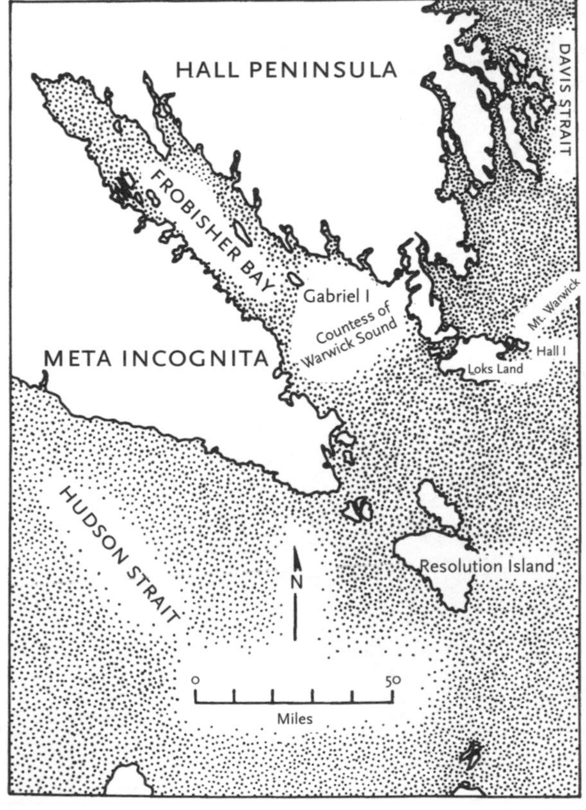

Frobisher Bay (From Kenyon 1975)

and assayer named Agnello, pronounced it to be gold-bearing, and that was enough for everyone concerned to forget about the Northwest Passage. Frobisher was quickly sent back for more gold, this time with actual financial participation by the queen. So delighted was Elizabeth, in fact, that she permitted him to kiss her hand before he left on May 15th of the following year (1577) with three ships, including a much larger one called the *Ayde,* 200 tons, to go along with the *Gabriel* and the *Michael* again, with sufficient stores for 143 men for six months. Their chief task was to bring back 200 tons of ore; only if time permitted could they go exploring for the route to Cathay.

By this time, late in the sixteenth century, England was excluded both from the southern routes to spices and other riches in the Far East and from any mineral wealth in the New World. But from the maps of the period, it appeared to English navigators that North America tapered to the north, just as South America tapered to the south, making a northern trade route possible; and of course if gold and silver were to be found in the southern Americas, why not in the north as well? Southern gold and silver, mined by enslaved Indians, had already begun to create an economic monster out of Spain—adding military strength to the Spaniards, which in turn added more control over the wealth of the New World, and so on in a threatening gyre. So Frobisher's (or at least Lok's) gold-rich ore became an understandably instant priority.

Even though Frobisher was a poor navigator and failed to "fix" his courses (with the result that it would take another couple of centuries for Englishmen to find their way back to Frobisher's Strait once he was finished there), he returned, reaching his destination in mid-July. Immediately a fracas blew up with some Inuits onshore, and Frobisher took an arrow in the buttock, fleeing, according to the chronicler Best, "rather speedily." Ten days later they found a small island, where they spent several weeks mining and loading ore, leaving the strait in late August with some 200 tons of ore and sailing into Bristol to a heroes' welcome. They brought with them three Inuit hostages, a man, woman, and child, all of whom thrilled the

English, the man performing feats in a kayak and with his hunting darts, but all three perished within two months of their arrival, the only sorry note amid a triumphant return. The investors immediately put up enough money for a third trip, consisting of fifteen ships and four hundred men, to leave the following May, charged with returning with 2,000 tons of ore, as well as leaving behind a hundred men in a permanent mining colony. So much, the English were telling themselves, for the vaunted hegemony of Spain.

And so, before the second expedition's ore had been any more than inconclusively assayed for its gold content, Frobisher set off again, this time with a gold chain placed around his neck by the queen and a grand flotilla under his command—in fact, the largest fleet to enter the Arctic until the Second World War, almost four hundred years later. The voyage soon proved treacherous, with Frobisher writing of "the yce comming on us so fast, we were in great danger, looking every houre for death." Soon thereafter they sailed into a dreadful mist, later "an horribile snowe." One ship collided with a whale, and they encountered a tempest and huge walls of ice, one of which sank the ship carrying a prefabricated house for the mining colony. The worst storm they had ever encountered left the fleet lost in Hudson Strait. Eventually they found their island, but it seemed too late to establish a colony without the prefab house, and the pilot of one ship instigated a mutiny on board and took his ship home. The remainder of the fleet left on September 1 with about 1,100 tons of black rock, lost some forty Cornish miners overboard in a terrible storm, and discovered that no one really cared about their return except for a few disgruntled investors, for by this time the company of venturers had learned that the black rock contained little or no gold. It was iron pyrite, or fool's gold. The company went bankrupt, and Michael Lok was left liable for the company's losses. He blamed Frobisher, who called his erstwhile backer a knave, and Lok went to jail personally bankrupt, leaving a wife and children languishing in poverty. Frobisher was reprimanded, went off to help put down a revolt in Ireland, then ably defended England against the Spanish Armada in 1588, for which he was knighted for his bravery. He died in 1594 battling the Spaniards on their own ground, laying siege to a fort.

What British explorers would find some three hundred years later was the remains of Frobisher's mining efforts on the small island, which lies within one of the large bays of southern Baffin Island, not a strait, and not the entrance of a northwest passage. It is now called Frobisher's Bay. He had not come anywhere near finding the passage, but he had helped keep the notion of it alive.

One breast alive with the dream of the passage was that of John Davis, a highly respected seaman and navigator who had been a childhood friend of Sir Walter Raleigh, and would later count among his acquaintances leading mathematicians and cartographers. Almost the opposite of Martin Frobisher, he was for the most part given to peaceful pursuits and nautical scholarship, producing a volume that would become the navigator's handbook for generations, inventing a standard device for measuring latitude, and writing a masterly summary of geographical knowledge of the world in 1595. From 1598 on, he

Canada's first mine. The great trench excavated for ore by Frobisher and his men (William W. Fitzhugh, Smithsonian Institution)

was in the service of the East India Company, discovering the Falkland Islands in the South Atlantic, charting the coast of Sumatra, and regrettably falling prey to Japanese pirates off Malaysia, dying at their hands two days after Christmas in 1605.

Before most of these deeds, however, Davis made the second notable English attempt to find the Northwest Passage, sailing first in a voyage financed by a consortium of merchants in 1585, six years after Frobisher's unpropitious final return from northern seas. In the poetically named *Sunneshine* (50 tons) and *Mooneshine* (35 tons, and which Davis oddly enough insisted on calling the *Moonelight* and which he outfitted with a four-piece orchestra), he reached Greenland and then the eastern coast of Baffin Island at 66° 40' N, before returning, convinced that the passage lay either west, up what is now called Cumberland Sound, or farther north. But before leaving, Davis' ships were spotted by a group of Inuits who, the English thought, howled like wolves. Davis had the orchestra strike up a tune and ordered his officers and seamen ashore to dance. The Inuits watched in fascination and offered the Englishmen pieces of their clothing. The next morning the Inuits were back, dancing to a drum.

The following year he returned with two additional ships and a pinnace. One ship and the pinnace were sent looking for the northward passage, but a massive buildup of sea ice sent them home. Another of the ships was lost in a storm, and yet another had to be sent home, as it was unwieldy in ice. All that was left was Davis' *Moonelight,* and she was halted by ice at 67° N and returned to England in October.

The following spring Davis set sail once again, with two ships and a pinnace. Encountering excellent conditions, he set the two ships to cod fishing to defray some of the expedition's costs and proceeded in the little pinnace along the west coast of Greenland to a farthest north of 72° 12' N before being turned back by the wind. Turning south down the Baffin Island coast, he charted numerous gulfs, inlets, and straits, including the entrance of the Hudson Strait (which he called the Furious Overfall, because of its fierce currents), and the shoreline of Labrador to boot. In all, it was a remarkable feat, sailing such a great distance through Arctic waters in what amounted to a sailboat, making the first effort at documenting ice conditions, weather, and terrain, and making sympathetic observations of the lives of the Inuit. In short, his was a scientific expedition as well as a voyage of exploration.

Ultimately unsuccessful in his quest, he remained convinced of the existence of the Northwest Passage, but his attentions, and those of England itself, were diverted from any further voyages seeking it by new troubles with Spain. But later, ten years after his last Arctic voyage, Davis wrote favorably of the nature of these northern lands and waters, saying that they were not at all uninhabitable: "I found the ayre very temperate, yea and many times calme wether marveilous hot; I have felt the Sunne beames of as forcible action in the frozen zone in calme neere unto the shore, as I have any time found within the burning zone."

He went on to praise the inhabitants as "people of good stature, shape and tractable conditions, with whom I have converced and not found them rudly barbarous, as I found the Caniballs which are in the straights of Magilane and Southerne parts of America."

While Davis' three voyages resulted in very little new country seen or new waters probed, it has been said that his efforts, particularly his assiduous charting, were what made it possible for the next two major seekers of the Northwest Passage to go as far as they did.

Henry Hudson, as we noted briefly before, made two voyages on behalf of English merchants seeking the Northeast Passage, both of which failed—and discouraged England from any further attempts to reach Cathay via the east. Hudson was a greatly respected navigator, and the English merchants concluded that if he couldn't accomplish such a voyage, probably no one could. Hudson came from a wealthy family (his grandfather was one of the founders of the Muscovy Company). He may have served in the battle with the Spanish Armada, and he may have sailed with John Davis on one of his voyages. In any event, by 1607 he was a captain, and in 1609 he was at sea again, this time for the Dutch East India Company, whose directors thought it worthwhile to make one more attempt at the Northeast Passage, especially since their rivals, the French, had begun talking to Hudson about mounting such an expedition on their behalf. The Dutch provided Hudson with a ship, *Halve Maen* (or *Half Moon*), an ungainly craft of some 80 tons that Hudson sought, unsuccessfully, to replace with one that was more seaworthy. Eventually, he sailed on the *Half Moon* with a crew of twenty men, half English and half Dutch, most of whom did not speak or understand the other language. Setting out in early April, they encountered headwinds, fog, and ice, and were unable even to reach the coast of Novaya Zemlya.

At this point there was a mutiny. It might have been led by a man named Robert Juet, a troublemaker whom Hudson had sailed with on an earlier expedition. (Hudson had a tragic and, it would turn out, fatal weakness. He was a very poor judge of character and was unable to control his men when an expedition was under stress—stress often caused by the men he misjudged.) Or the mutiny could have been caused by the Dutch sailors, who were unaccustomed to sailing in the cold. Hudson hauled out some maps of the New World that he had been sent by Captain John Smith of the Jamestown colony in Virginia and persuaded the crew that they should sail west to North America and a warmer climate.

By early July the *Half Moon* was off the coast of Newfoundland, having survived several violent storms, one of which swept the foremast into the sea. Hudson sailed as far south as Chesapeake Bay but did not visit John Smith. Instead he went north, looked in on Delaware Bay, and sailed into New York Harbor, claiming the area for Holland.

In the following days the *Half Moon* encountered some local Indians, who traded with the crew, but soon a few fracases broke out, in one of which a crew member was killed with an arrow through his throat. In response, the crew captured two Indians as hostages; one of them was later released, and the other escaped. Sailing up the river that would eventually be named for

Hudson, they encountered other Indians, these being friendly, and the crew got a couple of them drunk on wine and aqua vitae, which they took to calling "hooch," a term that apparently derived from the local Indians' word for hard liquor, *hoochenoo*. After sailing 150 miles upriver, reaching present-day Albany and shallow water, they headed south and were later attacked by about a hundred Indians in canoes. Hudson ordered that the guns be fired, and several Indians were killed. Once out of the river, Hudson left for England, arriving there in November.

After being forbidden by the English government to work again for a foreign government and being put under a modified house arrest, Hudson convinced several English merchants and the Prince of Wales to back yet another voyage, this one specifically to seek the Northwest Passage. Once again, and for unknown reasons, Hudson included Robert Juet in the crew, and this time he unwisely added a man named Henry Greene to the ship's complement. Greene had been a guest in Hudson's house and had a reputation as a gambler and troublemaker. When the *Discovery* was off Iceland, Greene got into a fistfight with the surgeon, Edward Wilson; Hudson intervened, defending Greene, while the crew supported the surgeon. Robert Juet then got into the act, saying that Greene had been hired to act as a spy on the crew. Hudson heard about this and decided to put Juet ashore but he was talked out of it and did nothing further about Juet's insubordination.

By August, after narrowly avoiding a mutiny, Hudson entered the Furious Overfall with its ferocious currents, and before long came to Hudson Bay, where he and Juet had yet another falling-out, with Hudson ordering a trial of Juet for mutiny. By way of punishment, Juet was demoted, and the *Discovery* sailed on. Warned of dangerous rocks near a shore, Hudson nevertheless ran the ship aground, losing face with the crew, and later, in the bleak subarctic waters of James Bay, they became iced in.

Tempers flared, and the crew began to suffer from scurvy. In mid-June the *Discovery* weighed anchor, and Hudson doled out the remaining stores of bread and cheese, only to be accused by the crew of hoarding. The ship got caught again in the ice, and somewhere in the middle of James Bay the men mutinied, led by Greene and Juet. Hudson was put on the ship's shallop (a small skifflike boat) along with several other men and his young son John. They were never seen again. Quite likely they died of exposure and starvation, but there is a tantalizing legend among the Inuit of the area that they once came across a small boat filled with dead white men and one live boy. Not knowing what to do with the boy, they chained him inside a house, where, presumably, he perished.

The mutineers hardly fared much better. Greene and several others were attacked and killed by what they thought were friendly Inuit; Juet later died of hunger after the crew had been reduced to eating bird bones fried in candle grease. Half dead, the remaining mutineers made it back to London in September, nearly a year and five months after they had set out. By the time they were tried, in 1618, several had already died, and the rest were let off mainly because the mutiny's instigators had all died on the way home. And, of course, they were helped by claiming to have found the Northwest Passage, making available Hudson's own chart that showed the east coast of Hudson's Bay. The London merchants were convinced and soon enough financed several more expeditions, one in 1612, by James Hall, who was killed by Greenland Inuit; another in 1613, by Thomas Button, who entered Hudson Bay, called it Button's Bay, and overwintered near Churchill; and a third in 1614, by William Gibbons, who spent the winter on the coast of Labrador. The latter two expeditions used Hudson's ship, the *Discovery,* and it was called into service yet again in 1615.

In a curious twist of irony, the 1615 expedition was captained by Robert Bylot, one of Hudson's mutineers, who had managed to pilot the *Discovery* back to England. His pilot for this voyage was William Baffin, one of England's most proficient navigators, self-taught in astronomy and mathematics, and already an accomplished Arctic hand. The expedition returned to Hudson Bay and circumnavigated it, and Baffin concluded that no passage existed out of the bay to the west. The following year Baffin sailed yet again on the *Discovery,* with Bylot in command, and explored 300 miles farther north than John Davis had, reaching 77° 45' N. No European would go farther north for another 236 years.

In his journal Baffin wrote of the Arctic summer: "It would be superfluous to write of the weather because it was so variable; there were few days without snow and was often freezing, insomuch that on Midsummer Day our shrouds, ropes and sails were so frozen that we could scarce handle them; yet the cold is not so extreme that it cannot be endured." Baffin clearly found the Arctic summer different from what John Davis experienced.

Baffin also charted the coast of Labrador and the shoreline of the bay that bears his name, including the entrance to Lancaster Sound, which Baffin did not realize was, in fact, the entrance to the Northwest Passage. Upon their return, Baffin's charts and his account were heavily censored, apparently because the merchant company sponsoring the voyage did not want any competitors to benefit from them. And it was a cruel fate that this last, highly successful exploratory trip by Baffin came to be thought of as too good to be true—in other words, a hoax—and Baffin Bay was removed from the maps of the time. It would not be found again until two centuries had passed and the European quest for the Northwest Passage resumed.

The attention of the English was beginning to turn to mining the unexpected riches of the Arctic. Henry Hudson had returned from his 1607 voyage with accounts of whales in the vicinity of Spitzbergen, and a major whaling industry sprang up almost immediately, in competition with the Dutch. Whales both live year round in Arctic waters and come there as summer visitors, feeding on upwelling blooms of plankton, with killer whales feasting on dolphins. Finback, humpback, blue, and sperm whales would form the basis of the Arctic whale fisheries of Europe and America.

Before too long the English were visiting Hudson Bay and inland in a grand geopolitical quest for riches of another sort—pelts. The Hudson Bay Company was founded some fifty years after Baffin's last Arctic voyage, and would for the next century play a major role in the competition among England, Holland, France, and Spain for hegemony in North America. The search for the Northwest Passage was largely abandoned.

By 1648, however, England was preoccupied by a different and far less happy circumstance than the fur trade. It was embroiled in the civil war that would, in due course, send the royal family out of the country and turn the nation over to the Cromwellian years of repressive Puritanism that would last till 1660.

Elsewhere in the year 1648, ninety Russian men set out in seven vessels from the Kolyma River with the intention of sailing east to find new territories and in particular to explore the country near the Anadyr' River, which was, Kolyma locals said, rich in furs. Most of the men on the voyage were hunters and traders, but a small group of representatives of the state went along, most notably a onetime Cossack named Semyon Ivanov Dezhnev. In the 1640s Dezhnev had served in Siberia and traveled widely in the north country.

Four of the seven vessels were wrecked along the Arctic coast, the crews either drowned or killed by natives. The other three passed around the eastern end of the Chukotka Peninsula, through the Bering Strait, and around the northeastern tip of Asia, reaching the Anadyr' River. By late September the three remaining ships were fighting the native people of the region, and in October a storm carried off two more vessels, which were never seen again, leaving only the ship with Dezhnev aboard. And that ship was wrecked south of the Anadyr', after which Dezhnev led the twenty-five survivors overland to the lower Anadyr', where they built the first Russian outpost on the river. Dezhnev apparently stayed in the area for another twelve years, eventually returning to Moscow, where he died. There were few records of the voyage. Dezhnev's own account languished unread in archives at Yakutsk until 1736, when it was uncovered by a German historian. But by then Vitus Bering had sailed through the strait that bears his name (and which is the western terminus of the Northwest Passage), not that of Dezhnev, who is its real, though forgotten, discoverer.

Vitus Bering was a Danish navigator who, after a voyage to the East Indies, was asked by Tsar Peter of Russia to join his naval service. Twenty years later, in 1725, in the waning years of his life, the tsar wrote to his admiral of the fleet:

> Bad health has obliged me to remain home. Recently I have been thinking over a matter which has been on my mind for many years but other affairs have prevented me from carrying it out. I have reference to the finding of a passage to China and India through the Arctic Sea. On the map before me is indicated such a passage bearing the name of Anian. There must be some reason for that. In my last travels I discussed the subject with learned men and they were of the opinion that such a passage could be found. Now that the country is in no danger from enemies we should strive to win for her glory along the lines of Arts and Sciences. In seeking such a passage who knows but perhaps we may be more successful than the Dutch and English.

This enlightened man, known to us as Peter the Great, would die before the expedition could get under way, but he had thought to select the leaders—Vitus Bering, along with Morten Spanberg and Alexey Chirikov as Bering's lieutenants. They were commissioned to find out if Asia and America were joined or separate and to map the northern shores of Siberia, as well as to look for the elusive Northeast Passage to China. It was an enormous effort, requiring five years in all, chiefly because they had to transport all of their supplies overland from St. Petersburg to Okhotsk, overwintering on the Yenisey River and at Yakutsk. It could be thought of as the Russian equivalent of the Lewis and Clark expedition through the Louisiana Purchase to the Pacific and back. The cold was, not surprisingly, vicious, and several men deserted, while two died along the way. When they finally reached Okhotsk in October 1727, local carpenters who had been previously commissioned there finished building a vessel, the *Fortuna*, which took them in two trips across the Okhotsk Sea. From there they passed the Kamchatka Peninsula.

The following August they came upon and named St. Lawrence Island and soon passed 65° 30' N, thus passing through the strait that would be named for Bering. But thanks to the continuous fog, they did not actually see the American shore and therefore lacked proof that Asia and America were separated. They spent the following winter on the Kamchatka Peninsula and returned to St. Petersburg overland from Okhotsk, arriving in March 1730. Bering was convinced he had passed through the strait, but others were not, and the matter required another trip. The next one would be more ambitious than the first, far more wide-ranging, with several parties and many more scientific activities to be undertaken. Collectively they were called the Russian Great Northern Expeditions.

In all, five parties were sent out simultaneously in 1733 to various parts of the Arctic, plus two others to regions of the Pacific. They were to map the Arctic and Pacific shores and to gather information on the flora, fauna, and geology of the region. Bering was in nominal command of all the parties, but practically speaking, he was in command of the Pacific section, in which Morten Spanberg was to survey the Kuril Islands south to Japan; Chirikov, with a French astronomer, Louis Delisle de la Croyére, was to head for the American mainland, and Bering, with a German naturalist, Georg Stellar, was to sail into

TABLE 2

RUSSIAN GREAT NORTHERN EXPEDITIONS, 1733 TO 1743

Region	Investigators	Dates
Arkhangel'sk to Ob River	Stepan Murav'yev and Mikhail Pavlov	1734–1736
Arkhangel'sk to Ob River	Stepan Murav'yev and Aleksey Skuratov	1736–1739
Ob River to Yenisey River	Dmitriy Ovtsyn	1734–1738
Yenisey River to Taymyr Peninsula	Fedor Minin and Dmitriy Sterlegov	1738–1741
Peninsula to Lena River	Vasiliy Pronchishchev and Semen Chelyuskin	1735–1737
Taymyr Peninsula to Lena River	Khariton Laptev	1739–1742
Lena River to Anadyr' River	Petr Lasinius and Vasiliy Rtishohev	1735–1736
Lena River to Anadyr' River	Dmitriy Laptev	1736–1743
Pacific Coast	Vitus Bering	1733–1743

(From Holland 1994)

the Bering Sea. All three succeeded, with Bering sailing along the Aleutian Islands chain as well and Stellar discovering the now extinct (and misspelled) Steller's Seacow, a seal-like creature that would soon be hunted out. The groundwork had been laid for a Russian presence on the northwest coast of North America, a presence that would eventually stretch as far south as Oregon.

But fate was not to be kind to the leaders of the Pacific section of the Russian Great Northern Expeditions. Bering, who with his crew was getting scurvy, was wrecked on an island off the coast of Kamchatka, and on December 8, 1741, he died there. In all, thirty members of his party died, the survivors building a boat and making their way back to Mother Russia.

The French astronomer, de la Croyére, died on board ship in 1741. Stellar was improperly arrested in Siberia on his way back to Moscow and died in prison. Chirikov contracted consumption in Siberia and died three years after returning to St. Petersburg. The exploratory phase of the expeditions was essentially over, but the scientific missions continued for several more years. Spanberg was ordered to stay on in Siberia to help manage these affairs, but he disobeyed and left in 1745. For this he was sentenced to death, but was later pardoned.

FIVE

Connubial Fidelity *and the* Vicar *of* Wakefield

EARLY IN THE NINETEENTH CENTURY the British navy did in truth rule the waves. In 1805 Nelson at Trafalgar defeated the combined navies of France and Spain. And once the British had laid siege to Baltimore and set fire to Washington in the War of 1812, there was little else for the navy to do. Most of the seamen were discharged, their numbers reduced from 140,000 to 19,000. Most officers were kept on, but nine out of ten had little or nothing to do and existed on half pay. At the time, the second secretary of the Admiralty, responsible for the navy's internal operations, was a man named John Barrow, who was also a founder of the Royal Geographic Society. Barrow was not a seaman, nor was he an explorer, but he had developed a geographer's zeal for the still mysterious Arctic and believed strongly that England should resume the Arctic explorations that had ended two centuries earlier with William Baffin's second voyage. The Northwest Passage remained to be discovered; the North Pole had never felt a human foot. And who better to undertake this work and achieve these goals than the world's greatest navy? New geographic and scientific knowledge, not to mention national prestige, would result.

Barrow was convinced, as many were, of the existence of an Open Polar Sea lying just beyond the pestiferous ice blockage at the Arctic Circle. He, like most others, also had a misconception about the northernmost part of North America. Essentially, it was thought that once you sailed past the first bend on the landform (which would soon be named Baffin Island), it would be clear sailing through to the Pacific. And so, with wondrous assurance, in April 1818 the British navy launched two expeditions, each with two ships. One expedition was under the command of David Buchan, with John Franklin as his second. Buchan's orders said:

> From the best information we have been able to obtain, it would appear that the sea northward of Spitzbergen [Svalbard], as far as 82-1/2, or 84, had been found generally free from ice, and not shut up by land. Should these accounts, in which several masters of whaling-vessels concur, turn out to be correct, there is reason to expect that the sea may continue open still more to the northward, and in this event you will steer north, and use your best endeavours to reach the North Pole.

Just what reports from whalers were being referred to in these orders is not known. In fact, the navy really did not have much interest in the reports of whalers and fishermen who almost certainly preceded the actual explorers to many parts of the Arctic, albeit anonymously. (Similarly, uncounted Vikings had no doubt preceded other Europeans into the far northern reaches as early as A.D. 1300, during a period called the Medieval Warm Period, an interval of warmth that was followed by what is known to us as the Little Ice Age, which in turn lasted into the nineteenth century.) One of the most widely traveled whalers—and one who was well known in his own time—was William Scoresby, who was publicly skeptical about the existence of an Open Polar Sea and had already made known his opinion that ice conditions in the Arctic varied so much from year to year that the Northwest Passage, if it existed, could have no real commercial value.

The other expedition was to be led by a seasoned captain, John Ross, with a bright young lieutenant, William Edward Parry, as second in command. These two ships were to sail across North America via the Northwest Passage. And in the Bering Strait, the two expeditions were to meet up with each other for a triumphant sail home, the Buchan and Franklin ships having crossed the top of the world. There were exceptionally precise orders to Buchan about fixing a rendezvous point in the Pacific with Ross, about the ordering of the chain of command once the ships met, and about various contingencies for ensuring that the "journals and despatches" of the expeditions be copied and returned safely to the Admiralty. For all the detailed managing, however, the navy largely ignored the early experiences in the record of such men as Davis, Hudson, and Baffin, and while the four ships were far superior to anything those men had sailed, the same cultural snobbery that made whalers and fishermen too low to consult made the Inuit too low, too barbaric, to emulate. And so, for example, the Royal Navy went forth in the wrong kind of clothes for the climate, evidently in the belief that they could bring their own climate with them. Inuit apparel, made exclusively from the skins and fur of local animals such as seal and polar bear, was worn fur side out in warmer climes and fur side in where it was colder. Such clothing worked for the Inuit in much the same way it did for the fur-bearers themselves, not only providing insulation from the extreme cold and the winds, but also tending to repel water and to dry out quickly when wet. The woolens of the English navy were less resistant to cold and wind, and once wet by a spill through the ice, they took far longer to dry out.

Buchan and company sailed north to Spitsbergen, where they ran into gales and pack ice. Putting into Fair Haven, an erstwhile whaling port, for refuge and to make repairs, they then sailed home, arriving in England on October 22, almost exactly six months after they left. Theirs was the first—and last—attempt by the Royal Navy to sail a vessel across the North Pole.

Ross and Parry sailed up through the Davis Strait, accompanied by some forty whaling ships, entered Melville Bay, and got as far north as Smith Sound. Cruising along the west coast of Greenland, they "rediscovered" Baffin Bay, and along the way encountered a group of Inuit. The meeting, captured in a drawing by John Sacheuse, was remarkable for the incongruity of the two cultures. Sacheuse was a Greenland native who had been educated in England and had come along as interpreter. In his drawing, the two English officers are shown in full dress attire, the naval equivalent of top hat and tails. A seaman, on the ship, is freezing in standard navy clothing, while the Inuit are dressed in furs of various kinds. At one point the Inuit turned to look at Ross' ship and said, "Who are you? What are you? Where do you come from? Is it from the sun or the moon?"

Ross and Parry proceeded to Lancaster Sound, between Devon and Baffin Islands, and sailed into it for fifty miles. Seeing what appeared to be a range of mountains stretching across the water, Ross assumed that the sound was in fact a bay with no way through it, so he had the expedition turn back to England even though it had been provisioned to stay in the Arctic for two years. They arrived in England in November, about three weeks after Buchan and Franklin's return. The young lieutenant, Parry, had not seen the mountains Ross saw, nor had anyone else aboard, and Parry was convinced they did not exist but had been a mirage of some sort visible only to Ross. The refractive properties of the northern seas, explorers would

Meeting of John Ross and William Edward Parry with Greenland Eskimos (Toronto Reference Library, Toronto)

eventually learn, often created wonderful optical illusions: Mountains would appear and disappear, the sun and its surrounding corona would suddenly become two suns and two coronas, and a greatly enlarged moon might become some other shape altogether.

Parry firmly believed that Lancaster Sound was the place to search for the Northwest Passage. He let this be known at the Admiralty, and the cautious Ross was soon retired at half pay, never receiving another naval command. The bold and intrepid Parry was promoted to be the leader of the next three of the navy's Arctic expeditions.

Boldness is often an advantage for an explorer, but there is also no substitute for good luck. When Parry set out in 1819, the Arctic was enjoying a particularly mild winter and the channels were clearer of ice than they had been for a decade. He made Lancaster Sound easily, arriving a month earlier than the previous year, and found it free of ice . . . until he reached its west-

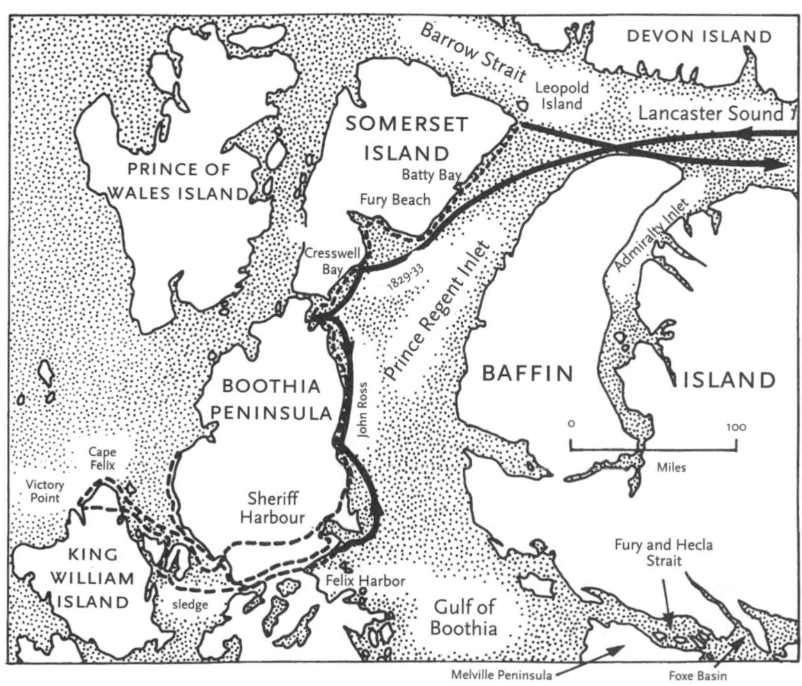

Geography of region investigated by John Ross and by William Edward Parry (From Berton 1988)

ern end. He detoured into Prince Regent Inlet and eventually made his way to the southern shore of Melville Island, where he overwintered as prescribed, in the gathering pack ice.

In addition to intrepidity and good luck, planning is also key. Parry set out with two ships, the *Hecla,* 375 tons, and the *Griper,* 180 tons. In all, the two ships carried ninety-four men. This was to be the first deliberate overwintering on board ship in the Arctic. In addition to scurvy (less of a threat now, since they knew to dole out daily rations of lemon juice), starvation, and exposure, a major danger for an overwintering crew was utter, mind-numbing boredom. It is not easy to imagine a group of men, presumably most of them not particularly well educated, having to spend some ten months stuck in the ice and cold and, for the most part, in the dark, where the passage of hours had virtually no meaning and there was nothing about but a vast, empty land—a bleak landscape of rock and ice, black, white, and gray, silent except for when the wind howled or, in the spring, when thousands of maniacally screaming seabirds would nest in the rocks that reached precipitously upward maybe five hundred feet. Tempers would flare, squabbles and fights would break out, and some men would simply drink themselves into total oblivion, or go mad.

To head off boredom and its attendant woes, Parry had the deck of the *Hecla* covered with a huge tentlike arrangement, providing a space out of the wind in which the men could exercise daily, which Parry made a requirement. He often entertained the men at night by playing his violin, and he arranged for theatrical performances once a week on the quarterdeck. *Miss in Her Teens, or The Medley of Lovers*, a farce, was the most popular of these. The crew could also anticipate the publication once a week for twenty-two straight weeks of a newspaper, *The North Georgia Gazette and Winter Chronicle*, which contained essays, poems, articles, and whatever might have passed for news. Providing this sort of entertainment worked, and the approach was emulated by later British expeditions, which would be relatively free of mutinous behavior or strife.

The polar gloom was implacable however, and men would

take walks in the silence, "the deathlike stillness," Parry later wrote, "of the most dreary isolation, and the total absence of animated existence." Only wolves and foxes made an occasional ghostly appearance in the murky landscape.

While the ships were trapped in the ice, Parry decided to trek across Melville Island and map its geography and topography. He took a party of twelve men, pulling a cart with some 800 pounds of equipment, even though he was well aware of the Inuit practice of using dogs to pull sledges. The cart was another Parry innovation but also an example of English patrician disdain rather than good planning.

As a nineteenth century chronicler wrote about Parry's expedition:

> The strong, flat-bottomed boats . . . had thus to be laden and unladen, in order to be raised over the hammocks. . . . Frequently the crew had to go on hands and knees to secure a footing. Heavy showers of rain often rendered the surface of the ice a mass of slush, and in some places the ice took the form of sharp-pointed crystals which cut the boots like penknives. But in spite of all these obstacles, they toiled cheerfully on, until at length, after thirty-five days of incessant drudgery, the discovery was made that, while they were apparently advancing toward the pole, the ice-field on which they were travelling was drifting to the south, and thus rendering all their exertions fruitless.

Once out of the ice—which took until August—Parry attempted to sail westward again through Lancaster Sound but got no farther than the previous year, so he returned home. On this one voyage he had passed the meridian of 110° W and discovered (and named) more new Arctic features than anyone before him—and more than anyone else would in a single voyage for another eighty years. The expedition, in particular the ships' surgeons, had gathered a good deal of information about the local fauna, dissecting and describing such exotic creatures as polar bears and walruses, and making some fairly good guesses about the migratory patterns of caribou and many bird species. Parry returned to London a hero, and the king gave him a reward of £5,000 for partial discovery of a northwest passage, as did Parliament. In addition, he received a lucrative contract for the publication of his journal, setting a trend that would continue in the world of adventuring and exploring to this very day.

Parry's book, *Journal of a Voyage for the Discovery of the North-West Passage from the Atlantic to the Pacific,* appeared in 1821, and April of that same year saw him back on the way north on the *Fury* and the *Hecla,* with George Lyon the captain of the second ship and the object of the three-year voyage being to penetrate the southern end of Prince Regent Inlet, thought at the time to be the gateway to the Northwest Passage. They found the outlet and named it the Fury and Hecla Strait, but they were unable to pass through it in either 1822 or 1823. In 1822 Parry purchased from the local Inuits a dog sled and some dogs as well as Inuit clothing for a short overland excursion. This was the first known instance of Europeans making use of native survival technology in the Arctic, though it would not catch on and be used as a matter of course until much later.

A symbiotic relationship with the dog was one of the Inuit's most important adaptions to the cold world they inhabited, along with a physiology and metabolism that permitted a more suitable circulation of blood, and the kayak, a fragile but seaworthy craft they made from driftwood and bone covered with skins. They used dogs, of course, to pull the sleds they built, also from driftwood and bone, and in this winter chore the dogs were usually assisted by both men and women. Not every Inuit had sufficient dogs to pull a sled—it took a minimum of five or six. But dogs could carry packs made of caribou skin and loaded with 25 to 30 pounds, and were frequently used this way as well. A hunter in pursuit of polar bear or caribou would typically be assisted by one or more dogs, and together they needed to be efficient, for besides feeding his family, a hunter needed to feed his dogs as well, and an adult dog would eat more than 850 pounds of meat and blubber annually. A good hunter looked after his dogs with great care—even to the point of making boots for them to protect their paws from sharp ice crystals—but the Inuit dogs were not all that different from the wolves they were descended from. A family typically kept its dogs tied up, one of the reasons being to keep their small children safe from attack. And their ultimate value lay in those all too frequent moments when starvation was stalking; one's dogs were the penultimate defense against that particular form of death, and were eaten without much in the way of sentimental turmoil on the part of their owners.

The central role of the dog in Arctic travel and survival could not have long been lost on European explorers, but it was not until Parry bought his first ones for a relatively short excursion that any European though to emulate the Inuit in this. Many others who came later would, for obscure reasons, eschew their use as well—almost always with ill effects.

The *Fury* and the *Hecla* overwintered twice on this voyage on the western shore of Foxe Basin, farther south than Melville Island, so there was more sunlight and, for some at least, a different kind of entertainment, provided by the Inuit people there.

Parry would later write (with classic nineteenth-century hypocrisy):

> I fear we cannot give a very favourable account of the chastity of the women, nor of the delicacy of their husbands in this respect . . . it was not uncommon for them to offer their wives as freely for sale as a knife or a jacket. Some of the young men informed us that when two of them were absent together on a sealing excursion, they often exchanged wives for a time, as a matter of friendly convenience; . . . the behaviour of most of the women, when their husbands were absent from the huts, plainly evinced their indifference towards them, and their utter disregard of connubial fidelity. The departure of the men was usually the signal for throwing aside restraint, which was invariably resumed on their return. For this event they

take care to be prepared by the report of the children, one of whom is usually posted on the outside for the purpose of giving due notice.

George Lyon, the second in command, also harrumphed in print about Inuit morals, writing that it "is considered extremely friendly for two men to exchange wives for a day or two, and the request is sometimes made by the women themselves. These extraordinary civilities, although known, are never talked of, and are contrived as secretly as possible. . . . Divorced women and widows, and even young and well-looking girls, are equally liberal of their persons."

A later explorer, Charles Francis Hall, would have a conversation with an elderly Inuit woman from this region named Erktua who claimed to have been the lover of first Parry and then Lyon, and said that Lyon additionally had left two Eskimo sisters pregnant. It is well established now that the later Arctic explorers, Peary and Stefansson among them, also left descendants in their wake.

Parry made another Arctic probe on the same two ships and with much the same commission: to pass through the strait he had named for the *Fury* and the *Hecla*. But they were beset by ice immediately on entering Lancaster Sound and obliged to spend ten months on the northwestern shore of Baffin Island—a barren, desolate, and deserted region and one without the comfort provided by friendly Inuit. Freed from the ice near the end of July, Parry was proceeding down the eastern shore of Somerset Island when he ran into a gale that drove the *Fury* ashore at a place still known as Fury Beach, where she was abandoned, lying heeled over in the ice under an enormously high rocky cliff. Stuck again for the winter, Parry kept the men busy with music, performances, scientific observations, and school classes. Thus they avoided ennui and the fact that all around was "dreary monotonous whiteness. Not merely for days or weeks, but for more than a half a year altogether. Which-ever way the eye is turned, it meets . . . inanimate stillness . . . a deadness with which a human spectator *appears out of keeping*." Indeed, Parry was often preoccupied with the "dreary solitude of this wintry desert."

The high cliffs kept the sun from melting the pack ice until later than usual. Early in July 1825 Parry ordered the men to saw a passage through the pack ice, and the expedition returned to England with both crews on the one ship, the *Hecla*.

Still the hero, Parry gave up on the Northwest Passage but made one final probe in 1827, this time going due north of Svalbard in an attempt to reach the North Pole across what he understood was a good deal of pack ice. Ever the innovator, he had two sledge-boats built that could be either hauled overland or launched in the sea. As with the cart he had used before, he hitched the sledge-boats up to twelve men each, but they encountered none of the hoped-for smooth ice. Instead, they ran up against the high walls of pressure ridges as well as ice hummocks—the rugged frozen terrain that would frustrate Arctic explorers until well into the twentieth century. Parry's progress was excruciatingly slow, and after more than a month on the ice, he perceived that the southward drift of the ice was nearly offsetting whatever northward progress he was making. He reached as far as 82° 45' N, a record that would last another fifty years, and spent more overall time on the ice—sixty-one days—than anyone else to date. He returned, still not quite forty years old, with four Arctic expeditions under his belt, one of the most proficient (and engaging) of the men who led people north to the Ultima Thule.

There were rumors at the time, and since, that Parry's voyages were not all harmonious. The ship's surgeon, for example, pointed out darkly that after Parry's second voyage he refused to take the same officers along from one trip to the next (except for a lieutenant named James Clark Ross, who was the nephew of the disgraced John Ross). There may also have been jealousies based on class between the several officers of Parry's ship and the others. And the old Inuit woman Erktua reported that when she switched her attentions from Parry to Lyon, Parry was irate and wildly jealous. But of course the Admiralty, to which all the records of these voyages were given, was tight-lipped about such matters, and one can imagine they saw to it that any memoirs of the trips were not an embarrassment to His Majesty's Royal Navy.

But after Parry's fourth effort, the attempt on the Pole, the navy lost interest in Arctic exploration for a while, and the initiative fell once again to private hands. John Ross persuaded a Londoner named Felix Booth to finance an expedition that would follow up on Parry's third voyage, finding the passage through Prince Regent Inlet to the coast of North America and thence to the Pacific. Felix Booth was a philanthropist whose fortune presumably arose from both of his professions—he was at once the Sheriff of London and one of the nation's major distillers, producing Booth's gin, still a favorite—and he wanted his name affixed to some Arctic features. Ross would reward him handsomely, putting Booth's name on the longest peninsula in the Canadian Arctic and its biggest gulf, along with attaching his Christian name to a harbor and his office of sheriff to another. This aggrandizement of expedition benefactors was done both before and after Booth, but never with greater flair than by the American explorer Robert Peary in the late nineteenth and early twentieth century (though a later commentator on the Arctic, the writer and fabulist Farley Mowat, found the practice reprehensible).

John Ross appointed his nephew, James Clark Ross, as second in command, and in May 1829 they sailed from London on the *Victory*, a ship of only 165 tons, and with a total complement of only twenty-three men—as opposed to Parry's third expedition, on two 375-ton ships with 128 men. The streamlining would prove fortuitous. The *Victory* bore the first steam engine to be used on a polar expedition (which proved a bit troublesome, as such new inventions often do, and was later beached) and the hopes of John Ross for the rehabilitation of his reputation. They reached Baffin Bay without much incident, entering the Lancaster Strait on August 6 and Prince Regent Inlet five days later. While there they visited the site of the wrecked *Fury* and its stores at Fury Beach and entered a gulf that Ross dutifully named Boothia, in the process sailing past a strait that was, in fact, the outlet from Prince Rupert Inlet to the Northwest Passage. This strait would later be found and named Bellot Strait.

With winter closing in, they put in at a place Ross named Felix Harbor, on the southeast shore of Boothia Peninsula. There Ross scuttled the steam engine, by then a useless "encumbrance." Ross and his nephew spent most of the next two years on land, venturing several times onto the peninsula. The next summer (1830) the ice pack allowed them to sail but a few miles from Felix Harbor to another, which they named Sheriff Harbor, and they again made exploratory trips across Boothia Peninsula when the weather allowed. Nephew James discovered King William Island (which he thought was part of the mainland) and—on June 1, 1831, at 8:00 A.M.—became the first European to stand on the north magnetic pole, which was then on the west coast of Boothia Peninsula. There, in what was otherwise a trackless frozen waste, he erected the British flag and claimed the surround in the name of Great Britain. (A hundred and fifty years later this pole was in western Greenland; it is constantly on the move and can thus be regularly "rediscovered.")

In the winter of 1832 Ross decided to abandon the *Victory* to the ice and trekked to Fury Point, where he and the crew spent the next winter in a rude shelter, surviving on the provisions that had been left behind by the *Fury* expedition under Parry. The next summer, in 1833, they sailed and rowed the small boats of the *Fury* out into Lancaster Sound and Baffin Bay, where they had the astonishingly good fortune to encounter a homeward-bound British whaler, *Isobella,* which took them back to England. Perhaps even more astonishing, *Isobella* was coincidentally the same ship that John Ross had captained on his first (and disastrous) expedition to the Arctic.

This expedition was the longest in duration of any known Arctic expedition before or since—four years from 1829 to 1833, with four overwinterings. It returned with twenty of the original twenty-three men, a considerable accomplishment that was owing to several factors. Their first three winters had been in Inuit country, and the natives supplied them with furs to replace their navy-issue wool clothing. The Inuit also provided them with fresh meat, particularly seal blubber, which we now know is rich in vitamin C, making it an excellent scurvy preventative. Without the Inuit, the explorers would almost surely have perished. Also, they were a small party with the flexibility to move in a coordinated manner as they trekked from the *Victory* to Fury Beach. And finally, they were just plain lucky to have a cache of boats and provisions available to them for the eventual escape. (It would be decades before Europeans had a true picture of the nature of the Arctic environment. In such a place, relatively few species of creatures exist—be they oceanic plankton, plants, or animals—although populations are typically large. But the individuals tend to be spread out far and wide or else are found in dense congregations that are either migrating or in the few areas that will support them at the right time of year. Similarly, Inuit bands were relatively small and typically moved far and wide. A single band of Inuit hunters might comprise about fifty men, women, and children, annually patrolling an area of some 30,000 square miles.)

Though the Northwest Passage still remained unnavigated, John Ross returned after four years in so challenging a region as a hero, his honor restored, and was knighted. More than a decade later, another Sir John went in search of a bracing victory over the Arctic to restore *his* honor. This was Sir John Franklin, who had sailed as second to Buchan in the quest for a straight shot at the North Pole. Before that, this career navy man had served at Trafalgar and other important moments in the British conquest of European navies. And subsequent to the failed attempt to sail across the Open Polar Sea to the pole, Franklin would soon lead two more Arctic expeditions for the English Admiralty—strangely enough, on foot.

Franklin's new expedition began in 1819 and lasted three years—years of frustration and ultimately catastrophe for a naval leader unaccustomed to the lubberly world of land exploration. Sir John had not hiked, canoed, or hunted anywhere in the Arctic, but he was assigned the task of traveling north from Great Slave Lake in northern Canada to the coast of Victoria

Island, in order to map the coast west to Alaska. This land was still plied by French-Canadian voyageurs and other north-country habitués in search of furs on behalf of major entrepreneurs such as the Hudson Bay Company and the North West Company. Why the Admiralty would have engaged in such a mission and, even stranger, would send someone without a landsman's experience is not at all clear.

The expedition made about 150 miles and then was forced to return, for they were near starvation and unable to kill sufficient game such as musk oxen for food. (The Inuit way of hunting herds of musk oxen was to chase them up to high ground, where the animals would form a protective circle. The hunters' dogs would hold the animals at bay while their masters picked the musk oxen off with arrows.) As Franklin's expedition trekked back toward Great Slave Lake, they were reduced to eating old shoes and other scraps of leather. Finally they were obliged to break up into three parties, one of which consisted of those men too weak to go any farther. Franklin's closest associate on the expedition, Dr. John Richardson, agreed to stay behind with these men. The second group of four men couldn't go much farther, and all but one of the four perished, the survivor—a French-Canadian voyageur named Michel Teroahaute—returning to Richardson's camp. (The third group, with Franklin, made it back to the lake).

Two days after reaching Richardson's camp, Teroahaute went hunting, returning with some fresh wolf meat, a reprieve against the killing hunger. All hands welcomed the meat, but it had a strange taste, and Richardson began to wonder if it was indeed the meat of a wolf, as Teroahaute said, or that of a missing crew member. A few days later, while Richardson and a colleague were out gathering lichens to eat, they heard a shot from back in camp. They returned to find Teroahaute standing and the only other man of that group who had survived up until then dead with a bullet hole in his forehead. Teroahaute said it was a suicide, but Richardson concluded that instead Teroahaute had executed him . . . for the sustenance of the survivors. Richardson reasoned that he himself might be next and took preemptive action, shooting Teroahaute. The party, now considerably reduced in number, was eventually rescued, but Richardson was never brought to trial for killing Teroahaute.

Eleven of the nineteen men who had set out with Franklin in 1819 returned alive—not a good record but evidently not enough to stigmatize Franklin as an inadequate overland Arctic leader. He was sent out again in 1825, again accompanied by Richardson. They and the rest of the expedition traveled by boat down the Mackenzie River from Great Slave Lake to the Arctic Ocean and then split up. Franklin headed west and mapped the Canadian and Alaskan shore for 500 miles; Richardson went east the same distance. Both parties fared well—for such expeditions—and returned back along the Mackenzie River. At one point, Franklin would later write, with starvation stalking his party, they encountered a herd of musk oxen. They sent out the best hunters, who took two hours to get within gunshot range of these unpredictable beasts. Their very lives depended on killing one of them. "In the meantime we beheld their proceedings with extreme anxiety, and many secret prayers were, doubtless, offered up for their success." The hunters opened fire; one cow fell and was promptly butchered. "The contents of its stomach were devoured upon the spot, and the raw intestines, which were next attacked, were pronounced by the most delicate amongst us to be excellent."

It was clearly a more seasoned John Franklin who embarked on this second overland expedition. Upon returning to England two years later in 1827, he was knighted—at the same time Edward Parry was knighted for his maritime explorations of the Arctic.

Now in his fifties and a widower, Sir John married a beautiful and intellectual London woman, Jane Griffin, just as his career was heading into eclipse. The Admiralty was reluctant to find a commission for him, finally offering him a year on a frigate in the Mediterranean. Nothing followed for a year after that, but then they offered him the governorship of Antigua, which he, and particularly his wife, found insulting. Soon the Admiralty offered him the governorship of Van Diemen's Land (Tasmania), which was bigger than Antigua, more populous and white, even if the population was mostly members of a penal colony. When young Lady Jane agreed that this was acceptable, Sir John took the position and for six years proceeded to make a hash of things. He was unable to deal with the politics of the place, which were too subtle for a forthright military officer, a man of action, and his wife did not help, being considered by most on the island an insufferable busybody in a day when women were supposed to be ladylike, quiet, and submissive. Eventually Sir John resigned amid a flurry of complaints, complaining himself that he was cut out only for a naval commission, and went home to seek one.

Then in 1843, out of the blue, the Admiralty again took up the notion of navigating the Northwest Passage. The way west halfway through it was well known by now, and the way north and east from the Bering Strait well along the coast of North America was also well known. Thus it was thought that this expedition, which would actually navigate the passage, could be little more than routine. At the time John Barrow, second secretary of the Admiralty and long the spark plug behind the navy's attempts in the Arctic, was eighty-two and near retirement. It would be a crowning achievement for the old man. A list of possible leaders was drawn up and, with a good deal of lobbying (no doubt urged on by Lady Jane), Sir John got his name on the list, albeit last. First, of course, was James Clark Ross, who, after probing about in the Arctic with the best of them, had also spent many successful years exploring the Antarctic, but he asked not to be considered. Others on the list were eliminated—either they did not want the assignment or they were thrown off for political reasons of one sort or another, mostly internal Admiralty politics. The process of elimination finally left Sir John Franklin, now fifty-nine years old, as the leading candidate.

Evidently Lord Haddington, First Lord of the Admiralty, objected to Franklin on the grounds of his age, but Franklin persuaded him that with age came wisdom, calm, and a bellyful of useful experience. And so, on May 19, 1845, Franklin left England in command of a two-ship expedition—the *Erebus* and the *Terror*, manned by 128 men. The orders were utterly straightforward, and the ships were almost overcautiously provisioned for a stay of three years in the Arctic. The stores for the two ships included some 2,900 books, plenty of scientific instruments, and hand organs for musical performances. The crews would not be bored in the long Arctic winters.

In July two whalers noted the expedition was in Baffin Bay, hooked up to an iceberg, waiting for the wind to take them north. Later it would be pieced together that the two ships entered Lancaster Sound, circumnavigated Cornwallis Island, and wintered at Beechey Island, off the southwest coast of Devon Island. The next summer they sailed south between Somerset and Prince of Wales Islands and were soon beset by ice off the northwest coast of King William Island. There they remained for the long winter of 1846–1847. When summer came, they were still unable to get free of the ice, and Franklin and several others died, evidently of scurvy. The remaining men overwintered yet again—their third winter—but by April the two ships had been crushed in the ice. The 105 surviving members of the expedition could do nothing but set out on foot with sledges, carrying whatever might be useful for a long trek south across the icebound sea and land.

They were never heard from again. The wrecked ships were never found. The expedition disappeared into the fog and mist, with no trace of it being found for several years, and then only accidentally.

Meanwhile, having heard nothing of the expedition by early 1847, Lady Jane grew fretful and asked the Admiralty about it. She was told not to worry and reminded that the ships were, after all, provisioned for three years. But by the end of 1847 the Admiralty was itself alarmed and sent out two ships, which promptly were caught in the ice and had to overwinter, returning with no word of Franklin's ships or men. Two more ships were sent the following year, with the same results. In all, some forty expeditions—mostly by sea, though two went overland, and mostly sponsored by the British navy—would go forth in the years following, all to no avail. Some of the search missions flew kites and balloons; others fired

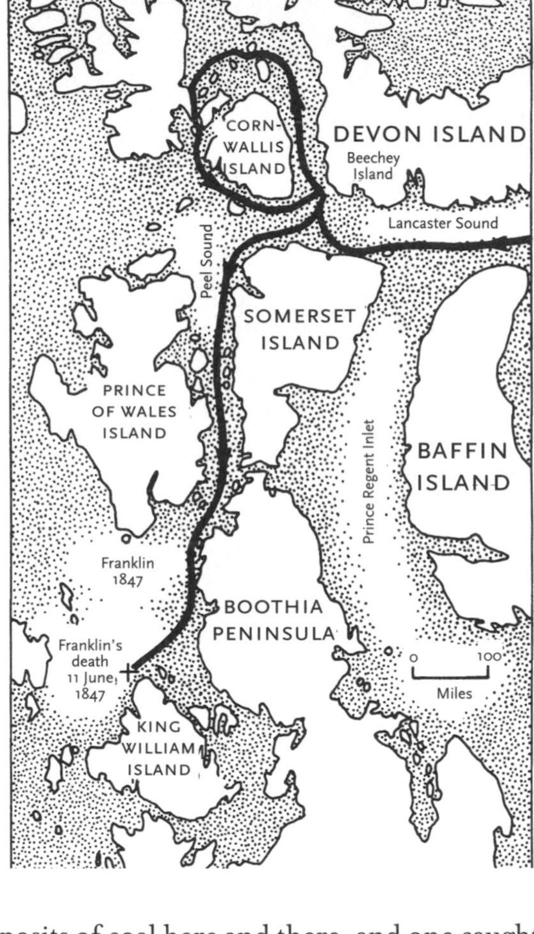

Franklin's last expedition, 1845–1847 (From Berton 1988)

rockets. Some left deposits of coal here and there, and one caught foxes and tagged them with directions to the coal deposits. Most of these expeditions were doomed to fail before they set forth, since the Admiralty focused virtually all the search parties west and south of Lancaster Sound, near Banks and Melville Islands, where in fact nothing was to be found. Also, Franklin's ships had sunk, leaving nothing above the water and ice.

For various reasons, Franklin's disappearance in the ice and cold captured the imagination of the English—and the Americans—as no one else who had ever been lost in the Arctic had. British pride was at stake, of course. This was an era of fervent belief in the excellence and power of scientific progress (of which exploration was an important part), and the loss of the Franklin expedition was akin to the twentieth-century losses of the *Titanic* or the space shuttle *Challenger*. The American interest was almost entirely the result of the continuing efforts of Lady Jane, who came to the United States early on. She had an audience with President Zachary Taylor, who promised that all of America would pray for her husband's safe return—which, of course, Lady Jane found a useless and contemptible response, and she demanded more of the president, who managed to get her out of the office, later referring to her as an insufferable bore. She went on a lecture tour and managed to persuade Henry Grinnell, a shipping tycoon, to put up $30,000 to buy two ships, which were put at the disposal of the U.S. government, which in turn was shamed into manning them and sending them off—without success. In all, this was the greatest search for missing men ever mounted before or since, and while all the voyages failed to find a trace of Franklin's expedition, they did succeed in learning more about the unexplored Canadian archipelago than all previous expeditions had done. New channels, new islands, and new shorelines all came to light; landmasses were crisscrossed; and all of the high Arctic south and west of the Parry Islands now could appear with some accuracy on maps and charts.

Half of the Admiralty's £20,000 prize for navigating the Northwest Passage, in the meantime, was given to one of the searchers, Robert McClure, and the men of *Investigator,* who had sailed through the Bering Strait in 1850, overwintered twice at Banks Island, and then proceeded overland to a point just west of where Sir Edward Parry had fetched up. Many felt that the award was inappropriate: The passage had not been navigated in the maritime sense of the word. But it was now known that a Northwest Passage did, in fact, exist—either through Bellot Strait from the Gulf of Boothia (when it was ice free) or down Peel Sound between Somerset and Prince of Wales Islands, then around the southern portions of King William, Victoria, and Banks Islands to the Beaufort Sea. On the other hand, by 1854, the British interest in such things had waned, thanks in part to the Franklin debacle and full realization that the passage had little or no commercial value. At the same time, Englishmen had begun dying in the Crimea, and the attention of the nation was to the south, where a sad and sorry war was being fought for obscure causes.

In 1854, given the utter lack of success in finding anything from the Franklin expedition after some forty attempts, the Admiralty gave up and declared all hands dead. Four months later the first clues came to light, thanks to John Rae, a surgeon, explorer, and civilian employee of the Hudson Bay Company. In 1853 his company had asked him to complete the surveying of a part of Canada's northern shores. In particular, he was to settle the question of whether Boothia was a peninsula, as thought, or an island, and whether King William was an island, as thought, or a peninsula. Rae was familiar with the techniques of traveling and surviving in the Arctic—that is, he knew the ways of the Inuit and other natives who plied these northerly regions. He trekked overland from Repulse Bay on Foxe Island to Pelly Bay on the Gulf of Boothia, where in 1854 he met, talked with, and traded with a few Inuit.

From them he learned that other Inuit, four years earlier, had seen forty white men traveling south over the ice of King William Island, dragging a boat and sledges. None of them spoke Inuit, but they had used sign language to help the natives understand that their ships had been crushed by the ice and they were headed south to find deer to shoot. They were thin and out of provisions, and bought some seal meat from the Inuit. Their officer, the Inuit reported, was a tall, stout man. At the end of the day they pitched tents, and the Inuit went on their way.

It was not at all uncommon for Inuit who found people lost and starving to feed them and help them along. But forty starving men would have been far too many for the Inuit to assist in any meaningful way without starving themselves. The Arctic is a vast place with a great deal of game, but—as noted—it is spread out very sparsely, for the most part, and no single area can support very many people. The British navy might have understood this from the success of Sir John Ross in making it back from a disaster with a relative handful of men who were helped by the

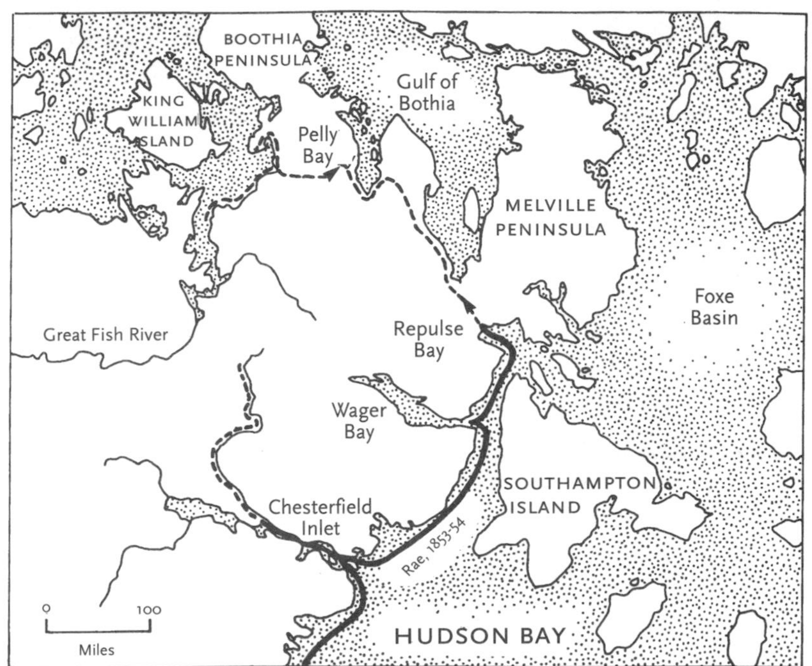

Sea and land travels of John Rae, 1853–1854 (From Berton 1988)

Inuit, but the Admiralty ignored that lesson in the case of Franklin—one of nearly uncounted examples of bad planning that underlay this greatest of polar tragedies. (Adventure, most experts say, is the last thing a professional explorer wants to have occur, but an expedition that goes without a hitch is simply not that interesting. Franklin's failure commands far more words in popular accounts of polar exploring than other, successful expeditions, and of course, in modern times the nearly fatal *Apollo 13* mission is far better remembered than the smooth *Apollo 14* mission that followed.)

In his account of his meetings with the Inuit, Rae wrote that later in the season, but before the ice broke up, the Inuit came across the corpses of about thirty people, some graves, and later, on an island, another five corpses. "Some of the bodies were in a tent or tents, and some lay scattered about in different directions. . . . From the mutilated state of many of the bodies, and the contents of the kettles, it is evident that our wretched countrymen had been driven to the last dread alternative as a means of sustaining life."

Rae went on to explain that there "must have been a number of telescopes, guns (several of them double-barreled), watches, compasses, &c, all of which seem to have been broken up, as I saw pieces of three different articles with the natives; and I purchased as many as possible, together with some silver spoons and forks, an order of merit in the form of a star, and a small silver plate engraved 'Sir John Franklin, K.C.H.'"

Rae carried his news to England in 1854, where he claimed and was given the £10,000 reward that Parliament had established for news of the Franklin disaster. With Rae's information, the Admiralty saw no reason to reopen the search for further information or artifacts—or bodies. But Jane Franklin was not so easily satisfied. After all, Rae's were secondhand reports, hearsay. The few objects Rae obtained could have been traded to the Inuit by members of the expedition. Rae had never visited the actual sites where these corpses were supposed to lie.

From what remained of her own money, and by public subscription, the determined and astoundingly faithful Lady Jane sponsored one last expedition (she had already financed several). It was now known where the search should be carried out: King William Island. And so in the same year (1853) in which Rae had set out to survey the Canadian coast, a British naval officer named Francis M'Clintock would later set out by sledge in search of any remnants of Franklin's expedition, traveling 1,338 miles in 105 days, a record for such treks. M'Clintock was an unusual British naval officer for the time in that he knew and emulated the ways of the Inuit when in Inuit country—something he had learned from James Clark Ross, for whom he had served as second officer. It was M'Clintock whom the Admiralty chose to command the *Fox* in Lady Jane's last attempt to pin down how her husband and his men had died. M'Clintock sailed in 1857, acquired dogs and an Inuit driver in Greenland, and was beset in the ice in Melville Bay in August. He would need to overwinter twice before setting three sledge parties loose on King William Island. There, in various places, they found a cairn with a message from the expedition that all was well, and then another cairn and message that reported the death of Franklin and the abandoning of the ships.

Along the southern shore of King William Island M'Clintock came across a sledge with a boat on top, in all a weight of some 1400 pounds, "a heavy load for seven healthy men." He and his men were amazed by what they found in the boat: "portions of two skeletons . . . five watches . . . two double-barreled shotguns—one barrel in each loaded and cocked—standing muzzle upright against the boat's side." They also found a half dozen books, "all of them scriptural or devotional works, except for the 'Vicar of Wakefield,'" along with seven or eight pairs of boots, silk handkerchiefs, towels and soap, toothbrushes, combs, and a gun cover. "Besides these articles we found twine, nails, saws, files, bristles . . . powder, bullets, shot, cartridges, wads, leather cartridge-case, knives, . . . needle and thread cases, slow-match, several bayonet-scabbards cut down into knife-sheaths, two rolls of sheet-lead, and, in short, a quantity of articles of one description and another truly astonishing in variety, and such as, for the most part, modern sledge-travelers in these regions would consider a mere accumulation of dead weight but slightly useful, and very likely to break down the strength of the sledge-crews."

Farther north, some three days' march from the point where the ships had been abandoned, they found yet another cairn and a pile of abandoned stuff the crews had evidently found it impossible to haul, however they might have been bent on leaving no possessions behind. They had abandoned four cooking stoves, shovels and pickaxes, old canvas, a copper lightning conductor, curtain rods, twenty-four phials of medicines, bar magnets, a small sextant engraved with the name Frederic Hornsby, and a four-foot pile of warm sailor's clothing.

One can only imagine that a certain kind of madness had settled into the feverish brains of the survivors, leaving useful material in a heap and pressing on with useless dead weight. It was not the first instance of insanity, and it would not be the last: There are many forms of insanity that have been inspired by the Far North.

SIX

Open Seas *and* Closed Minds

THE DREAMS OF MEN COME AND GO, replacing old and worn-out themes and impossible goals with fresh endeavors, new madnesses, or, as we often prefer to call them, challenges. Foolish or not, the quest for the Northwest Passage came to an end for the British Admiralty with the loss of the Franklin expedition, and it never much interested the Americans, whose passage to Cathay started perfectly conveniently in Seattle or San Francisco. And before too many years of the twentieth century went by, the passage so long sought by Spanish conquistadors, French voyageurs, British factors, and other geographic dreamers—an easy, direct route through the Western Hemisphere to the Orient—was built by main force through the Isthmus of Panama. No longer did men think they needed to obey the actual configuration of the Earth: indeed, there was once talk of a new and improved Panama Canal that would be gouged out of the land by nuclear explosions. For a time before the collapse of the Soviet Union, there was a good deal of talk about turning the flow of some of its rivers backward so that they would run from north to south, that is, they would run inland from the Arctic Ocean. Happily, sometimes people wake up before the dream takes hold.

The new, post-Franklin dream of those with an eye on the Arctic was in two parts: (one) reach the Pole (two) by sailing across the Open Polar Sea that was still thought to exist. But governments in Europe and America saw nothing much in it that would justify an expenditure from their treasuries, and so the new dream was left, for the most part, to be fulfilled or not by private citizens. These would turn out to be mostly Americans, encouraged and impelled largely by fledgling nongovernmental scientific institutions. The seeds of organized American scientific institutions were planted about the same time that Franklin's expedition disappeared, with the founding of the Smithsonian Institution in Washington, D.C., in 1846 with a noted physicist, Joseph Henry, at its helm. Before long, science in America was less a case of lone individuals and haphazard networking and more a matter of scientific societies devoted to the advancement of the sciences as delineated fields of knowledge, with centers of scientific research beginning to develop, notably in Boston, New York, Philadelphia, and Washington, D.C.

Many American scientists of good standing—and most Arctic explorers—stoutly insisted that the Open Polar Sea did indeed exist, even though no one had ever come close to seeing such a thing. Today we know, of course, that there is no such thing. So how is it that this notion could hold on in an age more given to science than any before? It has a great deal to do with the very nature of science itself, and also the state of science at the time. At the turn of the millennium, in a world where the technological fruits of science are virtually ubiquitous—where communication, healing, transportation, agriculture, and practically all other aspects of daily life are hastened along thanks to the stupefyingly rich findings of science—it is hard to imagine how very little scientific understanding of the world existed in the late 1840s.

By way of setting the scene, what follows is a very short and selective list of things that no one knew of, had conceived of, or had seen at the time: the principle of conservation of energy, storage batteries, oil wells, anthropology as such, germ theory, the measurement of the speed of light, the connection between electricity and magnetism, dynamite, Cro-Magnon man, the revolver, the periodic table of elements, taking accurate soundings at sea, typewriters, telephones, phonographs, electric light, psychoanalysis, the motion picture camera, rabies vaccine, and radioactivity. And in 1850 no European had been farther north than about 80° N, some 700 miles from the North Pole.

What this means, of course, is that there were no defining data on the matter of the Open Polar Sea at the time. Defining data are those pieces of information that pull a matter of scientific inquiry out of the realm of mostly speculation and into an area where a reasonable hypothesis can actually be put to a test. For example, we know today that carbon dioxide has increased in the atmosphere over the past thirty years (1958 to 1998) by 11 percent. The assumption is that a large increase (and 11 percent is certainly large) in this and other greenhouse gases will lead, as in a greenhouse, to higher temperatures for the terrestrial and oceanic Earth. But the only absolutely certain thing we know is that there had been the 11 percent increase; as many a scientist has said, we are going through a global geophysical experiment today the likes of which the Earth and mankind have never seen before. We have amazingly sophisticated computer models of climate into which we can plug in a vast host of variables and play out the future, and they produce all kinds of futures to contemplate. But in the absence of more data, defining data, we simply don't know which, if any, of the models is accurate.

In 1850 the only defining data available on the polar sea was that north of the Arctic Circle one encountered sea ice. So based on whatever assumptions one wished to make beyond that simple fact, one could conjecture that the Arctic Ocean was solid or liquid, and one could hypothesize the existence, or nonexistence, of landmasses up there. Such conjecturing and hypothesizing can be perfectly logical, perfectly reasonable, based on what is known at the time, but even the most logical progression of thought can go completely awry if you start off with a wrong assumption.

In what are called the hard sciences—mainly physics and chemistry—it is pretty easy to settle such matters. It can usually be done by framing experiments that either prove or disprove the hypothesis. Other people can do the same experiments the same way and see if they say what the first ones seem to say.

When inquiring about matters as messy as the Earth, biology, or human behavior, however, the scientific method is not so straightforward. You can't control all the variables, and in many cases you can't frame an experiment or repeat one that happened before. In such sciences, which in the mid-nineteenth century included a host of data-poor fledgling disciplines such as oceanography, there is plenty of room for speculation. Typically, the more room there is for speculation, the greater the determination to defend one's position against all comers. This is not as extreme a tendency in science as it has been in, say, religion, but it is a matter of human nature, in which almost every scientist shares. And in such instances in the history of science, the opinions that prevail are generally those of the most prominent, best-known persons in the field—at least until new information, defining data, arrives to make their position untenable. This was the case in the mid-nineteenth century concerning the nature of the Arctic Ocean.

Just as Mercator was the preeminent cartographer of the sixteenth century, a German named August Petermann was the preeminent cartographer of the nineteenth. He served for eight years, from 1847 to 1854, as the queen of England's physical geographer, and in 1874 a British explorer of Australia, Ernest Giles, named a mountain range there after him. In 1854 Petermann returned to Germany and began producing a yearly series of exquisitely illustrated volumes, *Petermanns Geographische Mitteilungen,* which gave the latest geographical findings from around the world. The series continues to this day as a geographical journal with the same title.

In 1852, while England was still involved in the search for Franklin's remains, Petermann held forth on the subject. "It is a well-known fact," he wrote, "that there exists to the north of the Siberian coast, and, at a comparatively short distance from it, a sea open at all seasons; it is beyond doubt that a similar open sea exists on the American side . . . it is very probable that these two open seas form a large navigable Arctic ocean." Until searchers entered this huge basin, he went on to say, there was no hope of finding any trace of the Franklin expedition. Forget for a moment the rhetoric Petermann employed to blitz any nonbelievers—"a well-known fact," "beyond doubt." He also had an answer for the reasonable question of where the heat came from that kept the ocean warm: the Gulf Stream.

A great Arctic current, he averred, that brought drift ice in from Siberian shores relaxed in the summer, and the Gulf Stream, which was hemmed in by ice in the spring and summer, then could head for the Siberian coast, carrying the drift ice

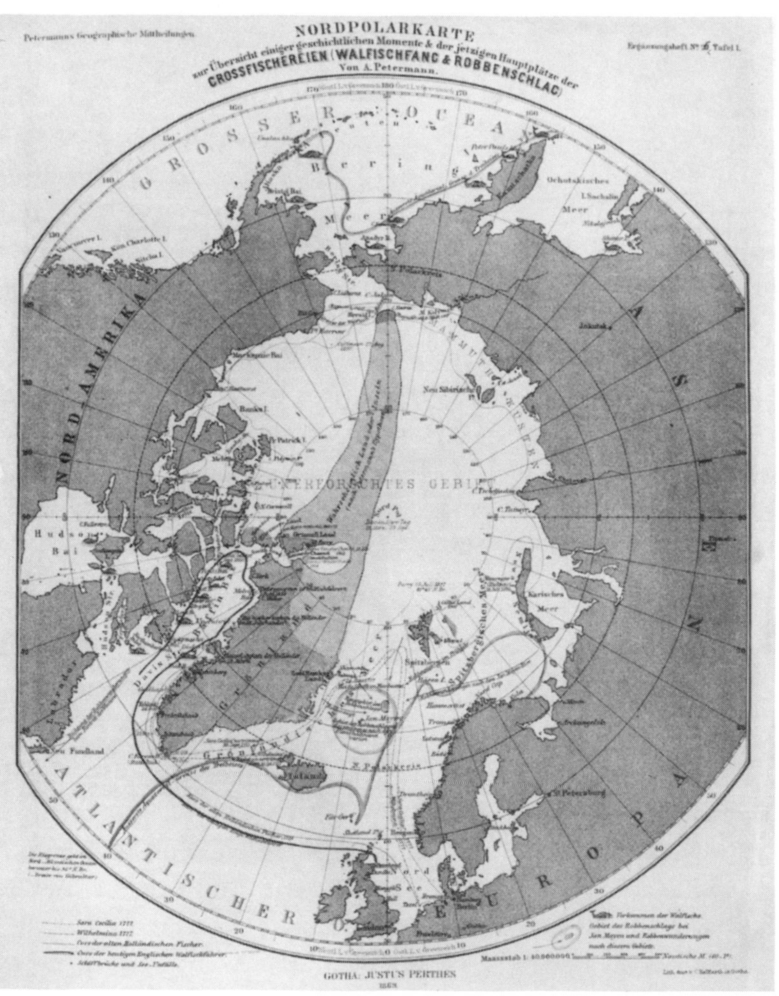

Map of the North Pole (Petermann 1869)

with it and clearing the way for "easy navigation." In fact, this is basically correct, but what is wrong about it is the assumption that the Gulf Stream transfers enough heat to the Arctic Ocean to keep it ice free.

Petermann also went on to suggest that there were two "poles" of cold (not associated with the North Pole) that moved around seasonally, in a sense creating an annulus or ring of ice around the warmer Arctic Ocean to its north. There was, of course, no data whatsoever to support such a notion. In an 1869 map Petermann did a splendid job of getting the details correct in the northern regions that lie south of the Arctic Circle. But above that, error crept in—for example, the projection of Greenland north across the Arctic to the Siberian coast, beyond its then known limits. Here again, most people didn't notice at the time that the old Spanish cartographers' rule—do not put a line on a map unless you know what's there—was being violated.

Another major supporter of the idea of an Open Polar Sea was a man who might be called the father of oceanography, an American naval officer who led a life that was at times as adventurous as that of any explorer. He was Matthew Fontaine Maury, a Virginian who circumnavigated the world as a midshipman, was promoted to lieutenant, and then was lamed in a stagecoach accident three years later, in 1839. Unfit for active service, he was put in charge of the U.S. Navy's Depot of Charts and Instruments, from which eventually arose the U.S. Naval Observatory and Hydrographic Office. He instructed U.S. captains on keeping certain records at sea, from which he compiled pilot charts of winds and currents, allowing ships to cut the time of various voyages. Eventually, with international information, he prepared wind and current charts of the Atlantic, Pacific, and Indian Oceans. He profiled the Atlantic Ocean bottom, showing that a transatlantic telegraph cable could be laid across it, and in 1855 he published the first modern oceanographic text, *The Physical Geography of the Sea.*

When the Civil War erupted, Maury went home and joined the Confederate Navy, serving as head of shoreline and river defenses and attempting to invent an electric torpedo. He was then sent as a special agent to Mexico and after the war remained there as Emperor Maxmillian's commissioner of immigration, hoping to establish a Confederate colony. When this scheme fell apart he eventually returned to Virginia as a professor of meteorology at the Virginia Military Institute. He was, in short, a man of action and a man of learning, a man above all to be respected when he spoke of matters oceanographic.

Part of Maury's thesis about the Open Polar Sea referred to observations of wind directions that indicated a lowering of barometric pressure toward the Pole, which he thought had to be the result of the liberation of latent heat. He asked, "[W]hence do those vapors come which liberate all this heat . . . if not from that boiling, bubbling pool of Gulf Stream water, which my observations show," and so forth. So convinced was Maury that he called chapter 7 of his masterwork on the oceans "The Open Sea in the Arctic Ocean," beginning it by recounting observations of harpoons from whaling ships in Baffin Bay that were found in whales in the Bering Strait. Being a careful observer, he admitted that this "did not prove the existence of an open sea there; it only established the existence—the occasional existence, if you please—of a channel through which the whales had passed." His main argument, like Petermann's, had to do with the transfer of heat from the Gulf Stream to the Arctic Ocean, noting that a relatively warm undercurrent passes through the Davis Strait from the Atlantic. There must be a place, he wrote, where the undercurrent stops flowing north and turns south as a surface current bearing huge quantities of salt. In fact, there is such a current—the Norwegian Current—which keeps the coast of Norway free of ice, but it is not warm enough to take care of the entire Arctic Ocean.

Maury also brought in what was then understood about the migration of birds and mammals in the Arctic, postulating that there had to be a warmer climate "somewhere in that inhospitable sea," because the birds and mammals were found at various seasons migrating north, "evidently in search of milder climates. The instincts of these dumb creatures are unerring," and the only thing that would make it milder to the north was a large open ocean. Of course, we know now that those migrations do not continue out into the barren Arctic ice pack. But thus, based on wholly inadequate data and considerable exercise of logic, was it demonstrated that there was an Open Polar Sea.

This kind of argument would be offered for several decades after the search for the Franklin expedition was called off—and of course not everyone agreed. Others adduced equally excellent logic based on the assumption that there was no Open Polar Sea and that the climate grew colder as you moved north to the pole—again, in the face of no defining data. Neither view, it should be pointed out, was absurd.

One of those who held with the notion of the Open Polar Sea was the first American to make an actual attempt to reach the North Pole, a remarkable man named Elisha Kent Kane. Born in 1820, Kane died when he was only thirty-seven years old, one of the earliest celebrities in a nation that would eventually turn celebrity into an industry. But unlike most of today's celebrities, who are created out of whole cloth, Kane deserved his renown (and notoriety), if for no other reason than that he accomplished more in his short life than most other men dream of.

Stricken at an early age with rheumatic fever, he lived with the forecast of a shortened life and reacted with the conscious decision to live his life to the fullest. He sought out a medical education and became a naval surgeon, and before he was thirty Kane had explored a volcano in the Philippines and traveled to other foreign lands from Brazil to Borneo, Nubia to China, Greece to the West Indies, and Persia to boot. In the course of these travels he contracted various other diseases, including tetanus and bubonic plague. During the Mexican War he was assigned by President Polk to carry a message to General Winfield Scott in Mexico City, a job that put him into contact with Mexican guerillas, one of whom wounded Kane with a lance. By 1850 he had settled down to a mundane and comfortable job with the Coast Survey in Mobile, Alabama.

This was when much of the English-speaking world was abuzz with the ongoing attempts to find the remains of the Franklin expedition, and it was the year that Lady Jane Franklin persuaded Henry Grinnell to buy two ships for the purpose and offer them to the United States government. This put the expedition under the aegis of the United States Navy, and when Elisha Kane heard about the expedition, he wrote the navy asking to be included and was selected as surgeon for one of the ships. Led by a naval lieutenant, Edwin De Haven, the ships entered Lancaster Sound in that same year, 1850, eventually drifting with the ice out into Baffin Bay. Attempting to sail north again in 1851, they were thwarted, and they returned to New York that September. This nondescript voyage, one of forty that all failed, would have been merely a footnote to history but for its effect on the young naval surgeon onboard.

Elisha Kane had caught a different kind of bug, the Arctic bug. He wrote a book about the expedition, a well-written account that sold well. For two years after the expedition's return he lectured and solicited funds for a second expedition. Meanwhile, he heard about a British navy captain who in 1852 had sailed into Smith Sound and reported that there was no problem with ice, and that he could have sailed even farther north except that he ran out of time. Here, then, Kane reasoned, was the way through the ring of ice that surrounded the Open Polar Sea. And if he were to sail to Smith Sound in search of Franklin, he could take the time to become the first man to reach the North Pole. He let on to his backers that, given the lack of success in finding Franklin west of Baffin Bay, the place to search now was to that bay's north. But he kept his plan for a polar dash to himself.

Kane persuaded Henry Grinnell to put De Haven's brig, the *Advance,* at Kane's disposal, and the navy agreed to provide ten men. The recently founded American Geographical Society, whose first president was also Henry Grinnell, supported the mission (and Kane as its leader, though he had no experience heading any sort of expedition). The *Advance,* a 140-ton brig (that is, a two-masted square-rigger), was originally designed for carrying loads of iron, and it had been strengthened yet more for the Arctic ice floes, which could crush less solid craft like flies. Cornelius Grinnell, Henry's son, was put in charge of outfitting the ship, since Kane was recovering from a bout of rheumatic fever at the time. With not enough volunteers to make up a full complement of seventeen (seven plus the ten navy men), Cornelius scoured the waterfront and came up with, among others, a couple of unsavory characters named William Godfrey and John Blake, along with a sailing master, John Wilson, who had no experience in the Arctic. Cornelius also provisioned the expedition with enough food for about a year, but not for two winters.

Kane would prove to be a brave and dogged explorer. He came close to death on several occasions, the result of scurvy and other illnesses, not to mention exposure and near starvation, but always managed to recover and forge on. Kane's dauntlessness can be perceived in a single diary entry for December 15:

> We have lost the last vestige of our midday twilight. We can see no print, and hardly paper; the fingers can not be counted a foot from the eyes. Noonday and midnight are alike; and, except a vague glimmer in the sky that seems to define the hill outlines to the south, we have nothing to tell us that this Arctic world of ours has a sun. In the darkness, and consequent inaction, it is almost vain that we seek to create topics of thought, and, by a forced excitement, to ward off the encroachments of diseases.

At the same time, he was no seaman—he was chronically seasick, nearly to the point of debility, whenever the ship was under way. And, it would turn out later, long after the journal of this voyage had been published and had cemented Kane's position as a major American hero, he wasn't all that effective as a leader. In fact, it seems he was a bit of a snob, taking a patrician's stance throughout much of the voyage. This was not the sort of thing to endear him to his men, nor was the favoritism

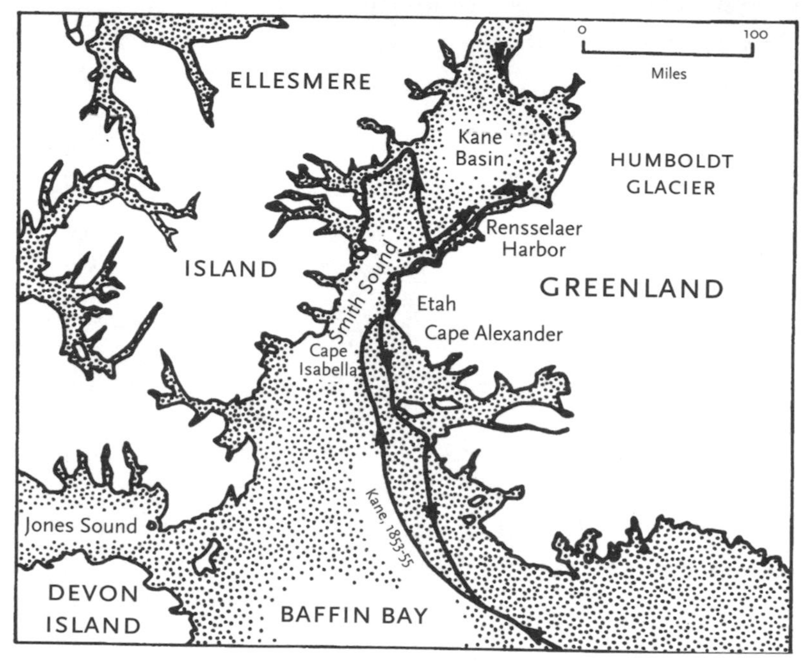

Geography of region investigated by Elisha Kent Kane (From Berton 1988)

he showed for William Morton, the personal servant he brought along. In fairness, Morton was possessed of great endurance and was a valuable man in a pinch, of which there would be a great many.

The expedition left New York on May 30, 1853, and made its way slowly into Baffin Bay and then north into the basin that now bears Kane's name. They encountered extremely dangerous ice floes and huge icebergs as the weather began to close in on them. Kane wrote on August 20, 1853, of the nautical nightmare of ice floes pressing, hurricane-force winds howling, and the ship's lines, anchored to an iceberg for protection, breaking loose:

> The manilla cable was proving its excellence. . . . We could hear its deep Eolianne chant, swelling through all the rattle of the running gear and moaning shrouds. It was the death song! The strands gave way with the sound of a gun:

and we were dragged out by the wild sea, and were at its mercy. . . . At seven in the morning we close upon the piling masses of ice . . . Down we went with the gale again, helplessly scraping along a lee of ice seldom less than thirty feet thick. . . . One upturned mass rose above our gunwale, smashed our bulwarks and deposited a half a ton of ice in a lump upon our decks. Our staunch little brig bore herself through all this wild adventure as if she had a charmed life.

Subsequently the *Advance* found itself among towering bergs, and the gathering floes shoved the craft up a sloping berg and heeled her over on her side. The crew could do nothing. Eventually, her timbers groaning, she settled back into the water. There was a deep silence, Kane wrote, before "the clamor of congratulation and comment could burst forth."

They were most fortunate to have with them two men of Inuit extraction, and the experience of one of them, Hans Hendrik, in navigating these hazards was essential. They overwintered at Rensselaer Harbor and spent the days in frigid tedium. As Kane would later write of the miserable hours: "We could keep no note of time and except by the whirring of the drift against the roof of our kennel, had no information of the state of the weather. We slept and cooked coffee, and drank coffee, and slept and cooked coffee, and drank again; and when by our tired instincts we thought that twelve hours must have passed, we treated ourselves to a meal—that is to say we divided impartial bites out of the raw hind-leg of a fox, to give zest to our biscuits spread with frozen tallow."

When spring came Kane sent out several sledge parties (powered mostly by humans, since most of the dogs he had obtained had died during the winter) to seek out the Open Polar Sea that he was convinced lay ahead. These sorties proved unsuccessful; two men died in the effort, and the others returned suffering from the onset of scurvy. Kane, normally an optimist, was covered with doubt, acutely feeling that he had failed: A year had passed and he had absolutely nothing to show for it. But then in early July his manservant, William Morton, returned from an excursion onto the Humboldt Glacier, along the northwest coast of Greenland. He told Kane that on June 24 he had stood upon the shore and seen "not a speck of ice." As far as he could see, he reported, "the sea was open, a swell coming in from the northward and running crosswise, as if with a small eastward set. The wind was due N—enough of it to make white caps,—and the surf broke in on the rocks in regular breakers." Morton had stood, he said, at 80° 30' N, the farthest north achieved by any white man, his feet upon the northernmost land on the face of the planet.

So here was success for Kane's expedition. He believed that if he was able to get his ship or perhaps just some seaworthy boats to that point, he could possibly achieve the Pole. But it was then that the expedition began a downward spiral. It became clear that summer that they would not be able to free the *Advance* from the ice in Rensselaer Harbor. They would be stuck there for at least another winter, because it was also too late in the season to try to escape south by boat. The crew, already fed up with the hardships of the voyage, grew mutinous. Kane called a meeting on August 24 and let everyone know that he would provide

William Morton's Open Polar Sea (From Kane 1856)

boats, provisions, and equipment to any who wished to leave and head south, however foolish an idea that was. To his astonishment and dismay, eleven of the seventeen men voted to go (only nine eventually left the ship). Among those who wanted to leave was the ship's surgeon, Isaac Israel Hayes.

Kane had lost control; his command was meaningless. In the book he would eventually write (*Arctic Exploration: The Second Grinnell Expedition in Search of Sir John Franklin, in the Years 1853, '54, '55*), Kane made little of this mutiny, but to his journal he confided: "I have washed my hands of them as a man and a Christian. . . . They have left the expedition and God's blessing go with them, for they carry not the respect of good men." Later he wrote in his journal that he expected some of them to return, seeking refuge, and he would provide it. But, he wrote, "but—but—but—If I ever live to get home—home! and should meet Dr. Hayes [and the others], let them look out for their skins."

The deserters fared poorly, returning to the *Advance* some three months later, exhausted and in poor health. In their travails, they had been watched and sometimes aided by the Inuit, who coveted the mutineers' knives and other equipment but feared their firearms. In an uneasy arrangement, the Inuit would barter food, enough to keep the deserters dependent on them. When the deserters finally realized that the Inuit were simply waiting for them to die off so that they could take their equipment, the sailors took matters into their own hands and forced the Inuit at gunpoint to sledge them back to the ship, where Kane took them back—but without forgiving them.

They survived the winter largely because of an oral treaty with the local Inuit, known then as the Etah Eskimos, wherein they provided the expedition with enough fresh meat to avoid starvation and the worst of scurvy. This treaty, which Kane took credit for arranging, was more likely the work of one of the Inuit men on their crew, Hans Hendrik, whose expertise in Arctic ways may well have made the ultimate difference between survival and doom for the entire expedition. Meanwhile, they were forced to dismantle the oak sheathing from the hull of their ship to use as fuel for fires against the ferocious cold, and finally the structural parts of the ship were burned as well, leaving enough wood to construct a couple of sledges long enough to carry the ship's boats.

Kane later wrote of the time when all the ship's timbers were burned and they used lamps for heat, like the "Esquimaux," whom they were imitating in all else as well. "Counting those which I have added since the wanderers [the mutineers] came back, we have twelve constantly going, with grease and soot everywhere in proportion. . . . Our beds and bedding are absolutely black, and our faces begrimed with fatty carbon. . . . I found an overlooked godsend this morning—a bear's head, put away for a specimen, but completely frozen. There is no inconsiderable quantity of meat adhering to it, and I serve it out raw [to the men who were sick with scurvy]."

In the course of the winter one of the mutineers, the troublemaker Godfrey, slipped off to go live with the natives. One day he returned to the ship with a dog sled loaded with fresh walrus meat, a most welcome gift. Kane, seeing the man as a deserter, ordered him to stay, but Godfrey simply turned tail and ran off across the ice. Kane ordered an armed companion to shoot the man, but the rifle misfired. Kane raced back to the ship, snatched another rifle from the gunstand, fired at the receding Godfrey, and missed. Not about to let Godfrey escape, he went to the Inuit camp at Etah and forced Godfrey to return at gunpoint.

On May 20, 1855, Kane and the crew abandoned the skeletal remains of the *Advance*, leaving a "memorial" pinned to its mast in which Kane wrote for any explorers who later happened upon the ship that he hoped "we have done all that we ought to do to prove our tenacity of purpose and devotion to the cause which we have undertaken." Escape by sledge across the southern ice was "an imperative duty—the only means of saving ourselves and preserving the laboriously-earned results of the expedition."

In fact, the results of the expedition were mostly chimerical except for the loss of three members of the crew and the crippling of several others from surgery for frostbite and the after-effects of scurvy and other hardships. They did finally make it out, leaving in three boats from Rensselaer Harbor, reaching civilization on the southwest coast of Greenland.

Elisha Kent Kane returned to the United States in the fall of 1855 to a hero's welcome, a major outpouring of public celebration. His first book had come out, and he was already famous, even before he returned from the expedition. While he had found no trace of Franklin (and indeed it was now clear he had never had any intention of looking for Franklin), he could say he had achieved a major first, a stupendous prize: He had found the Open Polar Sea.

It is difficult from this distance in time to appreciate the intensity and breadth of the popularity Kane enjoyed. Some two hundred thousand people bought his book, which was published in 1856. That is equivalent to two million people today, the kind of instant audience that greets a new Tom Clancy or Danielle Steel novel. The nation's most prominent historian, W.H. Prescott, called Kane's book "one of the most remarkable records I have ever met with . . . No man has probably done more than Dr. Kane to lift the dread veil of mystery which hangs over the Arctic regions." The orator Edward Everett enthused that the book would "secure him an abiding-place on the rolls of honest fame among the heroes of humanity." The statesman and antislavery spokesman Charles Sumner said it was possessed of "all the attractions of romantic adventure elevated by scientific discovery."

Kane's book made him a small fortune, which, unfortunately, he had very little time to enjoy. On a doctor's advice, Kane moved to Cuba to try to recover his failing health, but he died there of a heart attack on February 16, 1857. The nation's grief was enormous. The funeral procession was more elaborate and longer than any ever before in the young nation's history and would be exceeded in the nineteenth century only by that of President Lincoln some eight years later. Kane's casket went from Havana to New Orleans by ship and then by steamboat up the Mississippi and Ohio Rivers to Cincinnati, with people in mourning on the levees and wharfs of every town along the way.

New-York Daily Times.

DR. KANE HOME AGAIN.

The Second and Third Arctic Expeditions Safely Ended.

Arrival of Propeller Arctic and Bark Release at New-York.

THE ADVANCE LEFT IN THE ICE.

NEW LANDS FOUND.

A Bridge of Ice from Greenland to the Continent.

AN OPEN SEA FOUND.

NO TRACES OF SIR JOHN FRANKLIN.

LATITUDE 82° 30′ N. REACHED.

LIFE IN THE FROZEN REGIONS.

ON SLEDGES FOR THIRTY DAYS.

Detailed and Interesting Account of the two Expeditions.

DR. KANE'S OWN ACCOUNT.

DR. KANE, the intrepid Arctic navigator, after having been given up as lost, has returned safe home, with the loss of but three men on his whole expedition. He left his brig frozen up in the Arctic Sea, on the 24th of May, 1855. went three hundred miles over the ice to the sea, and then in open boats thirteen hundred miles to Upernavik in Greenland. After waiting for

VOL. V.....NO. 1269

from the fact, that the entire circuit of Smith's has been effected, and its shores completely cha

THE OPEN POLAR SEA.

But the real discovery of the Expedition *open Polar Sea.* The channel leading to these was entirely free from ice, and this feature w cered more remarkable by the existence of r solid belt of ice, extending more than o dred and twenty-five miles to the southward. sea verifies the views of Dr KANE, as expre the Geographical Society before his departure

The lashing of the surf against this frozen ice was, we are assured, impressive beyond tion. Several gentlemen with whom we hav versed, speak of it with wonder and admirati

An area of three thousand square miles wa entirely free from ice. This channel has been after Hon. JOHN P. KENNEDY, late Secretary Navy, under whose auspices the Expedition wa

The land to the north and west of this chan been charted as high as 82° 30′. *This is the land to the Pole yet discovered.* It bears the Mr HENRY GRINNELL, the founder of the ex which bears his name.

THE WINTER OF 1854–'55.

The extreme severity of the previous season evident that the brig could not be liberated be Winter set in. She was fast imprisoned in th of a large field of ice. The provisions, a abundant, were not calculated to resist scur the fuel, owing to the emergencies of the Winter, was deficient in quantity.

Under these trying circumstances Dr. KANE party of volunteers, on an attempt to reach th of Lancaster Sound, in hopes of meeting the expeditions, and thus giving relief to his ass passed in an open boat over the track of B travel, riding out a heavy gale. They found a terrupted barrier of ice, extending in one grea shoe from Jones' to Murchison's Sounds, ar forced, after various escapes, to return to the

Front page of the New York Daily Times, October 12, 1855 (From Corner 1972)

The body went by train from there to Philadelphia, again with mourners crowding the tracks at every town and small city where the train stopped. It lay in state briefly at the larger cities en route, such as Columbus, Louisville, and Baltimore, and was finally buried in Philadelphia on March 14.

Only later would the more unseemly parts of Kane's expedition be revealed—the mutiny and other avoidable difficulties. And what of Morton's sighting of the Open Polar Sea? In the first place, he was not near 80° N when he saw whatever he thought was that much fabled phenomenon, but much farther south. And he may have seen a polynya, a Russian term for a large area of open water in a sea of ice, and somehow—out of exhaustion or the delirium that was not uncommon among Arctic trekkers, especially if they were ill and underfed, or perhaps out of the faithful servant's desire to please the boss—expanded it into an ocean. But in 1857 not only were there "scientific" reasons to think the Open Polar Sea existed, but it had been seen.

All that remained was to cross it. The idea of being first to reach the North Pole, now clearly thought of as accessible, became something of a fixation for Americans, and later for the British as well.

The next person to try just that was Isaac Israel Hayes, the surgeon aboard the *Advance* who had deserted. Hayes had lost some toes to frostbite, but his enthusiasm for Arctic adventuring was intact. Less persuasive than the heroic and dashing Kane, he was unable to persuade the aging Henry Grinnell to come up with two ships and had to settle instead for a 133-ton schooner he named the *United States.* Convinced along with "many learned physicists that the sea about the North Pole cannot be frozen," he set out in 1860 with the plan to push his little schooner to the 80th parallel through Smith Sound and then haul a boat over the ice to the open sea, whence the Pole beckoned.

Of course, it was not so easy. At one point they anchored to an iceberg that promptly began to disintegrate and then to plunge and heave, seeking a new equilibrium and threatening the *United States* with disaster. They ran into blizzards, fogs, gales, and rapidly forming ice, finally reaching Etah, where they had to overwinter. Hayes sent sledge parties out north across the ice cap of Greenland, and things began to go wrong. A man froze to death when he fell through the ice. The sled dogs they had picked up earlier from Upernavik died in an epidemic. Hayes claimed to have reached as far north as 82° 30' N before he had to turn back. While he didn't actually see the Open Polar Sea, he maintained that it was just beyond the final point reached by his expedition, and he titled the book he wrote several years later *The Open Polar Sea.* In it he wrote, "[S]uffice it here to say that I stood upon the shores of the Polar Basin, and that the broad ocean lay at my feet; that the land upon which I stood, culminating in the distant cape before me, was but a point of land projecting far into it, like the Ceverro Vostochnoi Noss of the opposite coast of Siberia; and that the little margin of ice that lined the shore was being steadily worn away; and within a month, the whole would be as free from ice as I had seen the north water of Baffin Bay."

Hayes' book would not appear until 1867, long after his return from the Arctic. While his predecessor, Kane, returned to instant national acclaim, Hayes' *United States* sailed back into Boston Harbor on a foggy day to the notice of practically no one, as the Civil War had begun. Hayes would spend the war as an army surgeon in a hospital in Philadelphia, and his book, as well as any sort of Arctic adventuring, was put on hold. Meanwhile, in 1862, one of the scientific backers of Hayes' expedition, Alexander Dallas Bache, wrote Hayes asking for the return of the scientific instruments he had loaned the expedition. Hayes was forced to reply that he had expected lectures to pay for the remaining costs of the expedition, but because the war had intervened, he had been forced to hock the instruments in order to pay his crew their accumulated wages. Worse yet, later expeditions would find that many of Hayes' physiographic descriptions were inaccurate, and his claim of a farthest north at 82° 30' N was no farther north than 80° 10' N, an error of 140 miles.

In the days when searching for Franklin's expedition was almost an Anglo-American obsession, an odd figure determined that he wanted to become part of the scramble, but he could not raise the funds for an expedition ship. He was Charles Francis Hall, a high-school dropout with no scientific background, no knowledge of navigation, and no other naval skills, but he had read virtually everything in print about the Arctic. He was in the newspaper business in Cincinnati at the time, with a family to support, but he came to believe that he had been called north by God. This insistent and often prickly man left business and family behind and, after spending months in the eastern United States trying to raise money to outfit his own expedition, wangled a free berth on a whaler to Baffin Island, where, in Frobisher Bay, he disembarked. His plan was to live alone with only the support of the local Inuit and eventually to sail to King William Island in a small boat he had bought with funds supplied by polar angel Henry Grinnell. But while still on the whaler, writing in his cabin, he heard a female voice behind him.

"Good morning, sir," the voice said.

He turned and to his amazement found an English-speaking Inuit couple standing there. Their names, he learned, were Tookoolito and her husband, Ebierbing. In the 1850s a whaling captain had taken them to England, where they had thrived, even to the point of having dinner with Queen Victoria and Prince Albert, eventually returning to Baffin Island. They in turn took Hall in hand, and through them he heard Ebierbing's grandmother tell stories that she had heard as a child about ships that arrived many years before—first one ship, then next year three, and then in the third year, fifteen ships. She spoke of coal, bricks, and iron that had been left behind. Here, of course, was an oral history of the Frobisher expeditions. He went to the specific locations the old woman had mentioned and there rediscovered—three hundred years after the fact—the remains of Frobisher's gold-mining venture. In 1862 Hall returned to the United States with relics from the Frobisher encampment and with Tookoolito and Ebierbing, who would come to be known to Americans as Hannah and Joe. He settled his Inuit friends in Groton, Connecticut, with a small grant from Grinnell, saw his family in Cincinnati for two weeks, and returned to the East Coast to seek funds for a second trip. And before too long, Hall would head back north.

At this same time, a Finn named Adolf Erik Nordenskiöld had begun to visit the Arctic.

He had been trained as a geologist and chemist at the University of Helsinki, but in 1855 he was fired from his junior position at the university and at the state mining administration for the seditious promotion of the reunion of Finland with Sweden. The Russian authorities in Finland branded Nordenskiöld a "dangerous rabble-rouser," and he was forced to emigrate to Sweden in 1857, where he obtained a similar junior position at the University of Stockholm and a year later was appointed chief of mineralogy at the National Museum of Natural History, a position he held for the rest of his life.

In 1858 the Swedish government sponsored—and local businessmen supported—an expedition into the Arctic, and Nordenskiöld was among the scientists on board. It was chiefly a scientific voyage, designed to make detailed geographic surveys as well as studies and collections related to geomagnetism, geology, botany, zoology, and marine biology. It would be the first of many voyages to the Arctic for this promising young mineralogist, and he, like Charles Francis Hall, would one day attempt to reach the Pole. But if Hall was one in the growing lineage of American amateurs in the Arctic, Nordenskiöld would, in a sense, be the father of a lineage of supreme professionals—most of these from the nations of Scandinavia. Before long, English eyes would take note of such efforts and find that the pride of Britannia was again at stake—the Arctic was, after all, really a British preserve, wasn't it? And several other nations of Europe, notably Germany and Austria, would see fit to join this new international competition—the race to reach the North Pole.

SEVEN

Anything Is Good *that* Don't Poison You

WHILE THE AMERICAN CIVIL WAR was raging to its bloody conclusion, Charles Francis Hall headed back into the Arctic, leaving in 1864 to stay again among the Inuit, along with his companions and mentors, Ebierbing and Tookoolito. In 1865 his book, *Researches and Life Among the Esquimaux* was published in the United States, having appeared the year before in England. He remained in the Arctic for five years, an accomplishment unequaled in the annals of Arctic exploration, and he journeyed some 3,000 miles by sledge. During this long sojourn he came upon and collected a few relics of the Franklin expedition and traversed the shores of the Gulf of Boothia and King William Island.

One unfortunate incident cast a shadow over this second expedition. In July 1868 Hall hired five men from a whaler to help him, and he soon got into a heated argument with one of them, a man named Patrick Coleman. Coleman had questioned the Inuit about one thing or another, and Hall believed that conversing with the native people was his exclusive bailiwick. In the course of the argument Hall came to believe that Coleman had threatened his life, so he went to his quarters, fetched a revolver, and shot Coleman dead. Like several men before him, from Henry Hudson's mutineers to Elisha Kane, Hall got off scot-free, in his case without even a trial. It was not so much that the Arctic was lawless as that it seemed ordinary laws didn't apply to so strange and remote a place.

One of Hall's accomplishments on this second sojourn was to prove to everyone's subsequent satisfaction that no members of the Franklin party were still wandering about in the frozen north among the Inuit. Upon returning to New Bedford, Massachusetts, in September 1869, again with Ebierbing and Tookoolito in tow, he handed over his Frobisher and Franklin relics to the Smithsonian Institution. In 1870 his book was reissued with a simpler title, *Life with the Esquimaux;* it detailed the lifeways of the Inuit in greater detail than anything before it had done. And herein lay Hall's chief contribution to Arctic exploration. He showed that someone from Europe or America could survive perfectly well in the Arctic if he was willing to take on the lifeways of the people who had lived there for millennia. He learned not only to live like an Inuit and eat what the Inuit ate, but to like it. He felt at home there—more so, it would seem, than with his family in Cincinnati. Had others before him, and several after him, learned the same lesson, easily available in his writings, a great many lives would have been saved.

By the time Hall returned to the United States, another expedition had been launched—this for the Pole by a consortium of European adventurers under the German flag. Two ships were to break through the girdle of ice by sailing north from northeastern Greenland. The two vessels were separated quite early, with one sinking in the ice pack. The crew drifted about on the ice through the winter and made it to southeastern Greenland the following summer in the ship's boats. The other ship made it as far north as 75° N, where it languished until they could launch a sledge expedition, which made its way to 77° N before turning back.

While the group accomplished little in the way of establishing the Germans as first-rate Arctic explorers, its effort did focus yet more American attention on the Arctic and especially the felt need to be first among the civilized nations to reach the Pole. And thus came about Charles Francis Hall's third Arctic journey, in 1871. In the annals of Arctic exploration it would be downplayed by historians and others with sensitive noses, since it resulted in a mysterious death, which has since been shown to be a murder, and a case of scandalous betrayal as well as one of the most terrible (and unnecessary) voyages of escape in all the history of humankind.

With congressional funds flowing for another attempt at the Pole, Hall was chosen to lead the expedition, and a 380-ton former tugboat was outfitted and renamed (with great expectation) the *Polaris.* Steam-propelled, she could also proceed by sail. The screw, or propeller, was arranged so that it could be withdrawn to protect it from battering by the ice, and the hull was reinforced with oak planking. Among its amenities was an organ, presented to the expedition by the Smith Organ Company to be used in Sunday services. Hall had hoped to sign on as sailing master a seasoned captain named George Tyson, but Tyson was otherwise committed, so Hall chose Sidney Budington, a whaler who had dropped Hall off at Baffin Island back in 1861. Then Tyson became available and signed on as second navigator. Most of the officers were Americans but the crew was mostly German, as was the chief scientist, a young physician and naturalist named Emil Bessels. William Morton, Kane's servant, was along, as were Tookoolito and Ebierbing.

The *Polaris* sailed from New London and made for Upernavik, Greenland, where they added the seasoned Inuit sailor Hans Hendrik (plus his wife and three children) to the roster. From there Hall pushed on through Kane Basin toward the place where both Morton and Hayes had previously reported the Open Polar Sea opened to the north. They proceeded to 82° 11' N, the farthest north for a ship, before being forced to turn back by the massive and solid ice that covered the Arctic Ocean. They overwintered at Thank God Harbor on Greenland, and Hall determined then that when spring came they would head for the Pole by sledge, but other members of the crew—especially Captain Budington and Bessels—thought that, having met so awesome a barrier, they should return home. Unpersuaded, Hall set out with Hans Hendrik and Ebierbing to reconnoiter the ice pack, returning to the *Polaris* on October 24. One of his first acts upon his return was to ask for a cup of

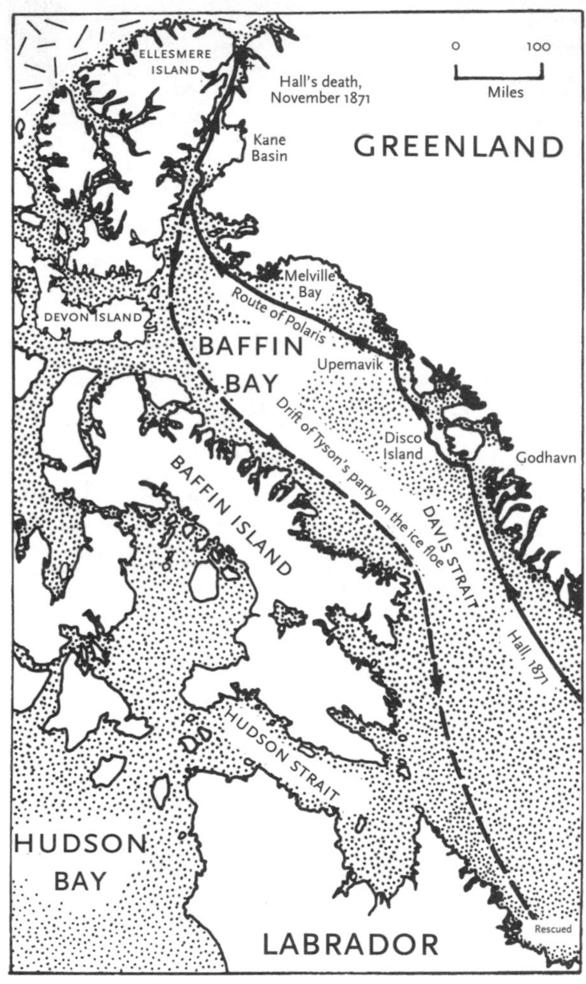

Route of *Polaris* and Charles Francis Hall to the north and drift of George Tyson to the south (From Berton 1988)

coffee, and on drinking it, he became violently ill. Over the next days he would seesaw between apparently good health and bouts of illness that included stomach pains, vomiting, dehydration, vertigo, and dementia. At times he confided to George Tyson that he thought he was being poisoned by crew members who were hostile to his plans. On November 8, two weeks after his return, he had a final relapse and died. He was given a solemn funeral and buried on shore at Thank God Harbor in a shallow, frozen grave.

Sidney Budington was now, by prearrangement, in charge of

the expedition, and he was determined to go home, but the ice kept the *Polaris* locked in place until August 1872. Meanwhile he armed the crew (except for Tyson), and they managed on the ship's stores and the occasional seal they were able to shoot. Once free, the ship began to drift south attached to one of the ice floes, and on October 15 the engineer came on deck with the cry that the ship was leaking badly and was being crushed by the ice. Eighteen people, including George Tyson and the Inuit, went onto the ice while the others hurled all readily available provisions and food supplies to them. It appeared that the ship's crew would have to spend the winter on the ice. But then the *Polaris* suddenly broke free and drifted off. To those stranded on the ice floe, it appeared that the men in command of the ship were not making much of an effort to retrieve them, and soon they set about facing a most uncertain and perilous future. With the help of Ebierbing and Hans, ice shelters were made in the snow, the Germans having one to themselves. In addition to the provisions they had off-loaded, they also had two of the ship's boats. Their drifting island was some five miles by one mile in dimension—an ample platform for the time being.

The *Polaris* at 82°11' N on September 1, 1871 (United States Naval Historical Center, Washington, D.C.

Theirs would be a long and harrowing voyage, drifting helplessly from Ellesmere Island south past Baffin Island all the way to the coast of Labrador over a period of half a year. Temperatures were regularly -40°F or lower, and many on the floe developed frostbite—one man lost both feet and most of both hands to this insidious enemy. Tyson, nominally in charge, kept everyone on short rations (and most of the men grumbled bitterly about this), but finally the ship's provisions ran out, and they had to rely on the two Inuit men to catch seals or dovekies (small seabirds). When all else failed, everyone was forced to chew on sealskin thongs and to eat the burned seal blubber from the lamps.

The German members apparently were reluctant to move out of their sleeping bags and also reluctant to allow the increasingly exhausted Inuit hunters a larger share of the seal, foxes, and other creatures they killed. Dissension was rife, and Tyson was largely powerless to enforce any regime against the armed crew. The Inuit children were constantly crying from hunger, the world was increasingly gloomy, and people began dropping off, racked by scurvy and other ailments, the cold, and starvation. Five men died (usually quite peacefully, Tyson reported, once they had all accepted that they had no future). Tyson, often delirious himself, simply entreated the men to die like men, not beasts—this in response to numerous instances of food theft. In spite of all they were doing to keep the crew alive, the Inuit knew full well that the German members of the crew were eyeing them as the first to be cannibalized—if it came to that.

With the coming of warmer weather, the ice floes began breaking up, and the expedition's ice island was fragmenting under their iglus and tents, finally leaving them with a platform so small that they could not all lie down at once. Gales brought huge seas washing over the floe, and the weakened, dying men nonetheless had to stand for hours in this weather, hoping to keep the one remaining boat, their only hope of reaching the land that was always just out of sight, from being washed away. They never did get to use it; instead, on April 29, they were finally rescued by a steamship within sight of the Labrador coast—after a voyage of horror that traversed at least 1,800 miles—one of the most astonishing episodes in the history of the Arctic or elsewhere.

Meanwhile, Budington and the others on board the *Polaris,* having in fact made no effort to rescue the people stranded on the ice floe, made for Greenland and reached the friendly Inuit settlement at Etah, where they were sustained through the winter by Inuit kindness, setting off in two boats in the spring, and subsequently were rescued by a whaler.

Later a Naval Board of Inquiry looked into Hall's death and the other unfortunate aspects of the expedition. It came out that as early as October 1871 Budington and Bessels were openly hostile to Hall and his plans. Budington was dead set against going farther north, and young Bessels considered Hall to be incompetent. According to testimony given by others, Budington had said of Hall's death, "There's a stone off my heart." Bessels was reported as saying, "Captain Hall's death was the best thing that could happen for the expedition." Such comments notwithstanding, the board of inquiry had little to go on and finally concurred with Bessels that Hall had died of "apoplexy," or what we call a stroke, and not poisoning.

One of the German officers on board gainsaid Tyson's reckoning of how far north *Polaris* had reached under Hall, further diminishing Hall's accomplishments, which in fact included taking a ship straight through the waters between Ellesmere Island and Greenland and reaching the edge of the polar sea—which Hall had established was icebound and not open, as so many had believed for so long.

The navy evidently wished to avoid the sort of scandal that would have ensued if Tyson's version of events had been believed. Later a great Scandinavian explorer, Vilhjalmur Stefansson, would point out that the continuing rumors that Hall had been poisoned, probably with arsenic, could easily be resolved by digging up the no doubt still frozen corpse in Thank God Harbor and testing its hair. But the suggestion was greeted with an icy silence until a century had passed and an

English professor at Dartmouth, Chauncey Loomis, undertook a biography of Hall that he entitled *Weird and Tragic Shores,* published in 1971. He took on the process of solving the mystery surrounding Hall's death and obtained permission from the Danish government's Ministry of Greenland to uncover the grave and take hair and fingernail samples for analysis. (Hall's body had mummified in the permafrost, with skin the texture of leather.) The samples were sent to the Centre of Forensic Sciences in Toronto, which reported that they revealed "an intake of considerable amounts of arsenic by C.F. Hall in the last two weeks of his life." So Hall died from arsenic poisoning, not a stroke, and there is little doubt where the arsenic came from: In the form of arsenious acid, it was a standard part of medical supplies in the 1870s for the treatment of headaches, ulcers, cancer, gout, and syphilis.

Hall, had he lived and not been so badly discredited, could have let subsequent explorers know that there was no Open Polar Sea, but it would have to be proven again. In the meantime, the oceanographer Maury had been replaced as the United States Navy's man in these affairs by Silas Bent, who stoutly defended the concept of the open ocean. But, unimpressed by the man's credentials or his arguments, Charles P. Daly, president of the American Geographical and Statistical Society, took Bent on in his presidential address of 1870. He said loftily that he was not about to comment on Bent's "deductions" from the laws of ocean currents, because "our knowledge of these laws is imperfect," and also because they were hypothetical and best left to those "who have made hydrographical studies a specialty"; beyond that, he added, what was called for were actual "facts and not theories." He pooh-poohed Bent's idea that the Gulf Stream and Japanese current provided warm-water gateways to the Pole, saying that no one knew for sure where the Gulf Stream went beyond the coast of Norway but that it *was* known to diminish and weaken in the Arctic, making it unlikely that it reached the Pole or had sufficient heat in it to affect the climate of the polar basin. Daly was not, by the way, a man of science; he was a judge.

Two years after Daly's skeptical address, the Austrians mounted an expedition under the leadership of Karl Weyprecht and attempted the Northeast Passage, but they became beset by ice, spending two winters in the Arctic and returning without much to show for it besides the discovery of a new land, which they called Franz Josef Land. Later, in 1875, Weyprecht would urge on a group of scientists the idea of a synchronous international exploration of the Arctic for scientific purposes, and not the inflated and unimportant stunts of finding new islands and racing one another to the Pole. What, he asked, is the nature of the Arctic climate? What drives it? How does it affect the weather of warmer latitudes?

Neither Hall nor Daly (nor Weyprecht) would be taken seriously by the British, whose national pride had been significantly piqued. The British believed that the Americans, despite little in the way of official backing on inadequate equipment, had gotten rather far north in their quest for the Pole, Hayes and Kane having actually come across the Open Polar Sea before returning. Surely the English boosters of an expedition, which included the leaders of the Royal Geographical Society and the British navy, could do better.

On May 29, 1875, flags fluttered in Portsmouth Harbor and people cheered. Sir George Nares was about to set out for the Pole, the plan being to pass between Ellesmere Island and Greenland, breach the annulus of ice, and sail triumphantly to the Pole. The London *Times* burbled that the enthusiasm of the assembled multitude "indicate[s] pretty clearly that a true chord has been struck, and that the sympathies of all, from the Queen downwards, go with" the expedition. Indeed, the crowd was aware that "the crews were about to enter upon a battle with Nature in her sternest aspects, and that it was the honour for the country that this should be so."

Sir George Nares was one of the few remaining men alive who had served in the Franklin rescue efforts. He was a seaman of unquestioned ability and had been called back by the Admiralty to take on this Arctic expedition from the ship *Challenger,* the first vessel to be equipped specifically for oceanographic

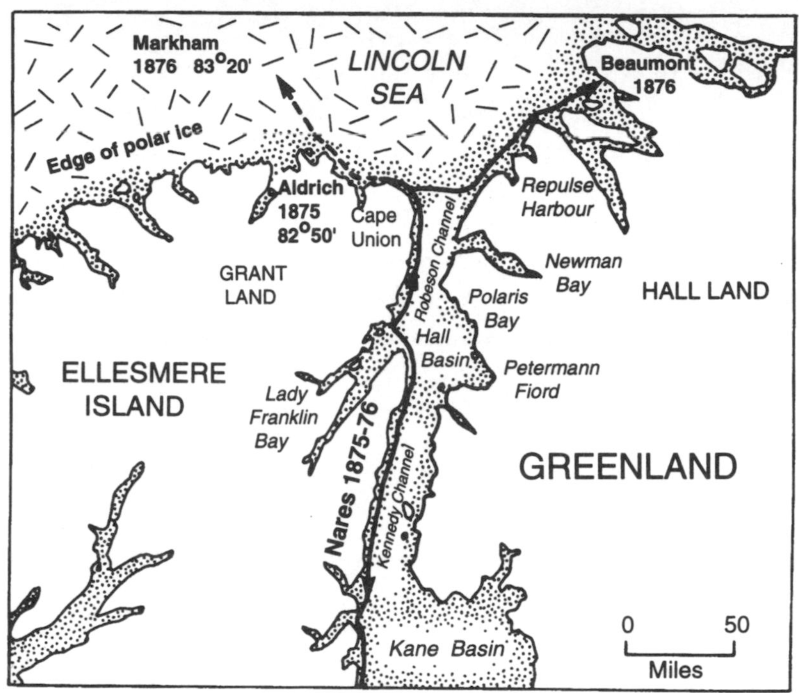

The Nares expedition, 1875–1876 (From Berton 1988)

science. Sir George was not a scientist but a close observer: He had earlier noted on the *Challenger*'s oceanographic expedition that the distribution of temperatures in the Atlantic showed that that ocean was divided down the middle by "one of a chain of banks with less than 2000 fathoms of water over them," this being the first mention anywhere of what we now know to be the Mid-Atlantic Ridge, where two tectonic plates are moving apart, with upward-flowing lava filling the gap. On his polar expedition, Nares was served by eager volunteer officers, "the Royal Navy suffering," as one historian put it, "from a slump in sea warfare," making an Arctic voyage the best game in town for obtaining promotions.

They all set out in two ships, the *Alert* and the *Discovery,* and before long both were beset in the ice, the *Alert* in Floeberg Bay at 82° 27' N, the farthest north any ship would go under her own power until the age of icebreakers in 1948. The other ship was beset in Lady Franklin Bay. Nares sent out several sledge

One of the Nares's sledge parties (National Maritime Museum, London)

parties from both ships, and one of these achieved a farthest north of 83° 20' N, the best effort to that date in the Arctic. Even with such achievement, the expedition was doomed—and it had been doomed from the start. Inexplicably, the Royal Navy had learned nothing from its own failed expeditions of the early 1800s, nor had it learned anything from people, such as John Rae (in England at the time), who had thrived in the Arctic. The Nares expedition was allowed to leave port with inadequate navy-issue clothing, improper food to prevent scurvy, and inadequate sledges to cross the hummocky terrain of the northern ice. They took no snowshoes and had no experience building houses out of ice; none of Nares' officers had ever even seen an iceberg. And, of course, seeking help from the locals was out of the question.

The result of all this was that by spring Nares had some sixty cases of scurvy on his hands, and several in the sledge parties had died. Though equipped to spend a second winter in the Arctic, Nares prudently returned early, reaching Portsmouth on November 2, 1876. The expedition was widely judged a disappointment among the English—who had been oversold in the beginning. A board of inquiry later took the expedition and its

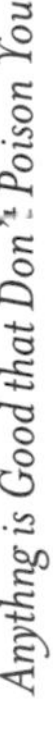

planners to task for all the lapses in plan that had led to such a sorry conclusion, pointing out, among other things, that two dogs can do the pulling of one man but eat less than one man and require no clothing. But they did achieve one thing: A bit redundantly, they proved that there was no Open Polar Sea, but instead a great frozen ocean.

Yet it was still possible, though barely, for diehards to believe in an open polar sea, thinking that Hall and Nares simply had not been looking in the right place. One possible way to the sea was still untried: the route of the Bering Strait between Alaska and Siberia. This was the route championed by Silas Bent, the navy's chief hydrographer, in the face of the skepticism of Judge Daly as announced in 1870. The idea was that the Kuroshio, a Pacific current that is the equivalent of the Atlantic's Gulf Stream, split near the Kamchatka Peninsula, with a northern branch proceeding through the Bering Strait—"a thermometric gateway to the Pole."

Amid the polar passion of the Americans and, however briefly, the English, an altogether dispassionate expedition took place designed to resolve a matter of Arctic exploration that was not so romantic as the Pole, but perhaps more commercially useful. We noted earlier that Adolf Erik Nordenskiöld began voyaging to the Arctic on scientific missions beginning in 1858. He made five more such expeditions and was the leader of the last four; on two occasions he attempted to reach the Pole but was turned back by the ice in each case. Even so, by 1868 he was well known by a world that was hungry for daring heroes. In times of relative peace, such adventurers were comparable to the first waves of astronauts and cosmonauts in our era. In Sweden Nordenskiöld was indeed not unlike John Glenn, being elected a member of the Swedish parliament, a position he would hold until 1893.

In 1875 and 1876 Nordenskiöld made two more Arctic trips, to the Barents and Kara Seas, expeditions designed to dredge for biological specimens and also to determine the feasibility of trade between Europe and Siberia via a northern ocean route.

With ships powered by steam as well as sail, they were able to improve on the records set by others in quest of the Northeast Passage, and pass south of Novaya Zemlya and up the Yenisey River.

Then in 1878 the Swedish Northeast Passage expedition left port, sponsored by the Swedish government and financed by a Swedish businessman, Oscar Dickson, and a Siberian counterpart, Aleksandr Sibiryakov. Its purpose was simple: navigate the Northeast Passage from the Norwegian Sea to the Bering Strait. Nordenskiöld was in charge of the entire expedition (which also had a scientific component, as did all such voyages) and the ship, the *Vega,* was under the command of Captain Louis Palander. On July 28 they passed south of the Novaya Zemlya, and on August 19 they passed south of Severnaya Zemlya, the northernmost part of Asia usually affected by ice. Nordenskiöld and company were the first to pass from the Kara to the Laptev Sea, and on September 28 they were obliged to stop and overwinter at Kolyichinskaya Guba, a mere 200 miles from their ultimate destination. The only unexpected complexities they encountered were some minor fracases with the local native population.

Ten months later, on July 18, the ice let them out, and the *Vega* reached Yokohama, Japan, on September 2. From there they made their leisurely way back to Sweden, passing through the Indian Ocean, the Suez Canal, and the Mediterranean. Regaled by well-wishers all along their journey, they reached Stockholm on April 24, 1880, acclaimed as heroes. Their expedition had been superbly planned and professionally carried out, without anything that could be considered a serious mishap. Such expeditions, unpunctuated by Sturm und Drang, do not usually make for very exciting reading, but Nordenskiöld wrote a two-volume account of the voyage that was sufficiently financially successful that he could buy a country estate and add to his collection of maps.

(In a footnote to a pleasant bit of Arctic history, the Swedes intended to celebrate the fortieth anniversary of the *Vega*'s expedition in 1920. Someone had the idea of inquiring about

Sibiryakov, the Russian merchant who had helped make the voyage possible. It was found that he had fled Russia after the Communist Revolution and was living in poverty in the southern coast of France. The Swedish government voted him an annual pension that sustained him comfortably until his death in 1933.)

In 1879 people could look at the great European cartographer Petermann's map of the north and see a final west-stretching arm of what he took to be a much larger, pole-crossing Greenland. This arm, which we know now is an island, was called Wrangle Land. One person who took this map at face value was James Gordon Bennett, owner of the *New York Herald,* which had enjoyed a splendid surge in circulation when its man Henry Morton Stanley found Dr. David Livingstone in darkest Africa. Bennett had grown interested in the Arctic and the race for the Pole. He bought a small yacht called the *Pandora*, renamed it the *Jeannette,* and persuaded the U.S. Navy to man it on a dash to the Pole via the Bering Strait. The leader of this voyage was a young

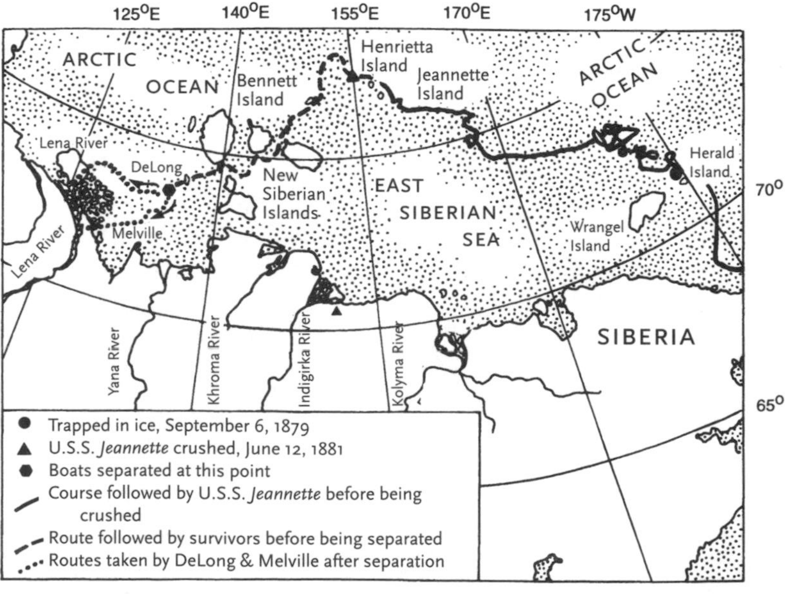

Track of the *Jeannette* and survivors in the East Siberian Sea (From Caswell 1956)

The *Jeannette* sinking (United States Naval Historical Center, Washington)

lieutenant, George Washington DeLong, who was instructed to sail as far north via the Bering Strait as possible, proceeding along the coast of Wrangel-Greenland, and to go overland by sledge along that arm of land to the Pole if necessary. Thus would Bennett bag the Pole for the United States of America. But by the autumn of 1879 the *Jeannette* was trapped in the ice, and she drifted about aimlessly in its clutches for eighteen months.

By then a disillusioned DeLong was convinced that Wrangel Land was an island, perhaps an archipelago. He believed, along with others, that warm ocean currents do not regulate the northern ice, but vice versa, writing that "if any warm current came through Bering Strait it would be the Kuro Siwo, and our sea temperatures indicated no such fact." He was, he realized, on a fool's errand. "No matter what the difficulties, or troubles, or accidents," he wrote in his journal, "the failure to do the specified thing stands out in bold letters. So with us. We started for the Pole; we are beset in the pack in 71 plus; we drift northwest; our ship is injured . . . : we drift back southeast."

In a cry of pain and disappointment, he wrote: " . . . [W]e have failed, inasmuch as we did not reach the Pole; and we and our narrative together are thrown into the world's dreary wastebasket, and recalled and remembered only to be vilified and ridiculed."

On June 12, 1881, the *Jeannette* was crushed in the ice and sank the next day. The crew escaped onto the floes near the New Siberian Islands and attempted to maneuver over ice, water, and land to the Lena River. They made their way overland to a land mass called Bennett Island and from there went south to the delta. A storm intervened, and one party was lost, never to be seen again. Others, in two boats, separately made it to safety—but DeLong was not one of them. Of thirty-three men on the expedition, only thirteen survived.

Three years later, on June 18, 1884, three Inuits out on the ice floes on the other side of the world, off southern Greenland, picked up a torn checkbook, a broken box, and a pair of oilskin trousers. The boxes bore the name *Jeanette*, and the oilskin trousers bore the name of one of that ship's survivors. This bit of serendipity would later give one of the Arctic's greatest explorers one of his greatest ideas.

Word of the DeLong fiasco didn't reach America until 1881, and by then the United States had embarked on another ill-starred Arctic expedition, this one under the command of Adolphus Greely, who was a lieutenant not in the navy but in the army. Several nations of Europe and the United States had taken up the idea originally offered by the Austrian Weyprecht for an international year of polar exploration. The U.S. Army had leaped at the idea and agreed to send a ship fully outfitted for scientific observations to one of eleven specified stations—the American station to be the farthest north of all. Greely evidently also was given secret instructions to make a dash for the Pole, which had up until then been the navy's province.

The plan was to leave in 1880, but the navy held things up, refusing to sanction the use of the ship, the *Proteus.* In the ensuing interservice feuding a fed-up Greely resigned, only to be rehired when the feud was resolved the next year, only two months before departure. The *Proteus,* as planned, dropped the men and their equipment off at Discovery Harbor (where Nares had overwintered), and the squabbles broke out almost immediately, with one officer resigning over his disgust at being asked to rise in the morning at the same early hour as the enlisted men. The *Proteus* left before this man was officially relieved, so he remained in an unofficial capacity—never something welcomed in a military situation. A supply ship was supposed to arrive the following year, and a relief expedition the year following that—1883. Greely named their encampment Fort Conger and that winter sent out dog sledge parties toward the Pole, one of these besting the record from the Nares push by four miles, reaching 83° 24' N.

More squabbles broke out after the resupply ship didn't show up. Greely never was completely in charge and seemed to be what today might be referred to as a minor-league martinet. The physician on board thought further sledge trips were a bad idea, using needed food supplies, and in a rancorous argument with Greely refused to sign up for another year. Greely arrested him, which seems an idiotic solution given the remoteness of their situation.

As the long Arctic winter set in, Greely cast about for some means of amusing the men. He had no musical instruments, no library, and we can assume, none of the theatrical bent of Edward Parry more than two centuries earlier. He decided to give "daily, a lecture of from 1 to 2 hours in length upon the physical geography and the resources of the United States in general; followed later by similar talks on each state and territory in particular." He spoke of grain and fruit production and gave an hour to mineral production, reporting that it "was interesting to note the lack of interest shown by the party regarding the production of gold and silver."

When no relief ship appeared by August 1883, they finally abandoned the *Proteus* and left in the ship's boats, which, it being too late in the season, were hemmed in by the ice. Plagued by indecision and storms (which destroyed much of the scientific equipment and records), they overwintered on Cape Sabine, 33 miles across the water from the Inuit village of Etah on Greenland. There, on diminishing rations, they squabbled and fought through the three months of sunless days, several men dying, the rest desperately netting krill from the sea, hoping to nab the occasional fox, and harvesting lichens from rocks. Jens Edward, one of the two Inuit hunters who were capable of hunting down seals, died when his kayak capsized—a major loss. In June one of the crew spotted Private C.B. Henry taking meat from some abandoned winter quarters and claimed it was human meat. Greely had him shot. People continued to die of starvation and the cold; the physician ingested narcotics from his medicinal stores and died, apparently a case of suicide.

Eventually the remaining few men were rescued by Newfoundland sealers commissioned by the U.S. Navy, and Greely went on to lay pipelines in the Philippines and to help oversee the cleanup of San Francisco after the 1906 earthquake leveled the city. Meanwhile, in America, the polar passion ebbed away for a decade, so calamitous and even macabre had the last three efforts been—those of Hall, DeLong, and Greely. But if the Pole seemed beyond the reach of mere men, and if the achievement of yet another farthest north hardly seemed worth the expense in lives lost and others ruined, there were other challenges remaining in the Arctic, and there were men interested in taking them on.

EIGHT

Three Faces *of* Ambition

BY 1880 IT WAS GENERALLY AND, AT LAST, assumed that there was no Open Polar Sea. Instead, the North Pole and much of the Arctic Ocean were understood to be covered with ice year round. There could be only two ways to achieve the Pole—by slogging over the ice with sledges, or by air (airplanes were decades away, of course, but there were hot-air balloons). But after Greely's aborted effort, the polar urge ebbed for about a decade. Everybody knew where the Pole was and could imagine what it looked like. No new and important knowledge would be added to the world's wisdom by actually reaching the Pole; no strategic advantage would accrue to the nation who first placed a citizen on it; and the patenting of the first zipper in 1893 would have a far more profound economic effect than any successful expedition to the Pole. It simply lurked up there as a challenge by which some individuals would one day again choose to measure themselves.

Along with the first navigation of the Northwest Passage, another, more modest (though highly perilous) goal remained unreached: No one, or at least no European, had crossed the Greenland ice cap, crouching atop this large island. Here on Greenland, three of the most remarkable men in the history of Arctic exploration would try out their survival skills from 1886 to 1892 in a prelude to their great race for the North Pole. One would die a clouded hero, one would do time for fraud in a federal penitentiary, and one would go on to win the Nobel Peace Prize.

* * *

In 1886, when polar exploits resumed, Robert Peary was thirty years old, a civil engineer in the United States Navy with the rank of lieutenant. His father had died when he was but three years old, and he was raised by his mother, to whom he wrote at age twenty-four: "I don't know whether it is my fortune or misfortune, or whether it is the sign of an ignoble spirit, but I cannot bear to associate with people, who, age & advantages being equal, are my superiors. I must be the peer or superior of those about me to be comfortable, not that I care to show my superiority, simply to know it myself."

From this curiously introspective young officer would eventually rise the most driven, even fanatical, Arctic explorer of all time. He would be a lifelong member of the navy, winning extensive leaves of absence for his much-publicized Arctic trips, of which he made eight—more than anyone else. His first one, in 1886, was quite modest—an attempt to cross the Greenland ice cap. He borrowed funds from his mother to travel by ship to the southwest coast of Greenland and headed north to Disko Bay, where he attempted to cross the big island from west to east along with a young Dane whom he had met, Christian Maigaard, and two Greenlanders. On foot, they got about 90 miles inland and reached an elevation of almost 3,000 meters, the highest to date and the farthest north, but were forced to return by foul weather.

Peary reported that he had penetrated the ice cap farther than had previously been achieved, but this, it turns out, was an exaggeration: Five years earlier some Lapps on an expedition across the ice cap led by Nordenskiöld had gone farther inland. But even with his actual achievement, not to mention his claim, Peary was well on his way to the fame he so desired. He wrote his mother soon afterward, confiding that his trip "has brought my name before the world and my next will give me standing in the world." His exploits would lead to "an enduring name & honor" and "social advancement . . . powerful friends with whom I can shape my future instead of letting it come as it will."

He went on, writing emphatically, "Remember Mother I *must*

TABLE 3

CHRONOLOGY OF THE EIGHT ARCTIC EXPEDITIONS UNDER THE LEADERSHIP OF ROBERT PEARY

YEARS	OTHER PERSONNEL	REGION
1886	Christian Maigaard	Greenland
1891–1892	Frederick Cook, Eivind Astrup, Matthew Henson	Greenland
1893–1895	Eivind Astrup, Matthew Henson	Greenland
1896	Matthew Henson, John Bartlett	Greenland
1897	Matthew Henson, John Bartlett	Greenland
1898–1902	Matthew Henson, Thomas Dedrick	North Pole
1905–1906	Matthew Henson, Robert Bartlett	North Pole
1908–1909	Matthew Henson, Robert Bartlett, Donald MacMillan	North Pole

have fame & I cannot reconcile myself to years of commonplace drudgery & a name late in life when I see an opportunity to gain it now & sip the delicious draught." Surely such was the motivation of most of the men who sought to triumph over the Arctic, not to mention most adventurers in general. In any event, Peary immediately began to lay plans for a return trip and another attempt to cross Greenland. But two years later, before he could get under way, his hopes were dashed to pieces.

Enter Fridtjof Nansen, a Norwegian man for all seasons and, indeed, a hero several times over. As a youth, Nansen grew tall and strong, an excellent skier, skater, hunter, and fisherman. At the university in Oslo (then called Christiana), he elected to study zoology, in part because it would keep him outdoors. In 1882 he shipped aboard a sealer for a voyage into Greenland waters and saw the Greenland ice cap from afar, thinking that it should be possible to cross it. In 1887 he announced his plan, which stood on their heads the notions of other such explorers—notably Nordenskiöld and Peary, both of whom had sought to cross Greenland from its inhabited west coast, thus having the option to return to some modicum of civilization if things went awry. Nansen, on the other hand, who had the most profound faith in his stamina and planning, decided that he could start from the uninhabited and barren east coast and, cutting off any useful line of retreat, force himself to press on. The major task in such a plan would be to get up over the ice-covered east coast mountain range. From its top, at an elevation of 8,920 feet, it would be downhill skiing all the rest of the way, with a wind behind them to boot. So he reasoned, but others thought the idea suicidal. And indeed, if Nansen was somehow wrong, his party could easily perish in the attempt.

Having completed his work for a doctorate in zoology, he left Norway aboard a sealer with five companions in May 1888 and arrived, after some difficulties with the weather, on the east coast of Greenland on August 15. Amid severe storms, the party snowshoed up the eastern mountain range, arriving at the top on September 5, and skied down the western slopes and across the ice cap, arriving on the west coast at Ameralik Fjord three weeks later, on September 26. Nansen had, among other things, answered a previously unanswered question: Did the ice cap extend all the way across Greenland? For this venture, Nansen had developed some light and flexible sledges with which dogs could haul provisions; these vehicles were based on both Inuit and Norwegian designs, came to be known as Nanseny sledges, and were used by subsequent explorers for decades to come. The party was forced to overwinter at the settlement of Godthåb, where Nansen spent his time learning more of the ways of the Inuit there.

It had been a flawless expedition, with little drama or melodrama. Later, in 1891, Nansen would write a book titled *Eskimo Life* about this journey, in which he included an odd incident—the sort of coincidental meeting that so often would occur in the vast Arctic region. The first European he met after reaching the west coast in Ameralik Fjord was a Dane in a tam-o'-shanter but otherwise dressed in the manner of the Inuit, who asked him if he was English or spoke English. Nansen replied in Norse and revealed that he was Fridtjof Nansen.

The Dane then said, "Allow me to congratulate you on taking your doctor's degree." Nansen wrote that, "to put it mildly, it struck me as comical that I should cross Greenland to receive congratulations of my Doctor's degree, which I happened to have taken just before I left home. Nothing, of course, could have been more removed from my thoughts at the moment."

The party returned to Norway in May 1889, and Nansen was acclaimed as a national hero. He had placed Scandinavia in ascendancy over the polar explorers of North America and the rest of Europe, and confounded the experts by going east to west. He was appointed curator of zoology at the university in Oslo, but without specific responsibilities. He was free, in other words, to do whatever he wished. And he had begun to develop a far more ambitious and innovative plan. He had read about the discovery of some of the relics of the failed American expedition under the leadership of George Washington DeLong in Baffin Bay, all the way across the world from where he had wrecked. They had to have been carried there by the drifting ice, Nansen reasoned.

Meanwhile, Robert Peary was in the midst of planning his second attempt to cross the Greenland ice cap when the world heard about Nansen's splendid performance. Peary was furious and accused Nansen of stealing his plans and of preempting him in a way that was inappropriate. Nevertheless, he needed to shift gears quickly, and chose a new objective—to determine the northern limit of Greenland. In 1888 no one knew how far it extended to the north or the east. Petermann's map, showing it reaching virtually to the Pole and its western arm being Wrangle Land near the Bering Strait, was still in use. So Peary announced an expedition to cross northern Greenland from west to east to chart its unknown northeastern shoreline and determine, if possible, its northern extent. Set to get under way in 1891, this would be a grander expedition than his first, and he obtained the sponsorship of the Philadelphia Academy of Natural Sciences and the American Geographical Society. Under the aegis of these august organizations, he was more easily able to raise the money for the voyage. Peary, as was the custom, put notices in newspapers that he was engaged in outfitting his United States North Greenland Expedition and seeking crew members for it.

Enter Frederick Cook, an American who had just (and barely) passed his examination to become a physician in 1890 after graduating from New York University. He had been raised in a poor family in Brooklyn and worked, among other places, in a dairy to put himself through medical school. He had just set up a practice in Brooklyn when he saw Peary's notice, and volunteered to serve as surgeon without pay. He was accepted and thus began his polar career, one that would eventually put him on a collision course with Peary himself. Nansen, Peary, and Cook would all in due course be—at least figuratively—at each other's throats. Nansen was already among those who pointed out that Peary had exaggerated the extent of his initial trek onto the Greenland ice in 1886.

Peary's new expedition included Cook as surgeon; a Norwegian named Eivind Astrup, who had, like Cook, responded to the newspaper notice offering to volunteer his time; Peary's black manservant, Matthew Henson; and Peary's wife, Jo. The ship *Kite* left them off in the vicinity of today's Thule Air Force Base on the northwest coast of Greenland at the head of Baffin Bay, where they were to overwinter and be picked up the following year by the *Kite.* Cook's presence on the expedition came in for early appreciation when Peary broke his leg on the voyage and needed medical attention. At this juncture, the two men gained a great respect for each other.

During the summer of 1892, his leg now healed, Peary, along with Astrup, made a tremendous overland traverse to the northeast of 500 miles of unrelieved ice, finally reaching a promontory that Peary named Navy Cliff. That, plus the return of another 500 miles, was the longest such trek ever undertaken in the Arctic and was a notable achievement in itself. Peary reported later that from Navy Cliff he saw a body of water to the east, which he called Independence Bay. Thus he had reached the northeastern coast of Greenland. Looking north, he saw a landform that he called Peary Land, separated from the mainland by a channel he called Peary Channel, thus determining the northern extent of Greenland. Peary Land was apparently an island, perhaps part of an archipelago that extended farther north.

It is impossible at this remove in time to determine what it

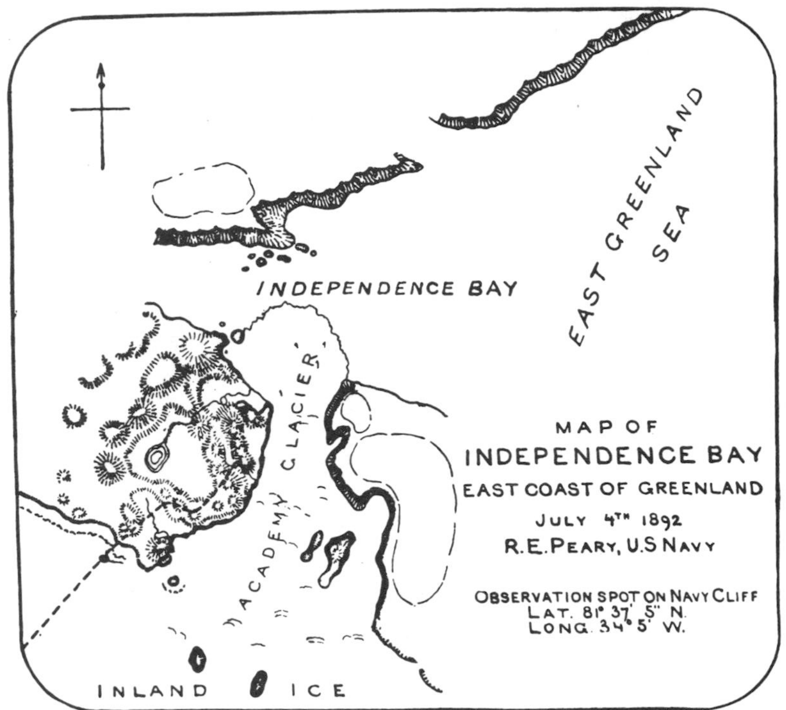

Sketch map of "Independence Bay," east coast of Greenland (From Peary 1898)

was that Peary saw (or didn't see). Independence Bay was not a bay, which is a broad indentation immediately adjacent to a coast, but a fjord, which is an elongated inlet with its head up to a hundred miles or more distant from the coast. Independence Bay is now known correctly as Independence Fjord. Overlooking this fjord, Peary was still some 200 miles from Greenland's northeast coast.

Also, there is no Peary Channel, and Peary Land is part of the mainland; no archipelago extends north. In his own report to Norwegian geographers, Astrup made no mention of the Peary Channel and said that no conclusion could safely be drawn as to what body of water extended to the east from Navy Cliff. The *American Geographical Society Journal* later reported the commentary of European geographers, one of whom found it "at least surprising" that Astrup made no mention of the discovery of the northern end of Greenland, "as if it were a matter

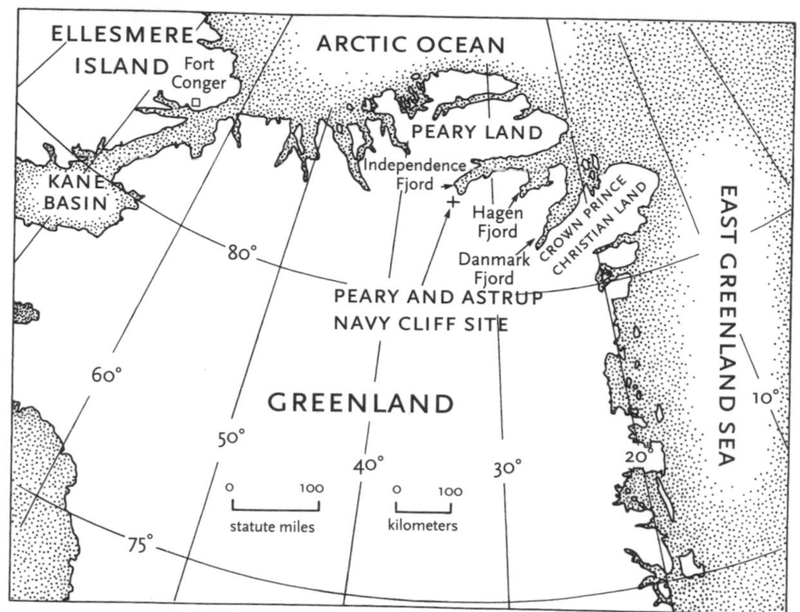

Map of northern and northeastern Greenland. The cross marks the Peary and Astrup Navy Cliff site

of secondary importance." Another said, "The Norwegians are for the most part truthful observers. . . . The American Polar voyagers, we regret to say, do not always inspire the same confidence, since the exaggerations of [Isaac Israel] Hayes."

Immediately upon his return to the United States in September 1892, Peary began planning another expedition for the following year, and Frederick Cook was offered and accepted the position as surgeon. But then a breach between the two men occurred. Upon returning, Cook lectured to medical societies about the lifeways of the Inuit, and decided to write a book about it. In this endeavor, he asked if Peary would let him use photographs that Cook himself and others had taken. Peary reminded Cook that he had agreed not to publish anything about the expedition of 1891 until a year after Peary's narrative appeared, and he refused to allow the use of the photographs. After all, the financing of Peary's next expedition depended on the success of his lectures and narrative, and indeed, Peary was an indefatigable lecturer, giving 165 of them in the 103 days after his return. Reasonable as the refusal was, Cook saw it otherwise. Deeply annoyed, he decided not to accompany Peary on his next expedition.

But Cook had the Arctic ambition. He spent the better part of the next two years on what were essentially frivolous expeditions. In the summer of 1893 he was hired by a Yale University professor to take his son on a sight-seeing trip to the Arctic, so Cook chartered a ship and crew and they traveled to Newfoundland, Labrador, and the west coast of Greenland. In 1894 he organized a hunting expedition of some fifty sportsmen to travel to northwest Greenland, chartering a ship called the *Miranda*. On July 17 the ship struck an iceberg and had to return to Labrador for repairs. Then, heading for Greenland, she struck a submerged ledge and eventually had to be abandoned. The crew and passengers were soon rescued by a fishing schooner and taken to Newfoundland. Not to be discouraged, on the return trip to the United States the assembled sportsmen decided on the basis of their shared experience to form a club. It was called the Arctic Club, and it would play an important role in the Arctic exploration in the future. (That august group exists to this day, meeting in New York City.)

While Cook was acting as Arctic guide in 1893 and 1894, Peary was on his way to what he hoped would be a new triumph. He left the United States for Greenland on June 26, 1893, with a party of fourteen that included Astrup and Henson again, as well as a doctor and nurse for Jo Peary, who was pregnant and delivered the Pearys' first child, Marie, on September 12 at their base camp, slightly north of Thule. Aside from Marie's arrival, the expedition was considered a dismal failure by all hands, including Peary himself. In the summer of 1884 they were able to force a traverse of no more than 128 miles to the northeast, beaten back by intensely bad weather, and Peary sent everyone back to base camp except for himself, Henson, and a young volunteer named Hugh Lee. In 1895 these three made it to Navy Cliff and nearly starved on their return trip, having to slaughter and eat their dogs. Peary was able to add nothing to his previous expedition, much less find a convenient route to the Pole.

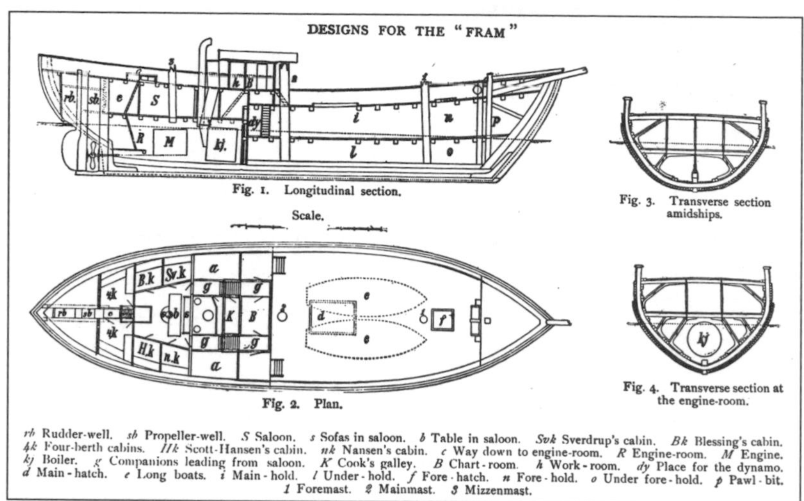

Designs for the *Fram* (From Nansen 1898)

For Peary, as for any other explorer, such a wholesale failure simply wouldn't do. He knew that many years earlier John Ross had mentioned the existence of three nickel-iron meteorites from which the Inuit made iron implements. Peary went south to Cape York, found them, and brought the two smaller ones back with him by sledge. *Small* is a relative term, of course; one weighed 300 pounds, the other 6,000.

Nevertheless, Peary felt himself to be at the nadir of his career. Indeed, he saw his dreams disappearing, his polar career at an end. On his return, he told the *New York Times:* "I shall never see the north pole unless someone brings it here. I am done with it." He went on to explain that such ventures required a younger man than he, "a trained man, a thorough athlete, and that I am not." He was in his forties at the time, "not an old man, as age is reckoned here, but I am too old for that sort of work."

Even so, Peary would soon recover his élan and his Arctic dreams. Perhaps the success of his rival Nansen had something to do with it.

In 1893, with the full financial backing of the nation's parliament and its king, Nansen set off on an extraordinary voyage, a passive reconnoiter of the Arctic. Based on the reported discovery of DeLong relics on the "wrong" side of the world, Nansen concluded that if he had the right sort of ship, he too could drift with the ice across the Arctic Sea. No one had ever even contemplated such a hazardous venture, but Nansen had the utmost confidence in his own abilities, his careful planning, and (of extreme importance) the scientific precision he brought to analyzing the situation he would face. Rather than refitting an existing ship, he needed a new ship with a totally new design—it should have a bathtub-shaped cross section so that it would ride up on the ice rather than being squeezed and crushed. But a ship with a flattened bottom was hardly oceanworthy. Nansen soon found a man who had designed maneuverable harbor pilot boats, and the two of them came up with a design that would permit the ship to sail to the ice margin and also to be carried upward and along with the floes. Once built, it was a compact ship with a displacement of 800 tons, a length at the waterline of 113 feet, a width of 34 feet across the beam, and a depth of 17 feet. Nansen named this sailing ship with an auxiliary engine *Fram,* which means "forward." She can still be seen in a refurbished condition at the Fram Museum outside Oslo.

The *Fram* left Oslo on June 24, 1893, with a crew of thirteen, including expedition leader Nansen. If Nansen had been at all wrong in his assumptions, he likely would have gone down in history as vain and foolhardy—and perhaps prematurely dead. The British humor magazine *Punch* saw fit to make some fun at Nansen's expense:

So Dr. Fridtjof Nansen's off!
Cynics will chuckle and pessimists scoff,
What a noodle, that Norroway chap,
Who'd drift to the Pole to—complete our map.

The *Fram* followed the same route as Nordenskiöld had with the *Vega* to the New Siberian Islands, and then, in late September, she became frozen fast in the ice. Drifting with the ice, she took a zigzag path to the northwest and then to the southwest, where she was released from the ice in July 1896—what amounted to three years in the ice. Along the way, there were scientific measurements and observations to be made (aside, of course, from confirming that the ice drifted from the New Siberian Islands to Spitzbergen). For example, the expedition established that the Eurasian side of the Arctic Ocean was a deep basin and not a shallow sea. Indeed, even Nansen had assumed the Arctic Ocean was relatively shallow throughout, and the cables he had brought along to sound its depths were nowhere near long enough, a problem he solved by unraveling the individual cables and stringing the pieces together. A six-volume scientific report, compiled at the voyage's end, contained information that is of value still on the oceanography, bathymetry, and bottom deposits of the Arctic Ocean; the natural history of Arctic birds, crustaceans, and plankton; astronomy; terrestrial magnetism and gravity; and meteorology.

NOTHING BUT ICE, ICE TO THE HORIZON. APRIL 7, 1895

Nansen on a pressure ridge near his Farthest North (From Nansen 1898)

Partway along, Nansen realized they were not going to pass near the North Pole, so he left the ship on March 14, 1895, with a companion, Hjalmar Johansen, twenty-eight dogs, three sledges, two kayaks for crossing open water, a tent and stove, skis and snowshoes, and provisions for a hundred days. They were to attempt a dash for the Pole, but as it turned out, the two men would be on the ice for nearly fifteen months.

At first the going was easy, but by March 29, only a couple of weeks into their trek, they were confronted with "great ridges of piled-up ice of dismal aspect," as Nansen wrote later. The following day they were stopped by "ugly pressure ridges of the worst kind, formed by the packing of enormous blocks," and the following day Johansen fell into the water as the ice broke under him. The open lead widened, and they had one man and a sledge on one side, two sledges and a wet man on the other. Later the lead froze over and they pressed on; after some level areas, they were again confronted with pressure ridges, and Nansen began to realize that the ice was moving south under them. By April 8 Nansen realized that "there is not much sense in keeping on longer; we are sacrificing valuable time and doing little." They were at 86° 13' N, the farthest north of any expedition so far. They headed south.

For almost the next three months they traveled south across the pack ice, sighting land on July 24. By now their twenty-eight dogs had dwindled to two, the weaker ones being fed to the others along the way. The sledges were being pulled by one man and one dog each. Now it was time to abandon the sledges and kayak across the water to what was Franz Josef Land. There was no room in the kayaks for the remaining two dogs, so they were killed. On August 24 the two men went into winter quarters on Franz Josef Land, essentially hibernating until the following May, surviving like Inuit in a hut of stone covered with walrus skins, eating the meat of seals, walruses, and polar bears they hunted, and using the blubber for fuel. After nine months they set out again in the kayaks. It was May 19. But where were they to go?

Spitzbergen, the nearest inhabited land, was more than 100 miles away, an absurdly long journey by kayak. Perhaps Nansen thought he might have been able to make it, but fortunately he never had to try such a journey. Still on Franz Josef Land on June 17, he and Johansen happened on a British Arctic expedition led by Frederick Jackson. Nansen's astonishingly good luck had held. As Jackson wrote later, "A more remarkable meeting I never heard of. Nansen did not know I was in Franz Josef land . . . and I had not the slightest idea he was within hundreds of miles of me; in addition, Nansen was very uncertain as to what part of the world he was in." Jackson pointed out that there were now 160 miles of practically open sea between Nansen and the nearest known land, not the kind of environment for "leaky canvas canoes," and he reported that "Nansen repeatedly remarks that nothing will ever induce him to undertake such a trip again."

Nansen and the *Fram* returned to Norway to unprecedented acclaim. He went on a lucrative lecture tour through Europe and the United States. His book on the expedition, *Farthest North*, became an instant best-seller. Scientific societies on both sides of the Atlantic showered the man with gold medals and prizes. He was suddenly independently wealthy as well as the darling of Norway. He did not make another polar attempt or another major Arctic expedition, though he thought hard about it at one point. Instead he moved gracefully back into the world of the academic scientist, writing much of and editing all of the six-volume report on the *Fram* expedition.

Here we will detour from the main story of Arctic exploration and follow the amazing trajectory of Nansen's life, since he was clearly the most extraordinary and variously accomplished of all men who ever sought adventure and knowledge in the Arctic region. Soon after the turn of the century, Nansen found himself in the thick of national politics, as a supporter of the movement (begun by Norwegian ship owners) for a peaceful separation of Norway from Sweden. For the previous century the two countries had been both separate and one, in that each had its own parliament, but both had the same king as supreme monarch, and foreign policy was run out of Stockholm. But Norway was a maritime nation, and her foreign interests were quite different from those of Sweden.

Negotiations had been under way for some time in 1905 when Sweden suddenly broke them off. Nansen began writing a series of provocative newspaper articles, which, given his hero status as well as his persuasive pen, revitalized the national spirit. He was sent abroad to convince the great powers of Europe and the United States to encourage Sweden to resume

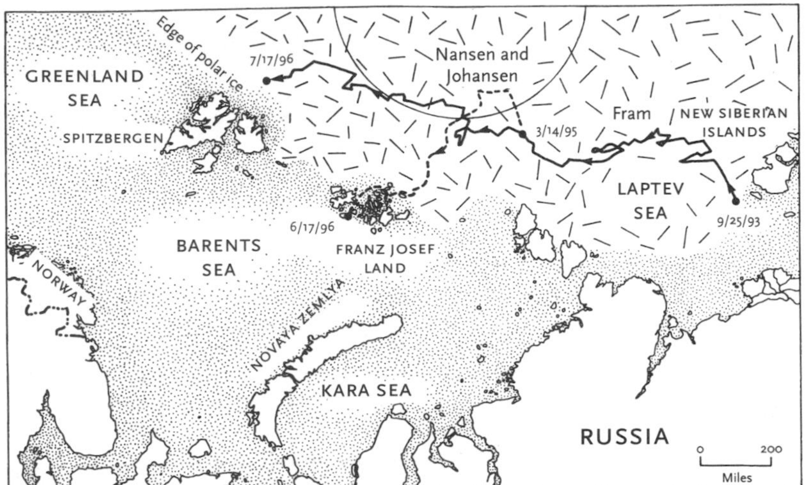

Drift of *Fram* through the Arctic ice and traverse of Nansen and Johansen across the Arctic ice (From Nansen 1898)

the negotiations. This finally happened, and a peaceful dissolution of the union was accomplished in that same year.

The new Norwegian government then sent him to be their first ambassador to the Court of St. James, in London, where he convinced England to sign the Integrity Treaty, guaranteeing the newly obtained independence of Norway. Following that, in 1908, he returned to Oslo, where he again took up the university life, now as a professor of oceanography. Up until World War I he made numerous oceanographic cruises, and invented the Nansen bottle for collecting samples of water at various depths in the ocean. A wire with a weight on it is lowered over the side of a ship by winch. At intervals along the wire, cylindrical bottles, initially open at both ends, are attached to the wire. When the bottles are at the desired depth, a weight called a messenger drops along the wire and hits the top attachment of the first bottle, which flips over onto the bottom attachment, closing off the bottle itself with a sample of water from that depth. At the same time, a second messenger is released from the first bottle and falls down the wire, repeating the process, and so on. In addition to inventing this device, Nansen also wrote and illustrated a book, *In Northern Mists,* a history of the early northern explorations of the Greeks, Vikings, and others, published in 1911 and still a classic. And if that were not enough, Nansen also illustrated the book.

A sketch of Fridtjof Nansen by himself (From Whitehouse 1930)

He came to the attention of the world again after World War I when he was appointed the Norwegian delegate to the Assembly of the League of Nations. Given his prominence (and the fact that he was from a neutral nation), he was then appointed by the League in 1920 to facilitate the return of prisoners of war—German and Austrian prisoners held in Russia, and Russian prisoners held in Germany. The Bolshevik government in Russia did not recognize the League, so he negotiated with them as a private citizen. Having arranged with both governments the return of these men, he then had to arrange through private sources for the money to pay for their return. In all, some 500,000 prisoners of war were thus repatriated under his aegis.

Meanwhile, thousands of Russians had fled their country after the Communist takeover in 1917, and they now were living abroad without permission and without the documentation necessary for civil functions or for travel. In 1921 the League of Nations appointed Nansen high commissioner of refugees to deal with just this problem, and his solution, agreed to by fifty-four nations and the League, came to be known as the Nansen Passport. It did not confer nationality; it simply gave the holder a title to existence. The concept of statelessness was now and for the first time enshrined in international law. By ensuring reentry, the document removed the main barrier to crossing borders, and the refugee was in effect under the protection of the High Commissioner, a kind of international consul. Nearly a million Nansen passports were issued in those years, and among their holders were Igor Stravinsky, Mare Chagall, Anna Pavlova, and Sergei Rachmaninoff.

In that same year Nansen would see to the raising of enough money to buy grain to send to some twenty million to thirty million starving Russians, saving a great number of lives (but incurring some opprobrium as a result of accusations of being soft on Communism, since many of the starving were Red Russians as well as the White Russians whose anti-Communist cause most of Europe supported). In the following two years his main task was to resettle peacefully some one million displaced persons, the result of Greco-Turkish hostility that was of centuries-old standing. Nansen was able to arrange with both governments that the Moslems left in Greece would settle in Turkey and the Orthodox Christians in Turkey would settle in Greece. And in 1922, in the midst of these negotiations, Nansen was awarded the Nobel Peace Prize. The citation said, in part:

> Work of an international character carried out by Mr. Nansen during these past years has brought him the Peace Prize. I might especially mention his work in the repatriation of prisoners of war, his work for the Russian refugees, his work in aiding the millions in Russia struggling against famine, and now his work for the refugees in Asia Minor and Thrace. Although this activity has been in progress for only a few years, its extent and significance are such that the Nobel Committee has felt it worthy of the great distinction of the Nobel Peace Prize.

Nansen died in 1930, a man of astoundingly diverse achievements and countless distinctions. Among these, he had also set a standard for grace and excellence in the exploration of the Arctic that would never be matched.

NINE

Amateurs, Pros, *and* Cons

THE YEARS FOLLOWING Nansen's *Fram* voyage, Peary's second expedition, and the beginning of the falling-out between Cook and Peary—that is, from 1896 to 1909—would see an unprecedented flurry of Arctic probes as well as Antarctic ones, some successful, some tragic, some almost tragicomic.

There is, after all, something almost comic about the notion of setting off in a balloon with the hope of reaching a particular destination hundreds of miles away. Anyone who has ever ridden in one knows that balloons are notoriously at the whim of the winds. A stiff breeze can send the balloon scudding off far too fast to make a safe landing, as well as simply send it in the opposite of the desired direction. No breeze at all leaves the balloon becalmed, able only to rise or fall in place. There may be no mode of travel that is less reliable, but this did not deter a Swede named Salomon Andrée, who was almost surely the first to have the idea of reaching the North Pole by air. Certainly he was the first to try it.

Andrée evidently was aware that the Arctic winds blow away from and around the Pole, not toward it. He planned to counteract this by retarding the balloon's motion by dragging ropes on the ground and then somehow "sailing" the balloon in a direction counter to the wind. He was a dreamer like Nansen, but Andrée's dream had little basis in reality. Even so, he was able to persuade several notable countrymen, including Alfred Nobel, to finance his venture. In the summer of 1896 he took his balloon to a small island off the northwest coast of Spitzbergen, where he intended to fill it with hydrogen he produced on the spot with a chemical generator. He needed a favorable southerly wind and waited for several weeks, but it never came, and so he had to abandon the venture for that season.

By another of the many, almost standard, coincidences that brought strangers or acquaintances together in the Arctic, Andrée met a Norwegian explorer, Otto Sverdrup, who was passing through Spitzbergen on his way home after spending three years aboard the *Fram* on her first voyage (1893 to 1896). Almost totally unsung in the years to follow, Sverdrup would spend more time in the Arctic than any of his fellow countrymen, including Nansen, and would discover more new Arctic land than all the combined discoveries of the forty Franklin search parties. Sverdrup is an example of how well-planned exploratory missions that go without a hitch do not make memorable legends.

The balloonist Andrée returned to his island off Spitzbergen the following summer, plans unchanged. A favorable wind blew, and on July 11 his balloon, carrying him and two companions, rose into the Arctic air. He kept a diary documenting the flight. At first they drifted to the northeast, but the next day the drift changed to the west, then to the east. A heavy fog weighed the balloon down, keeping it from gaining altitude; soon the cab was simply bouncing along the ice pack. By the end of this second day "aloft," Andrée realized they had no chance of reaching the Pole. He opined in his journal that they could have thrown some ballast overboard and made it to Greenland but instead decided to land and get some rest. But Andrée knew the adventure was over. "How soon, I wonder, shall we have successors?" he wrote. "Shall we be thought mad . . . I cannot deny that all three of us are dominated by a feeling of pride. We think we can well face death, having done what we have done. Isn't it all, perhaps, the expression of an extremely strong sense of individuality which cannot bear the thought of living and dying like a man in the ranks, forgotten by coming generations. Is this ambition?"

On July 14 the three men abandoned the balloon, heading south on foot with the hope of reaching Franz Josef Land and then setting a course for Spitzbergen. In early October, at a camp on White Island, the diary entries end. The men were not seen until thirty years later, when a Norwegian expedition came across their remains and Andrée's diary, still intact.

In 1898 the tireless Otto Sverdrup was back aboard the *Fram* on an exploratory and scientific mission that left on June 24 and would be at sea for four years, until September 1902. Three hundred years earlier, William Baffin had noted three waterways out of the northern end of the bay that came to have his name: Lancaster Sound, later plied by Parry, Ross, Franklin, and others; Smith Sound, explored by Kane, Nares, and Hall; and Jones Sound. It fell to Sverdrup to penetrate Jones Sound. He and the fifteen members of the crew went on to explore and map the south and west coasts of Ellesmere Island and the north coast of Devon Island. He discovered and mapped new lands west of Ellesmere, in particular Axel Heiberg Island, Amund Ringnes Island, and Ellef Ringnes Island, collectively known now as the Sverdrup Islands (Heiberg and the Ringnes brothers were the financial support of this expedition). In all, Sverdrup discovered more than 100,000 square miles of new territory in this four-year expedition, most of it traversed in two-man, dog-drawn sledges during the spring and summer months.

Of the three ambitious explorers—Nansen, Peary, and Cook—only Peary would continue in the early part of these years with a single-minded focus on the Arctic. His next two expeditions were, once again, in aid of interplanetary salvage: He sought the third meteorite at Cape York, this one weighing 33 tons. His expedition in 1896 failed, but the following year he succeeded, returning with this huge chunk of nickel-iron. He loaned all three meteorites to the American Museum of Natural History in New York, and much later his wife, Jo, sold them to the museum. The largest of the three has been for many years a stunning attraction just inside the door of the Hayden Plane-

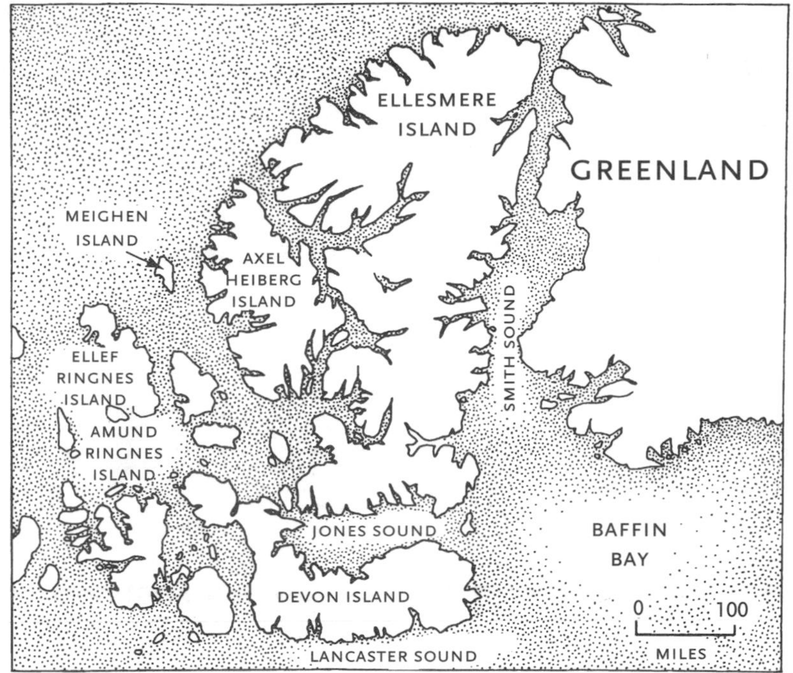

Map of Ellesmere Island and the Sverdrup Islands (Axel Heiberg, Amund Ringnes, and Ellef Ringnes (From Central Intelligence Agency 1978)

tarium, where generations of students and tourists hand-polished it to a high sheen. In 1897 Peary petitioned his employer, the United States Navy, for another leave of absence, five years in all, to continue his polar explorations, and it was duly granted, the navy deciding that even though the Spanish-American War was brewing (or being deliberately brewed), their purposes would be better served in this largely naval campaign if Peary could attain the Pole under the navy's flag.

Meanwhile, Nansen was, as noted, off on scholarly pursuits, and Frederick Cook, the doctor, shipped as medical officer and surgeon for an expedition to the other side of the world, Antarctica. The ship was named the *Belgica,* and this was the Belgian Antarctic Expedition of 1897–1899, under the leadership of a Belgian named Adrien de Gerlache. De Gerlache had spent three years raising the funds for the expedition, largely from private sources but also, in the end, from the Belgian government. The crew was half Belgian and half Norwegian, and one of the Norwegians who signed on as mate was named Roald Amundsen.

The purpose of the expedition was to put a four-man scientific party ashore on Victoria Land to make various measurements, but the ship was almost immediately locked in the ice in the Bellingshausen Sea, a long way from Victoria Land, where it remained for nine months.

Young Amundsen would recall that the highlight of the voyage was meeting and working with Cook, whose previous polar experience with Peary on Greenland in 1892 put him in the position of teacher to the pupil Amundsen. Together they made numerous trips into the Antarctic highlands using Nansen-type sledges. The Belgians had provisioned the expedition with, among other things, canned meat, but Cook knew what the result of that would be: scurvy. He insisted that the crew eat fresh seal and penguin meat, finally prevailing over the protestations of the ailing commander, de Gerlache. Later Amundsen would recall of this trip that Cook won the respect and devotion of all hands, and deserved it: "From morning to night he was occupied with his many patients, and when the sun returned it happened not infrequently that, after a strenuous day's work, the doctor sacrificed his night's sleep to go hunting seals and penguins, in order to provide the meat that was so greatly needed by all."

Long afterward, Amundsen's affection for the genial and dedicated doctor would put him into a most precarious position.

Peary's next expedition was to set out in 1898, while Cook was hunting and doctoring in the Antarctic. Peary was spurred on by reports in the fall of 1897 that Otto Sverdrup and the *Fram* were going to make an attempt on the Pole via the west coast of Greenland. In fact, Sverdrup had no intention of going to the Pole, but instead planned to map the north coast of Greenland. As we have seen, he did not even do that, but instead went west to Ellesmere and beyond. In any event, Peary wrote Sverdrup in

November 1897, drawing attention to information in the newspapers about his forthcoming attempt on the Pole and saying that Peary had already announced similar plans to the American Geographical Society, his preparations were well advanced, and he wished Sverdrup "to give me the authority to deny the statements." He ended the letter by saying, "With sincerest regards and the highest admiration for the masterly way in which you brought the Fram home, I am" and signed it.

A month later Peary got a letter from Sverdrup that said, "I beg to tell you that you are in a mistake when you mean, that I intend to reach the pole. My expedition has only a scientific purpose and is going to make scientific explorations in the north of Greenland and to study the paleocrystal [ancient] ice." Sverdrup then congratulated Peary on his intention of reaching the Pole "by that way, which I do not think difficult."

Peary wrote back some time later, saying that "I cannot believe" Sverdrup's intention to do science in north Greenland when Peary's own presentation to the American Geographical Society the previous year had included such scientific work as part of its mission. "I am sure you will pardon me if I remind you that such action on your part, in entering a field in which I have been at work for several years and assuming objects which I have formally proposed for my own work, will be without precedent in the annals of Arctic Exploration."

Indeed, Peary had so far devoted his professional life to mapping and other discoveries in northern Greenland and to finding a route to the North Pole. It was, in fact, considered ingracious of one to burst in on someone else's turf and reap potential rewards based on that person's groundwork. Explorers and exploration scientists still feel that way, whether the turf in question is a piece of the ocean bottom, the East African highlands, or space. As it turned out, Peary's and Sverdrup's paths would cross, but their aims and accomplishments would not overlap.

In 1898, what would eventually become known as the Peary Arctic Club came into being—not to be confused with the Arctic Club that had arisen on the sportsmen's voyage led by Cook.

The new group was relatively small and exclusive, made up of wealthy and influential individuals who elected to support Peary's efforts and in the process see their names affixed to various pieces of Arctic geography. Prominent among the members was Morris Jesup, president of the club and a noted philanthropist, a founder of the American Museum of Natural History, and a president of the American Geographical Society. The club also included Thomas Hubbard, vice president of the group and a prominent New York lawyer; Herbert Bridgman, the club's secretary, who was business manager of the *Brooklyn Standard-Union*; and George Crocker, a substantial contributor to Peary's efforts and a director of the Southern Pacific Railroad. Peary had parlayed his exploits into the friendship and admiration of the finest in society. The club financed the bulk of Peary's final expeditions, with Jessup, Crocker, and Hubbard putting up $120,000 (almost $2 million in today's dollars) for a properly built and outfitted ship.

Peary's sixth expedition left New York on Independence Day, 1898, aboard the *Windward*. They made their way to a winter base all the way north to Cape D'Urville on the east coast of Ellesmere Island, where they were frozen in. Slightly south of Cape D'Urville was Cape Sabine, and it was here that Otto Sverdrup on the *Fram* had to put in for the winter. One day in December Peary arrived at Sverdrup's camp on a sledge with an Inuit driver. He gave Sverdrup a terse hello and immediately left, suspicions swirling through his mind. He was now convinced that Sverdrup was planning to one-up him in an attempt at the Pole, so he immediately instituted a forced march north to the Fort Conger site to establish a base camp there before Sverdrup could. Fort Conger was 200 miles north of where Peary was, it was now the season of nearly total darkness, and the temperatures along the way were below -50°F.

Even so, with Matthew Henson, a doctor named Thomas Dedrick, and four Inuit, Peary left Cape D'Urville on December 20 and reached Fort Conger on January 6, 1899. On the way Peary fell, and his right arm and hand were partly paralyzed by the impact. But worse, his legs had become frozen up to his knees.

Upon their return to the *Windward,* Dr. Dedrick had to remove seven of Peary's toes because of frostbite; eventually an eighth was removed as well, leaving Peary with only his two little toes.

The pain of frostbite and of amputation was extreme. Peary could ski or snowshoe only with great difficulty, and then only for short distances. Most men would have given up, gone home, and rested on their laurels, but Peary, with almost superhuman willpower and endurance, stayed on for the three remaining years of the expedition (and later went on two more). In the annals of Arctic exploration there are numerous examples of astounding fortitude, and Peary's is near the top of the list.

For understandable reasons, little was accomplished during the exploration season of 1899. Peary returned to Fort Conger, attempted to cross Robeson Channel but couldn't, returned to the *Windward*, and completed a survey of Princess Marie Bay. Then he sailed to Etah, where his summer supply ship, the *Diana,* met him. In August both ships sailed for home, leaving Peary and his party to overwinter in Etah. In 1900 explorations were more successful. Peary undertook a major sledge journey along the north coast of Greenland to its northernmost point which he named Cape Morris Jesup, and from there traveled north of the Arctic ice to 83° 50' N. He arrived back at Fort Conger in June and overwintered there.

Robert Peary in London, 1910 (Rauner Special Collections Library, Dartmouth College)

Earlier Peary had sent a letter describing his physical condition, including the loss of his toes, home to his wife with the departing

Diana. Jo Peary decided to go north and bring her husband home, setting out during the summer of 1900 on *Windward*. The ship became locked in the ice in Cape Sabine, where she spent the winter of 1900–1901 while her husband remained at Fort Conger to the north. She was conditioned to spend a winter in the Arctic, but she was not prepared for what she soon met in another of those chance meetings that so often took place in the vast Arctic expanse—this one a meeting that Peary surely wished would not happen.

An Inuit woman named Allaksingwah boarded the *Windward* one day that winter. Jo Peary immediately recognized her as the nude woman lying on the rocks in a photograph in Peary's 1898 book, *Northward over the Great Ice*. The photograph bore the strange caption, "Mother of the Seals."

The woman was the mother of more than seals. Allaksingwah boasted that she was Peary's wife, and she had a baby with her to prove it. (She meant no real harm; she was utterly unaware of the differences in mores between Eskimo and American cultures.) Jo, on the other hand, had lost her second child at seven months, and now had this staggering blow to deal with as well. She wrote her husband a letter, dated August 28, 1900, in which she said, with restraint that one cannot imagine today: "You gave me three years of the most exquisite pleasure that can be had; after that the pleasure was pretty evenly divided with the pain until now is all pain, except the memory of what has been." Peary and his wife would meet briefly in August 1901, and they remained married. But both Peary and Henson fathered children in Etah, and their descendants still live there.

In 1901 the Peary Arctic Club resolved that it needed to act. It had heard nothing from either Peary, and so it sent out a second relief ship, the *Erik*, with Harry Bridgman aboard, along with Frederick Cook, now seasoned by Arctic and Antarctic experience. At the end of August both ships left for home, and Peary, Henson, and Dedrick were left to overwinter at Cape Sabine. The next spring Peary and Henson went north to Cape Hecla, on the northern coast of Ellesmere Island, their progress hampered by polynyas and hummocky ice, and halted by a final barrier that would plague Peary on his next two expeditions as well: what he called the Big Lead. The Big Lead is a shear zone between continental shelf ice to the south and Arctic Ocean ice to the north—a channel of gray-black water that is ice free for much of the summer and some other times as well, but otherwise frozen like the sea beyond. One needs to cross it in the early spring, when it is frozen, and return before it opens up, lest one become stranded on the Arctic Ocean ice.

On April 12, 1902, Peary reached a personal farthest north of 84° 17' N before being turned back. It was short of Nansen's personal record by almost 2° of latitude and, he would later learn, more than 2° short of a new record claimed for 1900 by an Italian explorer, Umberto Cagni.

So for four years in the Arctic, Peary had little to show except for acts of heroic personal endurance. He had not come close to the Pole; he apparently had no prize to bring home. But in 1899, in his survey of Princess Marie Bay, he had reached the top of the adjacent Ellesmere glacier. From its summit he saw Greely Fjord, which had been discovered previously, and a new fjord, which he named Cannon Bay after Henry Cannon, a founder of the Peary Arctic Club and president of Chase National Bank. As shown on his original sketch map, he also saw a landmass off to the northwest of his position, which he labeled Jesup Land. But in a written report to the club in August of that year, he made no mention of Jesup Land. Then, in late 1902 and early 1903, Otto Sverdrup's findings began to see the light, and on Peary's 1903 map of the area, Jesup Land got moved to the *west* of Peary's site atop the glacier—which is to say that Jesup Land was now located where Axel Heiberg Island is, thus giving Peary a prior claim to the discovery of the island.

Was this self-deception or sleight of hand? In any event, the international geographic community didn't take Peary's claim seriously. Jesup Land vanished, and the island became known by the name Sverdrup gave it. Peary returned to America in 1902 and immediately began planning his next expedition. The planning was meticulous. He decided his next assault on the Pole would start from Cape Hecla, with a fresh group of people

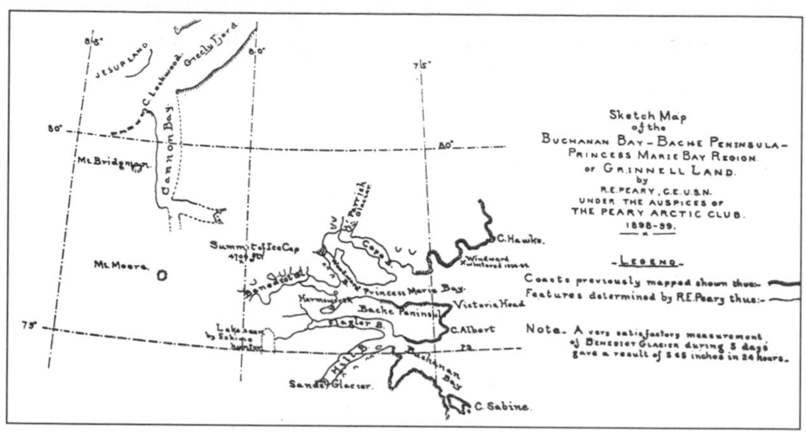

Sketch map of Princess Marie Bay region, including "Jesup Land" (From Rawlins 1973)

and fresh supplies. He wanted to avoid the exhausting sledge trips up the northeast coast of Ellesmere from Cape Sabine to the Arctic Ocean. And he wanted a special ship with which he could plow his way through the Kennedy and Robeson Channels to Cape Hecla. The Peary Arctic Club happily put up the money for the expedition and the ship—it was named the *Roosevelt,* after that great adventurer and outdoorsman (and president of the United States), Teddy Roosevelt. Other than the *Fram*, it was the only ship specially built for Arctic work and, like the *Fram*, the cross section of its hull was U-shaped, so it would be able to ride up on the ice.

The expedition left New York on July 16, 1905, with a twelve-man company, stopped briefly at Etah to pick up several Inuit families and their dogs, went through the Kennedy and Robeson Channels, and overwintered at Cape Sheridan, on the northeastern tip of Ellesmere Island—a promising beginning. The following year, on March 6, 1906, several sledge parties set out for the Pole, but were slowed by the many pressure ridges that barred the way and forced lengthy detours. On March 26 they reached the Big Lead, at a latitude of 84° 38' N, having traveled 124 statute miles at an average rate of 6 miles per day. Peary had taken no longitudinal measurements along the way but instead had simply headed north. On March 26 when he got out his instruments, he discovered that he had been offset to the west by *80 miles*. The ice drift to the west had been almost as great as his northward progress. Why Peary had imagined he could operate without his instruments and by dead reckoning is anybody's guess.

He was delayed at the Big Lead for more than a week, waiting for the temperature to drop sufficiently to attempt to cross the young ice. Then at 85° 12' N, at a location he appropriately named Camp Storm, he was pinned down for another week by a blizzard. Above the Big Lead, the ice drifted in the opposite direction, and during the week of the blizzard, Peary drifted 62 miles to the east. Finally, on April 13, he could start north again, having lost seventeen valuable days. He had hoped to set up advance supply depots, but these plans were torn asunder. Nor did he have enough time to get to the Pole and back in time to cross the Big Lead before it opened up for the summer months. It seemed that all he could do was seek another farthest north.

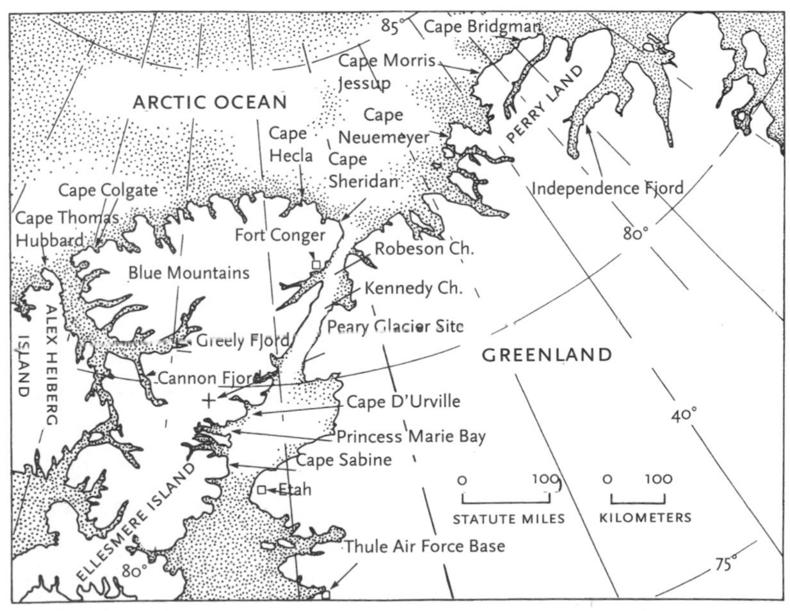

Map of northern Greenland and Ellesmere Island. The cross marks the Peary glacier site (From Central Intelligence Agency 1978)

He sent everyone back except Henson, six Inuit, and two sledges with dogs.

Peary was next seen at Cape Neumeyer on Greenland on May 9, four weeks after he had left with his small and mobile team. He reported that in that interval, on April 21, he reached a farthest north of 87° 06' N and then made a beeline back to Camp Storm and thence to Cape Neumeyer. At one point he and his party were blocked by a lead a half mile wide and were finally forced to eat their dogs and burn their sledges. Eventually, when the lead was two miles wide, it began to freeze over, and the party could wait no longer, even though the ice was so thin it could be crossed only with snowshoes, if at all. Twice Peary's snowshoes broke through and he thought he was a dead man, but he shuffled on, and everyone made it safely across.

In all, Peary would have made this round trip of 404 miles in twenty-six days, less the two days he reported being delayed—meaning an average speed of 18 miles per day over a region strewn with pressure ridges that had to be climbed or detoured around, and open leads that had to be avoided. Eighteen miles per day is three times Peary's normal speed of 6 miles per day, and far in excess of speeds registered by any other Arctic explorers of that era. This in itself makes it difficult to conclude that Peary actually reached very far north of Camp Storm, or that he achieved a new farthest north. Circumstantially, his claim is not made any more credible by the fact that during the entire trip of twenty-six days from Camp Storm to Cape Neumeyer, he recorded only the one statement of latitude: he made no other detailed observations for the northernmost point he said he reached, and made no latitude or longitude observations for any of the rest of the trek. For explorers of this era, such behavior was unheard of.

Meanwhile, other explorers were in the Arctic, seeking other goals. Frederick Cook wanted to be the first person to climb Mount McKinley, which, at 20,320 feet, is the highest peak in North America. And the Norwegian he had met and become friends with in Antarctica, Roald Amundsen, had his eyes on being the first person to actually navigate the Northwest Passage.

Upon returning from Antarctica, Amundsen had set about getting the backing of some Norwegian shipowners for his expedition. He left Oslo on a rainy night in June 1903 in a small fishing sloop 70 feet in length and equipped with an auxiliary engine. He had six crew members with him and was provisioned for five years. He left port surreptitiously, in order to avoid a merchant who was threatening to stop the expedition for lack of payment for supplies he had rendered. (Amundsen was plagued by financial problems throughout his life, his ambitions always outrunning his ability to pay for them. In this he closely resembled his American friend Frederick Cook.)

Amundsen was, however, what we would call a professional. He had wanted the Northwest Passage since he was seventeen years old (he was twenty-nine when he set out in 1903). He was in superb physical shape, was a regular long-distance skier, and had read every book and journal on the Arctic, noting two common problems in Arctic exploration that caused discord and often failure. First, the commander often had no navigation experience, so Amundsen went to sea and soon gained his captain's license. And since there had often been dissension between the scientific staff and the crew, he went to Hamburg and studied the theory and practice of magnetic measurements.

He knew that a small expedition could live off the land, whereas a large one couldn't; that eating seal prevented scurvy; that loose-fitting Inuit-type clothing prevented exposure. He would, in fact, survive two winters on the southern shore of King William Island and grow fat in the process—at the exact location where the Franklin personnel had perished. His expedition was without much by way of incident; he arrived on the southeastern shore of King William Island in September 1903 and built a shelter there for his magnetic and meteorological equipment, carrying out measurements for two years while living among the local Inuit. The following year, in 1906, he completed the Northwest Passage, arriving at the mouth of the Mackenzie River, where he overwintered, sailing the next year around the Alaskan Peninsula and reaching San Francisco in October.

He returned home to the expected hero's welcome—and to a pile of debts. Immediately he petitioned Nansen for use of the *Fram* for an attempt on the North Pole, using Nansen's proven technique of drifting with the ice. His idea was to sail around South America and north to the Bering Sea, setting the ship in the ice off Point Barrow, Alaska, and when the *Fram* drifted near the Pole, he would make a dog-pulled sledge dash for it. Nansen initially had other plans for the *Fram*, believing that the South Pole was a simple goal for someone with his skill in Nordic cross-country skiing; given his duties as Norway's ambassador to England, however, he gave up his South Pole plans and let Amundsen take the *Fram*.

In 1903, the same year that Amundsen had set out for the Northwest Passage in his little sloop, Frederick Cook had made a reconnoitering trip to the base of Mount McKinley. It was not until 1906 that he undertook the climb, thanks to a promise of $10,000 (more than $160,000 in today's dollars) made by Henry Disston, an heir to a Philadelphia saw manufacturing business, on the condition that Cook would arrange to take him hunting near the mountain in the autumn, after Cook's attempt on the summit. The expedition included two men, Belmore Browne and Herschel Parker, who would become eminent mountaineers, and Edward Barrill, a blacksmith and horse handler. They left for Alaska in early summer and spent two months on the mountain without finding an accessible route to the summit. In August they repaired to Seldovia, Alaska, to meet Disston.

Disston was not there, and after two weeks waiting for him, they received a message from him on August 25 saying that he wouldn't be coming at all. Of course, Cook was in hock. He had made purchases of equipment, contracts for horses, and promises of salaries to some in the party, all on the assumption of getting funds from Disston. He was broke, headed straight for bankruptcy.

On August 27 Cook announced that he and the blacksmith,

Barrill, were returning to the mountain to explore the foothills for the following year, but not to climb the mountain. On September 22 the two men returned to camp and Barrill said, "Go back and congratulate the Doctor. He got to the top." Later Cook produced a photograph of Barrill standing on the summit. Despite this triumph, Cook was still in hot water. A lawsuit in Seldovia for breach of contract on horse rentals kept him there for another month, He was found in default and obliged to pay $600 (about $10,000 today), an amount he had to borrow, sending him yet further into debt.

But upon returning to the mainland United States, he was widely and enthusiastically feted. He lectured at the Explorers Club and was elected its next president. He was a guest of honor at the American Alpine Cub and spoke at the national dinner of the Arctic Club. On December 15, 1906, the National Geographic Society put on a gala dinner attended by four hundred guests, including President Roosevelt and Washington's elite, to honor both Robert Peary's return with a farthest north of 87° 06' N and Cook's summiting of Mount McKinley.

In 1907 an article in *Harper's Magazine* by Peary and his book *Nearest the Pole* both appeared, in which he recalled the day on his last expedition that he stood on the peak of Cape Colgate (named after another member of the Peary Arctic Club) 2,000 feet above sea level. From there he saw the western land he had called Jesup Land, "though Sverdrup has later given it the name of Heiberger [sic] Land." From there, to the northwest, "it was a thrill that my glasses revealed the faint white summits of a distant land."

Crossing over to Axel Heiberg Land (his Jesup Land), he saw the snow-clad summits more clearly. "My heart leaped the intervening miles of ice," he wrote, "as I looked longingly at this land and in fancy trod its shores and climbed its summits, even though I knew that this pleasure could be only for another in another season."

He named this new and distant land Crocker Land, showing it on his map at the latitude 83° 40' N and at a longitude of

103° W, with a lateral dimension of about 60 miles. This, he said, was the second most important result of his 1905–1906 expedition. Yet, curiously, he made no mention at all of this mysterious land in his field journal or in any telegrams sent back to the Peary Arctic Club. In cairns left at the two sites from which he said he had viewed Crocker Land, which were discovered later, he made no mention of this land. And, indeed, there is no Crocker Land.

That same year, 1907, Peary was all set to head out on another voyage; a farthest north and a new piece of territory was not enough. He needed the Pole, the big prize. But he ran into a problem—money. His principal financial supporter, Morris Jesup, had died (without an island to call his own, it should be remembered). *Nearest the Pole* flopped, selling only 2,230 copies instead of reaping the vast sum in royalties he had anticipated. The lecture tour that he and Robert Bartlett, captain of the *Roosevelt*, took on raised little money, and Bartlett went back to Newfoundland to go seal hunting. Peary's exploration plans had to wait.

In 1908 he would finally obtain commitments for funds to pay off his debts *if* he reached the Pole. If not, he would be bankrupt. Peary was fifty-two years old, hobbled by the loss of his toes and by his financial burdens, but determined.

Here, then, were Peary and Amundsen, two of the most prominent seekers of the North Pole, facing what was surely to be bankruptcy if they didn't pull off the big one.

In 1907, while Peary was rounding up the conditional promises of funding, Frederick Cook was invited by a professional gambler and co-owner of a casino, the Beach Club, in Palm Beach, Florida, to accompany him on a hunting safari to northwestern Greenland. This was John R. Bradley, a millionaire from very successful gambling, who had just returned from hunting in northern Mongolia. He bought a ship (which he named for himself), engaged a crew, and put his guest, Cook, in charge of the outfitting. Cook, of course, had more than a hunting trip in mind; he envisioned a try for the Pole. He broached the idea to Bradley, and Bradley agreed to supply the extra equipment with the admonition not to say anything to anyone about it.

On June 3, 1907, they left for the Arctic. In September, after the hunting, Bradley and the crew left for home, with Cook remaining at Etah in northwest Greenland. On February 19, 1908, he left on his polar dash with two Inuit, two sledges, and twenty-six dogs. The party crossed Ellesmere Island, traveled northwest along Axel Heiberg Island, and thence to the Pole, which Cook reported reaching on April 21. Via the Ringnes Islands, he reached the north coast of Devon Island, where he overwintered, arriving back in Etah on May 20, 1909. The Pole was his!

While Cook was en route south to Etah on the last day of February 1909, Robert Peary and his party started out across the ice from northern Ellesmere Island. The Big Lead held him up from March 5 to March 11, and twenty days later he reached a new farthest north site, called Camp Bartlett, at 87° 47' N. On April 1 he took off across the ice with Henson and four Inuit, reaching 87° 57' N, which is essentially the Pole. The Pole was his! He was back in Camp Bartlett on April 9.

A month after that, as noted, Cook pulled into Etah, where he ran into a man named Harry Whitney, who had traveled north as a guest of Robert Peary and had stayed behind to do some hunting. Cook told Whitney that he had reached the Pole and left with Whitney a cache of instruments and, Cook said, notes. Then, triumphantly, he left by boat and sledge for Upernavik, Greenland, and thence by ship to Copenhagen, where he arrived on September 4, 1909. News of his achievement had run ahead of him, and he was greeted with enthusiastic acclaim. The Royal Geographical Society awarded him a gold medal on September 7, and the Danish university gave him an honorary degree two days later. Cook dined with the king before taking ship for the United States, where he arrived on September 21. A hundred thousand people cheered him as he passed by in a parade organized for him in his native Brooklyn. A reception followed, attended by five thousand admirers, and two days later the Arctic Club threw a grand dinner for more than a thousand guests to honor him.

By now Peary knew of Cook's claim. He had arrived in Etah on the *Roosevelt* on August 17, where he got the news. He was utterly convinced that Cook could not have reached the Pole, given his limited resources. But he also knew that Cook would be widely acclaimed and that he himself would be relegated to the role of also-ran—which was unthinkable. He would have to establish his own claim and destroy Cook's. On September 6 he sent out a telegram claiming the Pole.

The battle was joined. Each man had his supporters. Later in September the *Pittsburgh Press* took a poll of more than 76,000 of its readers. Only some 2,800 believed that Peary discovered the Pole in 1909 and that Cook hadn't actually gotten there the year before. More than 73,000 believed that Cook's prior claim of discovering it in 1908 was authentic, and of those, about 58,000 believed that Peary had never reached the Pole. No respondent thought both claims were invalid.

Polls, of course, are merely matters of opinion—in this case, uninformed opinion. But doubts about Cook's veracity began to loom on the horizon like thunderheads. Encouraged by Peary's financial supporters, Edward Barrill, the blacksmith

The Arctic Club of America's banquet to honor Dr. Cook at the Waldorf-Astoria, September 23, 1909 (Library of Congress, Washington, D.C.)

companion of Cook's on the climb of Mount McKinley, made a sworn statement that he and Cook had never reached the summit. Further, he swore, his diary entries for September 9 through September 18 were left blank at Cook's insistence and then dictated to him by Cook after the fact.

But which Barrill was one to believe—the earlier version or the later one? Then the other climbers, Browne and Parker, weighed in. Both had had doubts from the outset and had vacillated between support of Cook and censure. They went to the Explorers Club with their doubts, based on the extremely short period of time Cook had been away from base camp, and on the nature of the photographs made at the summit. The club arranged a confrontation for October 17, 1909, which Cook attended, but he declined to testify and instead asked for a delay. Then, a month later, he disappeared from New York and was not seen again for ten months, until he turned up in Munich, Germany.

The McKinley claim was easily settled: Browne and Parker returned to Mount McKinley under the auspices of the Explorers Club, carrying with them copies of Cook's photographs of the summit. They did not attain the summit, but instead on June 28, 1910, reached the place where Cook had photographed Barrill at the "summit." It was a rock ledge located less than 6,000 feet up the mountain, which they named Fake Peak.

The McKinley claim was clearly a fake, and Cook, in his absence, had nothing to say about it. His polar claim came under fire also, with people noting that he had claimed speeds over the ice of 17 miles per day when conventional speeds were more on the order of 6 miles per day. Peary advocates made a great deal of this until it was pointed out that Peary himself had claimed speeds in excess of 17 miles per day on his final dash. But there was more that damaged Cook's claim. According to his narrative of the achievement, he sighted Peary's Crocker Land on his trek north—but there is no Crocker Land. Beyond Crocker Land, Cook said, he sighted a new landform he called Bradley Land, but there is no Bradley Land. Near the Pole itself, he said, he sighted a submerged island, but there is no land or ice island, submerged or no, near the Pole. All of these locations, however, were shown on Cook's sketch map.

And another island was missing. In 1916 a small island west of Axel Heiberg Island was discovered. It is called Meighen Island. No one had seen it up until then, and it does not appear on Cook's map of his traverse in 1908. But if we are to take Cook's map at face value and believe that it shows his return route, he would have passed close enough by Meighen Island to see it. Yet he makes no mention of sighting the island.

The principal thing that dashed Cook's claim, however, was that he never could produce any data showing that he had made the trip north from Axel Heiberg Island and back. For eighty-eight days there are no notes showing that any celestial naviga-

Sketch map by Cook of his attainment of the Pole (From Cook 1913)

tion was done. They were asked for in both Copenhagen and New York, but to no avail. Cook claimed in the newspapers after his return to New York that he had left navigational equipment and his "proofs" (that is, his measurements) with Whitney at Etah, and a year later the equipment was found in a box at Etah, but there were no papers, no measurements, no proofs. Then in November 1909 an insurance agent named George Dunkel approached Cook with the proposition that a Norwegian sea captain named Loose would supply Cook with a fake set of astronomical observations for $4000 ($64,000 in 1990 dollars). Loose dutifully delivered the calculations, and Dunkel went up to Bronxville, New York, where Cook was staying, to pick up the $4,000. But Cook did not pay him, and he disappeared two days later, eventually fetching up in Munich. In December 1910 Cook came back to the United States and told a reporter, "I still believe I reached the Pole although I am not sure I did." Later still he reverted to his previous position, insisting he had bagged the prize in 1908. But very few could continue to champion him, and most explorers put as much distance as they could between themselves and Cook. He had been a founder and president of the Arctic Club, a member and president of the Explorers Club, and a founding member of the American Alpine Club. By the end of 1910 he had been expelled from all three organizations, with his polar and Mount McKinley claims judged fraudulent.

Frederick A. Cook (From Cook 1913)

A tragic event had occurred in 1908, the year before Peary's dash to the Pole, the result of some misinformation about the

One of Peary's sledge teams crossing a pressure ridge (From Peary 1910)

nature of northern Greenland that arose from Peary's account of his expedition there back in 1887. A 1908 Danish expedition to Greenland was to proceed up its east coast and then across the southern shores of what Peary had seen as Independence Bay and the Peary Channel, to the north coast of Greenland. When they reached the latitude of Peary's sightings, they found to their dismay that the land went off to the east, not the west, as Peary had it. They trekked along the shore of what is now called Crown Prince Christian Land until it finally turned west, but no clear route emerged. Instead they ran into two uncharted fjords. They turned back but perished. The following spring a relief party found the body of one of the Danes, a detailed map of their journey, and a commentary that the other two had perished in the fjords.

In a report on this tragedy, Adolphus Greely, by this time a major general in the United States Army and one-time polar expedition leader (however unsuccessful), wrote that the Danes' "explorations conclusively show, however, that Peary was mistaken, and his point of view at Navy Cliff was on a waterway a few miles wide and not on the sea, there more than a hundred miles distant, while Greenland extended to the east twenty-two degrees of longitude, or about a hundred and ninety miles."

To this day, people still argue about which of the two Americans made it to the Pole, and Peary usually wins out. He had many distinguished, wealthy, and very influential supporters both while he was alive and after his death, and he has come down in the public mind as the man who discovered the North Pole. (One of the few who would support Cook's claim even into the latter half of the twentieth century was the Canadian adventure writer Farley Mowat, best known for his book *Never Cry Wolf*.)

Today there is no reason to believe Peary reached the Pole. In the first place, in the interval from April 1 to April 9, when he, Henson, and the Inuit made their push, there is no navigational data of any sort—no latitudes and no longitudes—except for the latitude note for the Pole itself. No one can navigate to the pole by latitude alone. Additionally, the distance from Camp Bartlett to 89° 57' N is 150 statute miles, which gives Peary an average speed of 38 miles per day. No one has ever achieved such speed over the ice before or since: the fastest was a 1968 polar achievement by snowmobile that averaged 11 miles a day.

And Peary's field journal raises severe doubts. On April 6 he makes no mention of attaining the Pole, and for the next two days he made no entries. Instead, a loose page was inserted (on clean paper and clearly not something written at the time) with the lead statement: "The Pole at last!!! The prize of 3 centuries, my dreams & ambition for 23 years. *Mine* at last."

This is not illusion or self-deception. It is sleight of hand. Here was a man who insisted that he achieved the goal of his lifetime, his dream and ambition, but he said nothing about it until September, when he learned of another man's claim. On April 6 he did not share his single latitude observation with Henson, which he usually did. It was normal for Henson to note such positions in his own diary, but not this time. There was no great hurrah back at the *Roosevelt,* no triumphant telegram sent off to the Peary Arctic Club.

For Peary, ambition always seemed to be one step ahead of his accomplishments, and in most cases the accomplishments eventually caught up. In 1886 he claimed the longest trek across Greenland, which was not the case; on the next trip he made the longest trek across Greenland. On that expedition, 1891–1892, he claimed to have reached Peary Land and the northernmost part of Greenland, which was not the case; on the next expedition he found Greenland's northernmost point. On the 1898–1903 expedition he sighted Jesup Land, which in fact was not a new land but instead merely a part of Ellesmere Island; on the next expedition he mapped the northwestern coast of Ellesmere. On the 1905–1906 expedition he claimed a new farthest north of 87° 06' N, which is difficult to accept; on the next expedition, he did reach a farthest north of 87° 47' N at Camp Bartlett.

And on his last expedition he claimed to have reached the Pole, which we have no reason to believe he did. But there would be no further expeditions. He died in 1930 after nine years of retirement from the navy, a man venerated by many but haunted by a particular kind of loneliness, walking through the last thirty years of his life without eight toes, forcing a peculiar gliding shuffle. He evidently grew tired of the version of himself that came through from his lectures. He began to close down, becoming dyspeptic and tyrannical.

Peary's actual Arctic accomplishments, however achieved, were in fact the greatest of any American explorer. "His determination," as author and Arctic trekker Barry Lopez would write in the 1990s, "the depth and power of this man's obsession, absolutely stills the imagination of anyone who has looked upon the landscape he traversed." What drove Peary to cripple himself in the quest for the Pole? As another polar trekker, a physicist and playwright named David Fisher, wrote in his book about a trip through the Arctic on a Russian icebreaker, it was not so much a jingoistic patriotism. It was not a desire to have the Stars and Stripes be the first flag planted there, though Peary spoke of this. Nor was it Peary's determination not to be beaten out by the hated Cook. It was, Fisher writes, "the passion Joan of Arc knew for God, the passion Paris and Menelaus knew for Helen, the passion of Faust for knowledge and power . . . simply *passion:* blind and unreasoning, indefatigable and ultimately irresistible."

As others have pointed out, however, it is an especially haunting and lonely feeling to wonder when one's untruth will be found out, and both Peary and Cook no doubt experienced this. As for Cook, he tried going into business, failed twice, and then formed a stock company called the Texas Eagle Oil and Refining Company with some other partners in 1920. Using his name for its celebrity, they mailed out a massive appeal that raised $800,000. But this effort soon failed as well, and Cook formed the Petroleum Producers Association, designed to salvage other failing or defunct oil companies. In 1922 postal authorities began an investigation that found the company had issued bogus stock. Cook and his partners were indicted in 1923 and tried later that year; Cook was sentenced to fourteen years in prison. The presiding judge sneered at Cook's "persuasive hypnotic personality," compared him to Ananias and Machiavelli, and said, "I know the men who defended you, defended you with their handkerchiefs to their noses. It smelled to high heaven."

In 1930, after seven years in Fort Leavenworth, Cook was paroled, and in 1940 President Franklin Roosevelt granted him a full pardon at the request of Cook's family and other explorers. But he was by then a sick man. He died in August of that same year.

TEN

From Polar Larks *to* Canary-watching

IF THERE WERE ONLY FOUR truly important firsts to be achieved in polar exploration, they would be the achievement of the two poles, north and south, and the navigation of the two passages, northwest and northeast. In 1910 both passages had been navigated, but neither pole had been reached. Neither of the two great American explorers, Peary and Cook, can be given the honor they both claimed with such fervor, with such a wholesale lack of proof, and with claims of overland speed never before or since attained or even closely approached. The two passages had been achieved, in each case by a Scandinavian, and it would be one of these, Amundsen, who would lay legitimate claim to the South Pole, while the North Pole would remain untrodden for decades.

In 1909 Roald Amundsen, with Nansen's backing, was in the midst of raising the money and laying the detailed plans for his own attempt on the North Pole—a journey he hoped to achieve by drifting nearby on an ice-bound *Fram*. But on September 1 of that year, while he was well along in his plans, with a sailing date only four months away in January 1910, the local papers announced that Frederick Cook (Amundsen's old friend from the Antarctic) had reached the North Pole the year before. And a week later he read in the same newspaper that Robert Peary had also recently reached the North Pole. His own effort would be utterly redundant—nothing more than a footnote, if it were successful. What did he do?

In July 1910 he sailed south as planned—the original idea having been to enter the Arctic via the Bering Strait. But Amundsen had an entirely different goal in mind now, about which he said nothing to anyone. He was now headed for the other end of the planet, the South Pole. He kept this a secret from Nansen, his mentor; from the Norwegian government; from his financial backers; and from his crew. The latter were informed of the new destination only when the *Fram* stopped at the island of Madeira off the coast of Morocco on September 9, from where he also sent a telegram to the English explorer Robert Falcon Scott, who had long since announced his plans to make a scientific expedition to Antarctica and to try for the South Pole.

Amundsen, of course, had announced *his* original plans as a purely scientific expedition to the Arctic, keeping the dash to the North Pole secret from his backers. Now he had decided to make a nonscientific, purely exploratory dash to the *South* Pole, later justifying this intrusion into Scott's announced business by saying that Scott had announced to *his* backers only the intention of doing some science in Antactica. In fact, Amundsen was, without much question, a sneak, but he would also reach more polar goals than anyone else in history, because, in an almost wholly uneventful trip, he would reach the South Pole, thus bagging his second of the four big polar achievements. And he would bag a third as well, though a third with an asterisk.

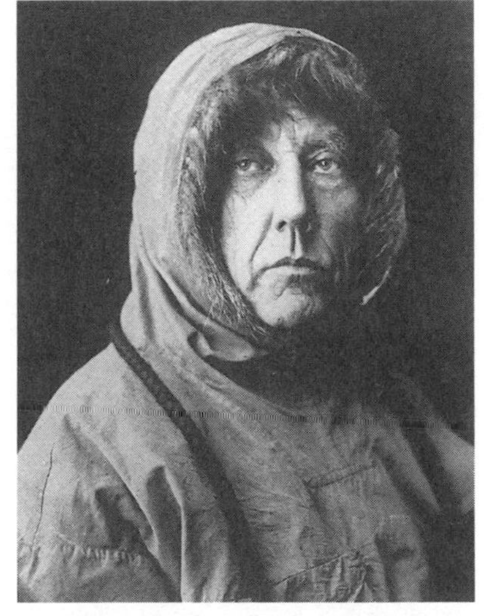

Roald Amundsen upon arrival of the *Norge* in Alaska (From Amundsen and Ellsworth 1927)

The *Fram* arrived in the Bay of Whales on January 14, 1911. After establishing depots along the way, Amundsen and a party of four others on skis with dog-powered sledges set out for the Pole on October 19. They reached it on December 14 and, after spending three days there, returned to the ship. The only difficulty the skiers encountered was the ascent of the Axel Heiberg Glacier to the Polar Plateau, where the geographic South Pole is located. On his departure he left a tent with a thirteen-foot center pole on which the Norwegian flag fluttered, and a letter for Scott.

Scott arrived a month later with a party of four; on their return without skis and with man-powered sledges, they all perished.

The British, of course, howled with cries of poor sportsmanship. No "gentleman explorer" would act as Amundsen reportedly had, usurping Scott's right of first shot at the Pole by changing his plans and rushing off to Antarctica—a cowardly deceit that, some opined, had forced Scott to speed up his planning, thus leading to fatal error. Scott's heroic death and his diaries, discovered a few months later, moved all of England. Amundsen's achievement and his careful planning counted for nothing in Albion: Scott had *also* reached the Pole, after all.

And there was the matter of the dogs. Had Scott used dogs and not crew members to pull the sledges, his party would almost certainly have survived. Amundsen had, in another ungentlemanly action, used sled dogs on his return and then had *eaten* them. Scott himself, on the other hand, had earlier expressed the British attitude to the grand game of exploration: "To my mind," he wrote, "no journey made with dogs can approach the fine conception" of men facing hardships unaided. "Surely in this case the conquest is more nobly and splendidly won."

In all of this the English were content to ignore the fact that Scott had used ponies on his trek to the Pole and had killed and eaten them at the foot of Beardmore Glacier. In any event, the English never were at all comfortable acknowledging Amundsen's first, nor were the Americans. By 1926 the geographic establishment in the United States had ruled that Robert

Peary's claim to the North Pole was legitimate and, conversely, that Frederick Cook's claim was not. Cook was by now, of course, languishing in federal prison for mail fraud. And in that year Amundsen, in financial troubles, as always, was on a lecture tour in the United States.

After his success (acknowledged with great fanfare by the Scandinavians while the British and Americans sulked), Amundsen had achieved sufficient wealth to establish a successful shipping business and, for once, was not in financial difficulty. He grew enamored with the notion of flying to the North Pole, a feat that at the time had not been accomplished, and in 1925 he ordered two Dornier flying boats from Germany and went to the United States in an effort to raise money to pay for them. He had the good fortune to meet Lincoln Ellsworth, who was not just an explorer but an explorer from a rich family. Amundsen received financing for the planes and the expedition, which left Spitzbergen on May 21, 1925. They flew northward for eight hours and landed on an open lead big enough for both planes, which they reckoned was the North Pole, but unfortunately they discovered they were 120 miles off. And then the lead froze up before they were able to leave, so they had to spend three weeks constructing a runway on the ice before they could take off, leaving one of the flying boats behind.

The following year Ellsworth put up the money to build a dirigible capable of flying across the Arctic from Spitzbergen to Alaska. The *Norge* was built in Italy and piloted by the Italian Umberto Nobile, with the overall expedition under the command of Amundsen. It left Spitzbergen on May 11, 1926, arriving in Alaska three days later, having circled the Pole several times.

It was a far from satisfying victory, and for two reasons. One was Richard Byrd, who would become one of the most celebrated explorers in American history. The other was Amundsen's expedition mate, Umberto Nobile.

On May 9, 1926, two days before Ellsworth and Nobile cast off for the North Pole in the dirigible *Norge,* Richard Byrd, with pilot Floyd Bennett, cranked up the engine of a Fokker trimotor aircraft and at 12:37 A.M. left King's Bay, Spitzbergen, expecting to be in the air for twenty-four hours, returning with the first overflight of the North Pole.

Byrd was from a prestigious Virginia family: The Byrds virtually owned Virginia politics for much of the twentieth century, with Richard's brother Harry being a U.S. senator from the commonwealth for decades. Richard Byrd served with distinction as a pilot in World War I and had been on one flying expedition over the Arctic ice when he determined to be the first to fly over the North Pole. The flight took less than sixteen hours, not twenty-four, since the plane had to return to King's Bay at 4:07 P.M. with a troublesome oil leak in the right engine. Byrd, who traveled as observer/navigator on this flight, as on others to come, and his pilot, Bennett, became the first to claim to have flown over the Pole. Byrd, who returned to a ticker-tape parade in New York City and was awarded the U.S. Congressional Medal of Honor for this achievement, would later become the first also to fly over the South Pole, and in his lifetime he did perhaps more than any other person to encourage and stimulate the exploration of Antarctica. When he died in 1957, at age sixty-nine, holding the position of officer in charge of U.S. Antarctic programs, he was an international hero, and was buried with military honors in Arlington Cemetery.

But he had never actually made the North Pole.

King's Bay, Byrd's departure point for that attempt, is 660 nautical miles from the North Pole, making a round trip of 1,520 *statute* miles, which Byrd covered in fifteen hours and thirty minutes—an average speed of 98 miles per hour. The Fokker trimotor, outfitted with skis for landing gear rather than wheels, had a top speed of eighty miles an hour, meaning that Byrd had to enjoy a tailwind of eighteen miles an hour from the south while headed for the Pole and a corresponding eighteen-mile-an-hour tailwind from the *north* on the return to King's Bay. Or he needed a tailwind of thirty-six miles per hour on the way to the Pole and no tailwind on the return, or some other combination of changing winds—but none of the meteorological conditions for these existed at the time, a fact since established from weather records.

Later Floyd Bennett confessed to fellow pilot Bernt Balchen that they didn't make the Pole. And in a 1979 book, *Antarctica, My Destiny,* by Finn Ronne, a captain in the U.S. Navy and a noted Antarctic explorer after World War II, the story came out that Byrd himself had admitted his fraud. Apparently Isaiah Bowman, then president of the American Geographical Society, had doubts after Byrd's return in 1926 that he had ever flown over the Pole. He asked for Byrd's compilations and navigational aids, but Byrd was "evasive" and claimed that no one should question his truthfulness. Bowman told Captain Ronne that he got his answer in 1930 after Byrd's successful return from Antarctica and the South Pole. "It was raining," Bowman said, "and after lunch we went for a walk . . . for almost four hours around the blocks of Broadway and 156th Street. By that time I managed to break down Dicky-Byrd, and the time it took was worth it. Byrd confessed . . . that he had not reached the North Pole, but had missed it by about 150 miles."

Bowman, later president of Johns Hopkins University, explained to Captain Ronne that if he had made this confession public, no one would believe him, so thoroughly was Byrd a national hero by then. But the arithmetic was confirmed, meaning that another feat by another American explorer turns out to have been a nonaccomplishment—in fact, a lie. This is a dreary way to have to end the tales from the heroic period of Arctic exploration—specifically the feats of the Americans, Peary, Cook, and Byrd, all three hoaxers. As a recent historian of such false claims, David Roberts, wrote, "One thing became clear to me about these men: the decision to fake an exploratory achievement determined almost everything about the rest of their lives. . . . The world was reduced to allies and betrayers. . . we cannot envy these men their declining years. They lived out their natural spans in bitterness and proud isolation, even when surrounded by the worship of a credulous public, even when decorated with honors. Exposure, one suspects, lurked like a wolf at the door."

Sadly, there is yet more, an unraveling in the life of even the most successful of the Arctic dreamers. Amundsen, it is now known, was the first to fly over the North Pole with his companions, but it was a bitter victory, for even as his claim appeared to make him second to Byrd, he felt that Umberto Nobile was taking more than his proper share of credit for the feat. Amundsen wrote a vitriolic book attacking Nobile and other real or imagined enemies. He was back in debt and had few friends, no family. He retired from polar exploration a bitter man and a loner, but not until he had made a last lecture tour to the United States, where he took a side trip to visit his old friend Frederick Cook in Leavenworth. Afterward he would attempt to justify the life and efforts of this now wholly discredited man, thus adding to the weight of distaste the American public held for him.

In 1928 his anathema, Nobile, made another Arctic expedition with a new airship, the *Italia,* in part to vindicate himself over Amundsen's aspersions. The airship disappeared. A search began with the Italian government asking for the help of the Norwegian government, but specifically requesting that Amundsen not be involved.

Amundsen chose to ignore this snub and accepted the aid of a Norwegian businessman who offered to buy a flying boat from France for his use. Arriving in Tromsø, Norway, in the French plane, Amundsen discovered that three other search planes were readying themselves for takeoff, one each from Sweden, Finland, and Italy. Nobile's location on the ice had by then been identified and it was now a matter of sending in a rescue mission, but the weather turned sour and the other three groups decided to postpone the rescue effort. They advised Amundsen to do likewise, but he refused their advice and, in an uncharacteristic action for a man renowned for careful planning, took off. It was Amundsen's last act—and a selfless one.

Nobile was eventually rescued along with seven crew members out of an original twenty-five, but the Italian pilot was publicly disgraced by a commission looking into the disaster. Amundsen's plane was never seen again, adding a coda, albeit a most tragic one, to this most romantic period of Arctic exploration, a period that had bloomed with such heroic promise (and promises) and which finally turned so tawdry.

* * *

By the onset of the 1930s it was generally accepted that the North Pole had been reached—by Peary on foot and by Byrd in a plane, as well as Amundsen, Ellsworth, and Nobile in a dirigible. Another trek overland—which is to say, over the ice pack—to the Pole and back was no longer something anyone needed to bother with. Other feats of endurance and exploration remained to be achieved: The summit of Mount McKinley was unclimbed, as was Mount Everest on the Tibetan-Chinese border, the highest place on earth, and K2, the world's second highest peak, on the Chinese-Pakistan border. Beyond that, the ocean depths awaited human eyes to peer at them, and the Moon still hung tantalizingly in the sky, only 240,000 miles away. And even in the 1930s, which we now think of as so far removed in the past, technology was about to take a front seat in the exploration business. Airplanes with longer ranges and capable of bigger loads were already flying; submarines were being launched. And the first man to try to reach the North Pole by sailing toward it under the ice was an Australian named Hubert Wilkins, now largely unsung and little recalled, but one of the most colorful and accomplished adventurers in the twentieth century.

By the time Wilkins had finished secondary school he had somehow picked up a good working knowledge of both electrical engineering and cinematography, and he took it into his head to see the world. To that end, he simply stowed away on a ship leaving Australia, destination unknown (unknown to him at least). He was eventually caught, worked to pay his way, and was discharged at the ship's first port of call, which was Algiers. There he managed to secure employment with an Italian agent investigating the smuggling of arms. At one point the two of them went to a meeting with some smugglers, were duped and drugged, and ended up as captives in a caravan to Tunis to be sold as slaves. Like a character in a romantic novel, Wilkins was rescued by a young Arab woman, who helped him escape.

Wilkins went on to England, learned to fly, and in 1912 found employment as a photographer and war correspondent, covering the Turco-Bulgarian conflict, a little-known war. At one point he was arrested by the Turks and held as a spy. Three times he faced a Turkish firing squad, but in each case all the others were shot while he was spared, since he refused to confess to being a spy. Finally, when an armistice was signed, he was released.

In 1913 he joined Vihljalmur Stefansson in an expedition to explore and map the northwestern coast and islands of Canada, remaining in the Arctic under the tutelage of this master until 1916. By the time he returned, World War I was well under way, and Wilkinson joined the British army, was wounded nine times, and was awarded the Military Cross and Bar for gallantry. After the war he attempted to win an Australian prize by flying from England to Australia but failed, being forced down near a Turkish insane asylum, where, some of his friends suggested, he belonged. Next he photographed the starvation conditions in Russia for the Society of Friends, crossing Nansen's path, and then led a biological collecting expedition to northern Australia.

In 1926 the Arctic bug bit him again and he returned to polar efforts, this time by plane. He and Carl Ben Eielson, the most famous of Alaskan bush pilots of that era, made a reconnaissance flight out over the Beaufort Sea, searching for new land but finding none. Next year the two scouted yet farther—some 550 miles—to the northwest and were forced down three times, the last time because they were out of gasoline. Thanks to Wilkins' previous experience with Stefansson, however, they survived a walk of more than 70 miles across the pack ice with its pressure ridges, hummocks, and bone-chilling cold. Undaunted, the two of them in 1928 made the first airplane flight all the way across the Arctic, flying from Alaska to Spitzbergen. Wilkins was knighted for this feat, and the two men went on in that same year to fly all the way across the Antarctic.

By now people had begun to think about the possibility of traveling to the North Pole under the ice. Wilkins and his colleagues Sloan Danenhower, Simon Lake, and Lincoln

Ellsworth became the first to do anything about such a notion, obtaining a submarine from the U.S. Navy for the nominal rental fee of $1 for five years. This was the *O-12*, built in 1918 and scheduled to be scrapped under the London Naval Treaty. They rechristened her *Nautilus*, after Captain Nemo's submarine in Jules Verne's *Twenty Thousand Leagues Under the Sea*. The new *Nautilus*, like all other submarines of that era, was not a true submersible but, instead, a surface ship that could operate submerged for a few hours, running on power generated by batteries. The batteries could be recharged only by running the diesel engines on the surface.

Overhauled and refit, the *Nautilus* had a safe diving depth of 200 feet, sufficient for Wilkins' purposes. At a slow speed of 3 miles an hour, it had an underwater range of 125 miles and enough oxygen in the form of bottles of compressed air to remain below the surface for three days. From his own and others' Arctic experience, Wilkins reckoned that about every 25 miles they would come across open water areas—polynyas or leads—big enough for the sub to surface, and the vessel was equipped with an observation area in the conning tower for spotting such open areas. She also had a special auger for boring upward through the ice.

There was a great deal of speculation involved here, of course. The distance from Spitzbergen to Alaska via the Pole was more than 2,000 miles, and little was known at the time about variations in the thickness of the ice in the Arctic Ocean. If they didn't find the open areas of water and if the auger failed, they would perish.

In the fall of 1931 they proceeded under the ice from Spitzbergen, found no open water, and learned that the auger did not work. They could not surface. After several unsuccessful attempts, Wilkins called off the project—wisely. It was a good idea, but about three decades ahead of its time. After this, Wilkins turned his attention chiefly to the Antarctic and served in a civilian capacity during World War II with the United States War Department. He died in 1958, but not before the first nuclear-powered submarine was launched, yet another

Nautilus—and this time a true submersible like Captain Nemo's. Here was the technology to take men to the Pole under the ice.

In a nuclear-powered submarine, the atomic reactor is a self-sustaining unit requiring no external fuel or oxygen. Euipped with various life-support systems, it can stay submerged for a month or more and can travel several thousand miles underwater in that time. But if you are submerged under the Arctic Ocean, how do you know where you are? The luxury of surfacing and getting a celestial, satellite, or electromagnetic fix is not available. You need a self-contained navigation system. The first inertial navigation systems were just that, and the earliest ones were installed on the *Nautilus* and its partner in polar probing, the *Skate,* in 1958.

An extraordinarily sophisticated instrument, an inertial navigation system is used for ships and aircraft, and as a guidance system for missiles. Its concept starts with velocity, the rate of change in distance. In an automobile we speak of miles we travel in an hour. If, for example, we drive a car at a fixed rate of speed in a straight line on a desert flat, we would easily know our ending position as a product of the speed and time driven. But if the speed varied over the drive, we would simply add up the time increments spent at various speeds, integrating the speed over time.

Velocity has both a magnitude (speed) and a direction. If we had a meter that could measure both speed and direction, we could integrate each component over time and determine our final destination—that is, where we are—after driving across the countryside by highways and byways.

The next problem is acceleration—the rate of change of velocity. We need a device to measure both the north-south and east-west components of acceleration and then we can determine our position at any given moment via a double integration that can easily be done by computer. Acceleration is pretty easy to measure in itself, since it is the equivalent of a force exerted; sensitive accelerometers are mounted in gyroscopes to maintain their orientation, and accuracies of less than a mile can be achieved over distances traveled of a few thousand miles.

The *Nautilus'* first polar attempt was under the command of William Anderson in 1957, when the ship did not have an inertial navigation system (though it was equipped with an inverted echo sounder to tell them by means of sonic echoes how far above them the lower surface of the ice was). Anderson had to rely on dead reckoning and gyroscopic and magnetic compasses, and when they had achieved 87° N, their gyroscopic compass failed and they had to turn back. In 1958, now equipped with an inertial navigation system, *Nautilus* undertook the assignment to traverse the Arctic Ocean from the Chukchi Sea to the Greenland Sea and immediately had to confront a major problem: the only deepwater passage into the Arctic Ocean is the Fram Strait, between Greenland and Spitzbergen. Elsewhere the ocean is bounded by a continental shelf with shallow water. Further, the ice beneath some of the pressure ridges extends 100 or so feet below the surface of the water, making formidable obstacles for a submarine passage, just as the pressure ridges held up explorers above on the ice pack. A nuclear submarine at the time was 50 feet high from keel to sail.

In June 1958 *Nautilus* made two attempts but was stymied by the thickness of the continental shelf ice. In July she returned after the ice pack had retreated off the shelf, and found a passage into a deep valley to the deep basin of the Arctic Ocean. Having submerged off Alaska on August 1, she reached the North Pole on August 3 and surfaced between Greenland and Spitzbergen on August 5. It was an astounding (and uneventful) voyage, and a momentous signal that a new age was upon the world: What would have taken months—even years—of struggling against the cold, the ice, the weather, and the frailties of the human body and the human spirit was achieved in a few days.

That same month and year, August 1958, the nuclear submarine *Skate,* under the command of James Calvert, was assigned the job of developing techniques to surface in pack-ice areas. It was the Arctic summer, and the open-water areas of the polynyas could be detected by the inverted sounder readings. The sub entered the Arctic basin through the Fram Strait, progressed to the North Pole, and went to the western edge of the basin before turning back and exiting via the Fram Strait. She surfaced nine times during the voyage, once near the Pole. In a sense, Calvert had accomplished just the sort of voyage Wilkins had contemplated back in 1931.

After his 1958 voyage Calvert gracefully took the time to visit Wilkins and Stefansson, then both in their seventies, to bring the old warhorses up to date and to seek their advice. And they had some advice, suggesting that the *Skate* go back in the winter to try the same thing. There would be no polynas but instead regions of recently frozen leads where the ice would be no more than two feet thick. (In December, shortly after Calvert's meeting, Wilkins died, no doubt happy to have been involved to the end.)

With its sail strengthened, *Skate* returned to the Arctic in March 1959, located regions of thin ice, broke through, and surfaced at several sites, including, again, the North Pole where, at Wilkins' request, Calvert sprinkled his ashes, a tribute to one of the greatest adventurers and explorers of the twentieth century. Indeed, one can say that a sense of honor had finally been restored to America's polar explorations.

At the same time, it should be pointed out that these astounding submarine efforts were undertaken not out of any altruistic interest in scientific exploration nor for any sort of adventurer's glory. They were for military ends, pure and simple. The Arctic is the nearest ocean to a number of targets in the former Soviet Union, and the need to be able to reach those targets was preeminent in the minds of the military as well as the U.S. Congress at this time, when the Cold War raged and the balance of the world hung on both diplomacy and the buildup of the most threatening arsenals in history. The Arctic ice also provided a safe haven where a submarine could lurk for extended periods, undetected by surface ships or aircraft. And with the ability to surface near a specified location in the Arctic, as *Skate* had done, the submarine becomes a convenient platform for launching ballistic missiles. So for most of the remainder of the twentieth century, the Arctic—so little known only fifty years before—was an integral component of the Cold War, a region of paramount strategic importance.

But still, no one had accomplished what Robert Peary and Frederick Cook had set out to do: cross the ice on foot and sledge and reach the Pole. And, after all, why bother? We had planes, submarines, and powerful icebreaking ships as well as all kinds of high-technology equipment to facilitate work in the Arctic. And the Arctic was no longer a place for the frivolity of mere adventure. It was serious business, and even in the 1930s, no country was more aware of this than the Soviet Union. The Soviets' northern border was the Arctic and of obvious strategic importance, and the Northeast Passage continued to be of great importance to the commercial interests in Siberia, where weather information and predictions were always vital.

As early as 1937 the Russians established stations in the Arctic to monitor the weather and other physical variables. The first Soviet drift station was flown to the North Pole in May of that year, and designated *SP 1* for *Severnyy Polyus 1,* or *North Pole 1*. It included a party of four—the leader, Ivan Papanin, two scientists, Eugen Fedorov and Pyotr Shirshov, and radio operator Ernest Krenkel. These were the first human beings to set foot on the Pole. But more important to them, it seems, was that they accomplished their scientific mission with skill and élan, paving the way for more such expeditions.

They remained in shacks on the ice for nine months, until February 1938, during which time the Transpolar Drift System had taken them across the Arctic to the coast of Greenland, where they were eventually picked up by a Soviet icebreaker. At the time of their rescue, they were inhabiting a slab of ice 100 feet long and 30 feet wide—shades of George Tyson. Along the way they had made daily observations of atmospheric and oceanographic conditions as well as geophysical measurements of gravity and magnetism, and on their return they were welcomed as heroes in Moscow—and justifiably so, being not only the first men on the Pole but the first to man an Arctic drift station for such a length of time, 274 days.

The leader, Papanin, a good Party member, sent off a message to Stalin, saying how pleasant it was to think that "we, four ordinary Soviet citizens, have justified the hopes placed in us by our Party, our Government and our beloved Stalin, who reared us and on whose initiative our Motherland has acquired a new waterway linking up the east and the west of the Union of Soviet Socialist Republics."

In the 1960s, once the *Nautilus* and *Skate* had breezed under the Pole, some people began to realize that the goal of getting to the North Pole via the ice, and not over or under it, had not been achieved. The next attempt to do just that would arise in a restaurant in Duluth, Minnesota, in 1966, where an insurance agent named Ralph Plaisted was drinking a few beers with a physician friend, Arthur Aufderheide. They decided to try for the Pole on snowmobiles. An indefatigable promoter and planner, Plaistead set about gathering funds and equipment, including the snowmobiles, from corporations, institutions and private individuals. Undismayed by being turned down by the Campbell Soup Company, for instance, he went around to Knorr Soup and talked them out of ample supplies. He also convinced a crew of five television people, including Charles Kuralt, to join the expedition.

In all, sixteen people departed from Ellesmere Island on snowmobiles in late March 1967, headed for the Pole. There has never been a more amateur expedition. None of them had ever spent even an hour on the Arctic ice: one was an instructor at a winter survival school run by the Royal Canadian Air Force, and another had been stationed for a while at the U.S. Air Force base at Thule, Greenland. Otherwise, like Plaisted, they were all utter greenhorns.

They ran into the usual array of pressure ridges and open leads, including the Big Lead that had so frustrated Peary, and also including what they called the Big Ridge, a pressure ridge of indeterminate length and some 36 feet high, which they had to hack their way through. Even though they were supplied by air drops and landings that allowed an exchange of personnel from base camp to field, they eventually had to abandon the project, stymied by an unrelenting six-day storm. Having reached 84° N, they were airlifted out.

But Plaisted was not about to throw in the towel. He had learned a great deal about what to do and not to do in the Arctic, and the following year he returned with a smaller crew aboard more powerful snowmobiles—Ski-Doos, manufactured by Bombadier Limited of Quebec. They set out from Ward Hunt Island in northern Canada, winding through jagged ice ridges in the last weeks of the Arctic winter, traveling 825 miles. The Pillsbury Company had contributed special food cartons, so the trekkers enjoyed 5,000 calories a day, as well as vitamin pills. On April 20, 1968, a bit more than a year before Americans set foot on the Moon, Plaisted and three companions became the first to reach the North Pole by an overland route.

Soon airlifted out, they got home to very little attention. No CBS team had accompanied them this time, and most of the media considered Plaisted's trek more of a stunt than the actual achievement it was. The *New York Times* reported it as a brief item on page 68 of the April 20, 1968, issue. Nevertheless, it was Plaisted, the amateur explorer and insurance salesman from Duluth—and not Robert Peary—who was first to reach the Pole over the pack ice.

The following year a Briton accomplished the same thing, except that he went by sledge and on foot. Wally Herbert had long had what he called an "obsessive ambition" to make a surface crossing of the Arctic Ocean via the North Pole. By 1969 he had logged thousands of miles of trekking in the Arctic, Canada, Greenland, and Antarctica, and had spent four years planning his crossing of the Arctic Ocean. His plan was to travel from the Pacific side of the Arctic to the Atlantic side, drifting with the ice as Nansen had done before him. On February 21, 1968, Herbert left Point Barrow, Alaska, with three companions and dog-powered sledges. They got as far as 85° N, 162° W in their first season and set up winter quarters. On February 24, 1969, almost exactly a year after leaving Point Barrow, they started out again, reaching the Pole on April 5 and Spitzbergen on May 29. This was a longer expedition than Plaisted's but like Plaisted's, it was supplied along the way by air.

Almost two decades later an American adventurer named Will Steger, who, like Herbert, had spent a lifetime trekking in the Arctic and Antarctic, determined to reach the North Pole in the same conditions under which Peary had made his attempt—that is, he sought to complete the journey without resupply by aircraft. With six other men and one woman (a physical education instructor named Ann Bancroft), he set out from Ellesmere Island on March 8, 1986, with five sledges powered by dogs. Fifty-five days later six of them reached the Pole—Bancroft becoming the first woman to try to do so and the first to succeed—and were airlifted out with their equipment and dogs.

Once Roger Bannister broke the four-minute mile, it fell to hundreds of other runners. Since the New Zealander Edmund Hillary climbed Mount Everest and the American Jim Whittaker did the same, people almost routinely climb to that highest of summits; it has been done by hundreds of people now. And since Plaisted, Herbert, and Steger reached the Pole, it is no longer an unusual accomplishment—though no one has yet done what Peary and others set out to do: reach the Pole over the pack ice and return over the pack ice with nothing but human and canine power. Instead people get there by air or by icebreaker. The North Pole, in that sense, has become something of an "extreme" tourist destination. In 1991, for example, the American physicist David Fisher came up with $30,000 to buy a round-trip ticket to the North Pole aboard a Soviet nuclear-powered icebreaker, the *Sovetsky Soyuz,* with about a hundred other people. Along the way they found the hut where Fridjof Nansen spent the winter on a barren island, and saw the last island visited by George Washington DeLong on his doomed expedition. Fisher, like other polar travelers before him, wrote a book about his trip, *Across the Top of the World* (1992), full of amusing episodes as well as polar exploratory history. Once the complement of tourists reached the Pole, many of them proceeded to dance in a wide circle around the Pole, insisting that they were now members of the elite group of people who have circled the globe and passed through every time zone on a single trip—this much to the annoyance of an extremely abrasive passenger who had bragged repeatedly about circling the globe at lower latitudes.

But the physicist sounded a cautionary note. Visiting the islands that the old explorers described as icebound, the passengers found them to be relatively free of ice. Was this just the kind of climatic variability that has always pertained in the Arctic—extensive pack ice one year, less another—or was this ominous evidence of global warming?

These days, by the way, a trip to the Pole aboard a Russian icebreaker costs about half of what Fisher paid.

Today by far the greatest interest in the Arctic is as a vital region for environmental research. Nowhere, for example, are the climatic shifts of the past more readable than in cores drilled and taken from the Greenland ice sheet, which preserves a record of atmospheric gas quantities, pollen, and other substances frozen into the layers of ice on a nearly annual basis going back thousands of years. From such cores, one can read (and date, like tree rings) the amounts of various gases and particulates that were present in the atmosphere and from this derive reams of climatological data. And the climate of previous times represents the initial conditions in the great experiment the human race is now carrying on with the planet—that is, the near certainty that we are creating a greenhouse effect by hugely increasing the amount of such substances as carbon dioxide in the atmosphere, a result of burning fossil fuels at an unprecedented rate. These gases, like greenhouse glass, let the Sun's heat in but prevent much of it from reflecting back into deep space; the result is to make things warmer on the Earth. But how warm it will get, and where it will warm up a great deal and where less, and what effects this patchwork change in climate and regional weather will have on such things as forest growth, ocean currents, sea level, and other matters are all unknown. Average global temperatures could rise anywhere from 2° F to

11° F, according to various estimates deriving from complex computer models. Many scientists concerned with this looming problem believe that, for several complex reasons, the temperature increase in the Arctic will be three times greater than the global average—and that most likely the effects of global warming will be seen *first* in the Arctic.

White snow and ice in the Arctic are a good reflector of sunlight and thus help to maintain the Arctic cold. When some of it melts in summer, it exposes patches of dark seawater that absorb sunlight and can cause yet more ice to melt in what is called a positive feedback loop. (A negative feedback loop is like the thermostatic control of heat in your house: When it reaches a certain preselected temperature, the thermostat cuts off the furnace, the house cools down to another preselected point, and the furnace is ordered to kick in again. In a positive feedback loop, it is as though the thermostat responds to an increase in heat by ordering up more heat, not less.)

If the temperature in the Arctic rises significantly, it could set off a series of positive feedback loops, including some that are wholly unpredictable. Would the fresh water locked up in the ice melt and make the seawater less saline and colder? Would that affect the nature of ocean currents such as the Gulf Stream, with their profound climatological roles? In fact, there is irrefutable evidence now that the Arctic ice *is* melting at an alarming rate. Indeed, in a recent trip to the Pole, scientists found the Pole itself free of ice. If more dark ocean water soaks up more heat, melting more ice, how long will it take to raise the world's sea level by two feet? Three feet? How much will it cost to put up Holland-like dikes around such island nations as the Maldives, or to wall off New Orleans, New York, and much of Los Angeles from the rising sea? How long would the Everglades and much of the Florida peninsula last? Would there be any beaches left?

What if the permafrost of the far northern tundra in northern Canada and Siberia begins to melt, freeing the carbon dioxide in the peat underneath to escape in vast quantities? Would this cause even more rapid global warming? Or would the net effect be to create a denser and more widespread cloud cover over much of the globe, thus keeping the sun's heat out?

After the first Soviet drift station was put in place in 1937, thrity more have been set adrift on the ice, the last being *SP 31*, which followed a clockwise drift in the Beaufort Gyre off the coast of Alaska from 1988 to 1991. In addition, the Soviets flew hundreds of temporary weather stations into the Arctic over the years. And there have been several international interdisciplinary research programs designed to discover such things as the factors that affect the motion and deformation of the pack ice, or what is causing the upper ocean today to be less saline and warmer than it was in 1975. In that year, the melt season implied an addition of 0.8 meters of fresh water; in 1997, the figure was 2.0 meters. Is this a natural variation, or is it man-made? We do not have the necessary database to answer such questions yet, and scientists will continue to swarm over the Arctic painstakingly and, one hopes, not too slowly, developing that necessary database. And they will be greatly aided in this endeavor by the fact that in 1997, with the Cold War over, the Russian and American governments agreed to share their vast quantities of previously classified research data amassed over the years.

When it comes to global warming, the Arctic may well be the canary in the mine, and we can also be grateful at least that this canary is being very closely watched.

Over the past century and a half, another kind of science has been progressing in the Arctic—the softer social science called anthropology and the related field of archeology (though archeology didn't begin in the Arctic until well into the twentieth century). The subjects of this research were, of course, the people who were called the Eskimos and who are now known mostly by their own name for themselves, the Inuit. They were the first native people in North America to be seen by Europeans—the Norse having been in their country, on and off, for more than a thousand years, and British and other Arctic explorers running into them before they reached such places as

New England. The early accounts by explorers, however sharply observed, basically fell into the category of travel writing, for these men were not by any means trained observers of other cultures.

Anthropological studies per se began about two decades before the turn of the century, with Franz Boas, an early founder of modern ethnography, visiting the Inuit of Cumberland Sound and east Baffin Island. In this endeavor, Boas traveled some 2,400 miles on foot, by boat, and by dog team, making the first charts of Cumberland Sound as well as describing the culture of the eastern Canadian Arctic in remarkable detail (with the help of travel accounts as far back as Parry). More studies followed throughout the entire 6,000-mile range of Inuit lands that range from Eastern Greenland through Bering Strait to the northeast coast of Siberia, the longest linear distribution of any single group of people in the world.

World War II and the years after brought numerous new incursions of the outside world into the lives of the Inuit. Military bases sprouted like thorns. Oil geologists were followed in some cases by large drilling installations and pipelines. Life was changing rapidly and radically for many of these people, who over the centuries had adapted with such skill to extremely hostile conditions in isolation from the rest of the world. Indeed, so remote were some of these groups that when in 1818 Sir John Ross came across what he called the Polar Eskimos, a group of Inuit living in western Greenland, they believed themselves to be the only people on earth. Their isolation had been so long that they had given up and since forgotten the use of bow and arrow, skin boats, and salmon spear.

Suddenly the silence of the Arctic was broken by the sounds of internal-combustion engines and jet planes, radio and television. New people had brought new wishes, new wants. As early as 1957 the ethnographer Margaret Lantis wrote, "The substance of the situation is that Eskimos are trying just as hard today to adapt as they did 500 or 900 years ago; the difficulty is that they are adapting not to the Arctic but to a Temperate Zone way of living." Today, in fact, there is only one community in the Canadian Arctic—a place called Umingmaktok—where no non-native people live.

But these people are, of course, the unsung heroes in a book about Arctic exploration. They had explored most of the Arctic themselves and had learned to live in it, making even physiological adjustments to the climate, not to mention subtle cultural adjustments. And had it not been for their usually benign attention, even more European wayfarers would have perished as they probed these strange and awesome new lands. A few Inuit, as we have noted, received the accolades of the European explorers, and some even had their names recorded for history. But for the most part, the various bands of Inuit go anonymous.

There is considerable justice, then, in the recent action of the Canadian government, which in 1982 held a plebiscite in which 53 percent of the people in the Northwest Territories voted in favor of creating a new Canadian province, and which in 1993 passed the Nunavut Act, giving birth in 1999 to Nunavut (the name means "our land"), a province of 895,000 square miles in the northeastern and eastern part of Canada, including most of the Canadian Arctic islands. In this vast area live some 22,000 people, of whom 17,500 are Inuit, and they will, of course, have the controlling interest in the national parliament over the affairs of the province. The word *Eskimo* will not much longer be heard in this province: It is a Cree word that means "eaters of raw meat," and is considered derogatory. Inuit will be the name of the people and of the language.

Nearly 60 percent of the people in this new province still depend on hunting and fishing for a living; a total of 12.5 miles of highways stretch across this land. Just as the word *Eskimo* will cease to be used, the map will change as well. Cambridge Bay is now called Ikaluktutiak. The names of some of those old explorers—and the names of their financial angels—will surely become things of the past.

References

CHAPTER ONE—THE NATURE OF THE PLACE

Ahrens, C. D., 1988, *Meteorology Today* (third edition), West Publishing, St. Paul, 582 pp.

Central Intelligence Agency, 1978, *Polar regions atlas*, U.S. Government Printing Office, Washington, D.C., stock number 041-015-00094-2, 66 pp.

Colony, R., and A. S. Thorndike, 1984, An estimate of the mean field of Arctic sea ice motion, *Journal of Geophysical Research*, 89, 10, 623-10, 629.

Dumas, D., editor, 1984, *Arctic: Handbook of North American Indians*, volume 5, Smithsonian Institution, Washington, D.C.

Herbert, M., 1973, *The snow people*, G. P. Putnam's Sons, New York.

Hibler, W. D., III, S. J. Mock, and W. B. Jackson III, 1974, Classification and variation of sea ice ridging in the western Arctic Basin, *Journal of Geophysical Research*, 79, 2735-2743.

Jackson, L., 1988, Ice island an ideal platform, *Canadian Geographic*, 108, 6, 38-49.

Maloney, E. S., 1978, *Dutton's navigation and piloting* (thirteenth edition), Naval Institute Press, Annapolis, 910 pp.

Parkinson, C. L., J. C. Comiso, H. J. Zwally, D. J. Cavalieri, P. Gloerson, and W. J. Campell, 1987, *Arctic sea ice, 1973-1976:*

Satellite passive-microwave observations, National Aeronautics and Space Administration, Washington, D.C., 296 pp.
Rodahl, K., 1953, *North: The nature and drama of the polar world*, Harper and Brothers, New York, 237 pp.
Vowinckel, E. S., and S. Orvig, 1970, The climate of the North Polar Basin, in Orvig, E., editor, *Climates of the polar regions*, Elsevier, Amsterdam, pp. 129-252.

CHAPTER TWO—SEA-LUNGS, GODLY COMMERCE, AND PROJECTIONS

Central Intelligence Agency, 1978, *Polar regions atlas*, U.S. Government Printing Office, Washington, D.C., stock number 041-015-00094-2, 66 pp.
Clark, K., 1969, *Civilization*, Harper and Row, New York, 359 pp.
Gad, F., 1970, *The history of Greenland, I, earliest times to 1700*, C. Hurst, London, 350 pp.
Harrisse, H., 1896, *John Cabot the discoverer of North-America and Sebastian his son*, Benjamin Franklin Stevens, London, 503 pp.
Holland, C., 1994, *Arctic exploration and development c. 500 B.C. to 1915, an encyclopedia*, Garland Publishing, New York, 704 pp.
Jones, G., 1986, *The Norse Atlantic saga*, Oxford University Press, Oxford, 337 pp.
Lamb, H. H., 1982, *Climate, history and the modern world*, Methuen, London, 387 pp.
Lucas, F. W., 1898, *The annals of the voyages of the brothers Nicolò* and Antonio Zeno, Henry Stevens and Styles, London, 233 pp.
Magnusson, M., and H. Pálsson, 1965, *The Vinland sagas: The Norse discovery of America*, Penguin, Harmondsworth, 124 pp.
Mercator, G., 1569, *Map of the world*, reprinted in the form of an atlas by the Maritiem Museum Prins Hendrik, Rotterdam, 1961.
Mirsky, J., 1948, *To the Arctic: The story of northern exploration from earliest times to the present*, A. A. Knopf, New York, 334 pp.
Morison, S. E., 1971, *The European discovery of America: the northern*

voyages, A.D. 500–1600, Oxford University Press, New York, 712 pp.

Nansen, F., 1911, *In northern mists: Arctic exploration in early times*, 2 vols., Frederick A. Stokes, New York, 384 pp., 420 pp.

Oleson, T. J., 1963, *Early voyages and northern approaches: 1000–1632*, McClelland and Stewart, Toronto, 211 pp.

Roberts, D., 1982, *Great exploration hoaxes*, Sierra Club Books, San Francisco, 182 pp.

Selmer, C., editor, 1959, *Navigatio Sancti Brendanis Abbatis*, University of Notre Dames Press, South Bend, 132 pp.

Severin, T., 1978, *The Brendan voyage*, Hutchinson, London, 292 pp.

Skeats, W. W., 1894, *The complete works of Geoffrey Chaucer*, volume III: *The house of fame, the legend of the good woman, and the treatise on the astrolabe*, Oxford University Press, Oxford, 504 pp.

Stefansson, V., 1940, *Ultima Thule: Further mysteries of the Arctic*, Macmillan, New York, 383 pp.

Sykes, E., 1969, *Nicholas of Lynn: The explorer of the Arctic, 1330 to 1390*, Markham House Press, London, 27 pp.

Whitaker, I., 1982, The problem of Pytheas' Thule, *Classical Journal*, 77, 2, 148–164.

Williamson, J. A., 1962, *The Cabot voyages and Bristol discovery under Henry VII*, Cambridge University Press, Cambridge, 322 pp.

CHAPTER THREE—FRIZADORES FOR CATHAYO, AND THE OPEN POLAR SEA

Anonymous, 1904, An old story of Arctic exploration, *Scottish Geographical Magazine*, 20, 415–423.

Barrow, J., 1818, *A chronological history of voyages into Arctic regions; undertaken chiefly for the purpose of discovering a north-east, north-west, or polar polar passage between the Atlantic and Pacific*, John Murray, London, 379 pp.

De Veer, G., 1609, *Three voyages by the north-east towards Cathay and China undertaken by the Dutch in the years 1594, 1595, and 1596*, reprinted in 1878 for the Hakluyt Society, number 13.

Gordon, E. C., 1986, The fate of Sir Hugh Willoughby and his companions: A new conjecture, *The Geographical Journal*, 152, 243–247.

Holland, C., 1994, *Arctic exploration and development c. 500 B.C. to 1915, an encyclopedia*, Garland Publishing, New York, 704 pp.

Kirwan, L. P., 1959, *A history of polar exploration*, W. W. Norton, New York, 374 pp.

Mirsky, J., 1948, *To the Arctic: the story of northern exploration from earliest times to the present*, A. A. Knopf, New York, 334 pp.

Willan, T. S., 1956, *The early history of the Russia Company, 1553–1603*, Manchester University Press, Manchester, 295 pp.

CHAPTER FOUR—FOOL'S GOLD, HOOCH, AND MUTINY

Asher, G. M., editor, 1860, *Henry Hudson, the navigator*, Hakluyt Society, London, number 27, 292 pp.

Best, G., 1578, *A true discourse of the late voyages of discoverie, for the finding of a passage to Cathia*, reprinted in 1867 for the Hakluyt Society, no. 38, 374 pp.

Bruemmer, F., 1966, Kodlunar Island's gold rush, *Canadian Geographical Journal*, 72, 2, 48–51.

Golder, F. A., 1914, *Russian expansion on the Pacific, 1641–1850. An account of the earliest and later expeditions made by the Russians along the Pacific coast of Asia and North America; including some related expeditions to the Arctic regions*, Arthur H. Clark, Cleveland, 368 pp.

Hogarth, D. D., and J. Loop, 1986, Precious metals in Martin Frobisher's "black ores" from Frobisher Bay, Northwest Territories, *Canadian Mineralogist*, 24, 259–263.

Holland, C., 1994, *Arctic exploration and development c. 500 B.C. to 1915, an encyclopedia*, Garland Publishing, New York, 704 pp.

Jackson, D. D., 1993, Hot on the cold trail left by Sir Martin Frobisher, *Smithsonian*, 23, 10, 119–130.

Kenyon, W. A., 1975, *Tokens of possession: The northern voyages of Martin Frobisher*, Royal Ontario Museum, Toronto, 164 pp.

Markham, A. H., editor, 1880, *The voyages and works of John Davis*, Hakluyt Society, London, number 59, 329 pp.

Markham, C. R., editor, 1881, *The voyages of William Baffin*, Hakluyt Society, London, number 63, 192 pp.

McFee, W., 1928, *The life of Sir Martin Frobisher*, Harper and Brothers, New York, 276 pp.

Morison, S. E., 1971, *The European discovery of America: The northern voyages, A.D. 500–1600*, Oxford University Press, New York, 712 pp.

Oleson, T. J., 1964, *Early voyages and northern approaches, 1000–1632*, McClelland and Stewart, Toronto, 211 pp.

Powys, L., 1928, *Henry Hudson*, Harper and Brothers, New York, 213 pp.

Shammas, C., 1975, The "invisible merchant" and property rights: The misadvantures of an Elizabethan joint stock company, *Business History (Great Britain)*, 17, 2, 95–108.

Stefansson, V., 1938, *The three voyages of Martin Frobisher in search of a passage to Cathay and India by the north-west, A.D. 1576–8*, Argonaut Press, London, 322 pp.

CHAPTER FIVE—CONNUBIAL FIDELITY AND THE VICAR OF WAKEFIELD

Beechey, F. W., 1843, *A voyage of discovery toward the North Pole*, Richard Bentley, London, 351 pp.

Berton, P., 1988, *The Arctic grail: The quest for the North West Passage and the North Pole, 1818–1909*, Viking, New York, 672 pp.

Delgado, J. P., 1999, *Across the Top of the World*, Facts on File, Inc., New York, N.Y., 228 pp.

Hartwig, G., 1874, *The Polar and Tropical Worlds: A Description of Man and Nature in the Polar and Equatorial Regions of the Globe*, C. A. Nichols & Co., Springfield, Mass.

Holland, C., 1994, *Arctic exploration and development c. 500 B.C. to 1915, an encyclopedia*, Garland Publishing, New York, 704 pp.

Lyon, G. F., 1824, *The private journal of Captain G. F. Lyon of H. M. S. Hecla*, John Murray, London, 486 pp.

M'Clintock, F. L., 1859, *The voyage of the Fox in the Arctic seas: A narrative of the fate of Sir John Franklin and his companions*, John Murray, London, 403 pp.

Mirsky, J., 1948, *To the Arctic: The story of northern exploration from earliest times to the present*, A. A. Knopf, New York, 334 pp.

Parry, W. E., 1821, *Journal of a voyage for the discovery of a North-West Passage from the Atlantic to the Pacific; performed in the years 1819–20*, John Murray, London, 310 pp.

Parry, W. E., 1824, *Journal of a second voyage for the discovery of a North-West Passage from the Atlantic to the Pacific; performed in the years 1821–22–23*, John Murray, London, 571 pp.

CHAPTER SIX—OPEN SEAS AND CLOSED MINDS

Bent, S., 1870, Communication from Captain Silas Bent upon the routes to be pursued by expeditions to the North Pole, *American Geographical and Statistical Society Journal*, 2, 31–40.

Berton, P., 1988, *The Arctic grail: The quest for the North West Passage and the North Pole, 1818–1909*, Viking, New York, 672 pp.

Caswell, J. E., 1956, *Arctic frontiers: United States explorations in the far north*, University of Oklahoma Press, Norman, 232 pp.

Childs and Peterson, 1856, *Dr. Kane's great work*, Childs and Peterson, Philadelphia, 8 pp.

Corner, G. W., 1972, *Doctor Kane of the Arctic seas*, Temple University Press, Philadelphia, 306 pp.

Daly, C. P., 1870, Annual address: Review of the events of the year and recent explorations and theories for reaching the North Pole, *American Geographical and Statistical Society Journal*, 2, LXXXIII–CXXVI.

Hartwig, G. 1874, *The Polar and Tropical Worlds: A Description of Man and Nature in the Polar and Equatorial Regions of the Globe*, C. A. Nichols & Co., Springfield, Mass.; Hugh Heron, Chicago, Ill.

Hayes, I. I., 1867, *The Open Polar Sea: A narrative of a voyage of discovery towards the North Pole*, Hurd and Houghton, New York, 454 pp.

Kane, E. K., 1853, Access to an open polar sea along a North American meridian, *American Geographical and Statistical Society Bulletin*, 1, 85–102.

Kane, E. K., 1854, *The U.S. Grinnell expedition in search of Sir John Franklin: A personal narrative*, Harper and Bros., New York, 552 pp.

Kane, E. K., 1856, *Arctic explorations: The second Grinnell expedition in*

search of Sir John Franklin, 1853, '54, '55, vols. 1 and 2, Childs and Peterson, Philadelphia, 464 pp., 467 pp.
Loomis, C. C., 1971, *Weird and tragic shores: The story of Charles Francis Hall, explorer*, Alfred A. Knopf, New York, 382 pp.
Maury, M. F., 1859, *The physical geography of the sea*, Harper and Brothers, New York, 389 pp.
Mirsky, J., 1954, *Elisha Kent Kane and the seafaring frontier*, Little, Brown and Company, Boston, 201 pp.
Petermann, A., 1852, *The search for Franklin: A suggestion submitted to the British public*, Longman, Brown, Green, and Longmans, London, 24 pp.
Petermann, A., 1869, *Pettermann's mittheilungen ergänzungsheft*, no. 26, 118 pp.
Wright, J. K., 1953, The open polar sea, *Geographical Review*, 43, 338–365.

CHAPTER SEVEN—ANYTHING IS GOOD THAT DON'T POISON YOU

Berton, P., 1988, *The Arctic grail: The quest for the North West Passage and the North Pole, 1818–1909*, Viking, New York, 672 pp.
Caswell, J. E., 1956, *Arctic frontiers: United States explorations in the far north*, University of Oklahoma Press, Norman, 232 pp.
Deacon, M., and A. Savours, 1976, Sir George Strong Nares (1831–1915), *Polar Record*, 18, 113, 127–141.
DeLong, E., editor, 1884, *The voyage of the Jeanette: The ship and ice journals of George W. DeLong*, Houghton, Mifflin and Company, New York, 911 pp.
Ellsberg, E., 1940, The drift of the Jeanette in the Arctic Sea, *American Philosophical Society*, 82, 889–896.
Guttridge, L. F., 1986, *Icebound: The Jeanette expedition's quest for the North Pole*, Naval Institute Press, Annapolis, 357 pp.
Holland, C., 1994, *Arctic exploration and development c. 500 B.C. to 1915, an encyclopedia*, Garland Publishing, New York, 704 pp.
Jackman, D. D., A ship's gallant attempt to solve the "Northern mystery," *Smithsonian*, 27, 12, 86–98.

Kish, G., 1973, *North-east passage: Adolf Erik Nordenskiöld, his life and times,* Nico Israel, Amsterdam, 283 pp.

Leslie, A., 1879, *The Arctic voyages of Adolf Erik Nordenskiöld*, Macmillan, London, 447 pp.

Loomis, C. C., 1971, *Weird and tragic shores: The story of Charles Francis Hall, explorer*, Alfred A. Knopf, New York, 382 pp.

Markham, A. H., 1878, *The great frozen sea: A personal narrative of the voyage of the "Alert" during the Arctic expedition of 1875–6*, Dalby, Isbister and Company, London, 440 pp.

Mirsky, J., 1948, *To the Arctic: The story of northern exploration from earliest times to the present*, Alfred A. Knopf, New York, 334 pp.

Mowat, F., 1967, *The polar passion: The quest for the North Pole*, Little, Brown and Company, New York.

Nordenskiöld, N. A. E., 1881, *The voyage of the Vega around Asia and Europe, with a historical view of previous journeys along the north coast of the old world*, volumes I and II, Macmillan, London, 524 pp., 464 pp.

CHAPTER EIGHT—THREE FACES OF AMBITION

Anonymous, 1895, Will never see the Pole, *The New York Times*, 2 October, p. 9.

Astrup, E., 1898, *With Peary near the Pole*, C. A. Pearson, London, 362 pp.

Berton, P., 1988, *The Arctic grail: The quest for the North West Passage and the North Pole, 1818–1909*, Viking, New York, 672 pp.

Bryce, R. M., 1997, *Cook and Peary: The polar controversy, resolved*, Stackpole Books, Mechanicsburg, 1133 pp.

Haberman, F. W., editor, 1972, *Peace, Nobel lectures*, volume I, Elsevier Publishing, Amsterdam, 450 pp.

Herbert, W., 1989, *The noose of laurels: The discovery of the North Pole*, Hodder and Stoughton, London, 395 pp.

Hulburt, G. C., 1894, The North Greenland expedition of 1891–1892, *American Geographical Society Journal*, 26, 74–77.

Huntford, R., 1997, *Nansen: The explorer as hero*, Duckworth, London, 610 pp.

Mirsky, J., 1948, *To the Arctic: The story of northern exploration from earliest times to the present*, Alfred A. Knopf, New York, 334 pp.

Nansen, F., 1890, *First crossing of Greenland*, volumes I and II, Longmans and Company, London, 510 pp., 497 pp.

Nansen, F., 1898, *Farthest north: Being the record of a voyage of exploration of the ship Fram, 1893–96, and of a fifteen months' sleigh journey by Dr. Nansen and Lieut. Johansen*, volumes I and II, Harper and Brothers, New York, 587 pp., 729 pp.

Nansen, F., 1911, *In northern mists: Arctic exploration in early times*, volumes I and II, Frederick A. Stokes, New York, 384 pp., 420 pp.

Peary, R. E., 1898, *Northward over the great ice: A narrative of life and work along the shores and upon the interior ice-cap of northern Greenland in the years 1886 and 1891–1897*, volumes I and II, Metheun and Company, New York, 521 pp., 525 pp.

Rawlins, D., 1973, *Peary at the North Pole: Fact or fiction*, Robert B. Luce, Washington, D.C., 320 pp.

Roberts, D., 1982, *Great exploration hoaxes*, Sierra Club Books, San Francisco, 182 pp.

Schlee, S., 1973, *The edge of an unfamiliar world: A history of oceanography*, E. P. Dutton, New York, 398 pp.

Sörensen, J., 1932, *The saga of Fridtjof Nansen*, W. W. Norton, New York, 372 pp.

Whitehouse, J. H., editor, 1930, *Nansen: A book of homage*, Hodder and Stoughton, London, 189 pp.

CHAPTER NINE—AMATEURS, PROS, AND CONS

Andrée, S. A., 1896, A plan to reach the North Pole by balloon, *Proceedings Sixth International Geographical Congress*, 211–227.

Anonymous, 1895, Will never see the Pole, *The New York Times*, 2 October, p. 9.

Anonymous, 1899, The Sverdrup expedition, *American Geographical Society Bulletin*, 31, 91–93.

Anonymous, 1909, Peary lands; refuses honors, *The New York Times*, 22 September, pp. 1–2.

Anonymous, 1909, Dr. Cook home; no proofs yet, *The New York Times*, 22 September, pp. 1–2.

Anonymous, 1909, Fraudulent observations made for Dr. Cook before his records sent to Copenhagen; sworn testimony of the men who made them, *The New York Times*, 9 December, pp. 1–3.

Anonymous, 1909, Cook's claim to discovery of the North Pole rejected; outraged Denmark calls him a deliberate swindler; having no original observations, he used Loose's "fakes," *The New York Times*, 22 December, pp. 1–3.

Berton, P., 1988, *The Arctic grail: The quest for the North West Passage and the North Pole, 1818–1909*, Viking, New York, 672 pp.

Browne, B., 1913, *The conquest of Mount McKinley*, G. P. Putnam and Sons, New York, 367 pp.

Bryce, R. M., 1997, *Cook and Peary: The polar controversy, resolved*, Stackpole Books, Mechanicsburg, 1133 pp.

Cook, F. A., 1908, *To the top of the continent*, Doubleday, Page and Company, New York, 321 pp.

Davies, T. D., 1990, New evidence places Peary at the Pole, *National Geographic Magazine*, 177, 1, 44–61.

Greely, A. W., 1909, Polar exploration during the year 1908, *Independent*, 66, 685–689.

Hall, T. F., 1917, *Has the North Pole been discovered*, Richard G. Badger, Boston, 539 pp.

Henson, M. A., 1912, *A negro explorer at the North Pole*, Frederick A. Stokes, New York, 200 pp.

Herbert, W., 1988, Did Peary reach the pole, *National Geographic Magazine*, 174, 3, 414–429.

Herbert, W., 1989, *The noose of laurels: Robert E. Peary and the race to the North Pole*, Atheneum, New York, 395 pp.

Hulburt, G. C., 1894, The North Greenland expedition of 1891–1892, *American Geographical Society Journal*, 26, 74–77.

Mirsky, J., 1948, *To the Arctic: The story of northern exploration from earliest times to the present*, Alfred A. Knopf, New York, 334 pp.

Peary, R. E., 1907, *Nearest the Pole: A narrative of the polar expedition of the Peary Arctic Club in the S. S. Roosevelt, 1905–1906*, Hutchinson and Company, London, 410 pp.

Peary, R. E., 1910, *The North Pole: Its discovery in 1909 under the auspices of the Peary Arctic Club*, Frederick A. Stokes, New York, 373 pp.

Rawlins, D., 1973, *Peary at the North Pole: Fact or fiction*, Robert B. Luce, Washington, D.C., 320 pp.

Roberts, D., 1982, *Great exploration hoaxes*, Sierra Club Books, San Francisco, 182 pp.

Stafford, E. P., 1988, Descendants of the expeditions, *National Geographic Magazine*, 174, 3, 414–429.

Sverdrup, O. N., 1903, The Norwegian polar expedition in the Fram, 1898–1902, *Geographical Journal*, 22, 38–56.

Swedish Society for Anthropology and Geography, editor, 1930, *Andrée's story: The complete record of his polar flight*, Viking Press, New York, 389 pp.

Washburn, B., 1958, Doctor Cook and Mount McKinley, *American Alpine Journal*, 11, 1–30.

CHAPTER TEN—FROM POLAR LARKS TO CANARY-WATCHING

Aagaard, K. et al., 1996, U.S., Canadian researchers explore Arctic Ocean, *Eos*, 77, 209, 213.

Ackley, S. F., W. D. Hibbler III, A. Kovacs, W. F. Weeks, A. Hartwell, and W. J. Campbell, 1973, *Investigations performed on the Arctic Ice Dynamics Joint Experiment, March 1971*, U.S. Army Cold Regions Research and Engineering Laboratory, Hanover, Research Report 315, 66 pp.

Amundsen, R., 1912, *The South Pole: An account of the Norwegian Antarctic expedition in the "Fram,"* 1910–1912, volumes I and II, John Murray, London, 392 pp. 449 pp.

Amundsen, R., 1927, *My life as an explorer*, Doubleday, Page, New York, 282 pp.

Amundsen, R., and L. Ellsworth, 1927, *First crossing of the Polar Sea*, George H. Doran, New York, 324 pp.

Anderson, W. R., 1959, *Nautilus–90–north*, World Publishing, Cleveland, 251 pp.

Anonymous, 1926, Amundsen in role of Cook's defender, *The New York Times*, 24 January, p. 2.

Anonymous, 1926, Amundsen back from lecture tour, *The New York Times*, 4 March, p. 18.

Anonymous, 1978, 4 men, in a 44–day trek, reach the North Pole in snowmobiles, *The New York Times*, 20 April, p. 68.

Balchen, B., 1958, *Come north with me*, E. P. Dutton and Company, New York, 318 pp.

Belt, D., 1997, An Arctic breakthrough, *National Geographic*, 191, 2, 36–57.

Bryce, R. M., 1997, *Cook and Peary: The polar controversy, resolved*, Stackpole Books, Mechanicsburg, 1133 pp.

Calvert, J., 1960, *Surface at the Pole: The extraordinary voyages of the USS Skate*, McGraw–Hill, New York, 219 pp.

Dumas, D., editor, 1984, *Arctic: Handbook of North American Indians*, volume 5, Smithsonian Institution, Washington, D.C.

Ellsworth, L., 1927, At the North Pole, *Yale Review*, 16, 738–748.

Fisher, D. E., 1992, *Across the top of the world*, Random House, New York.

Grierson, J., 1960, *Sir Hubert Wilkins: Enigma of exploration*, Robert Hale, London, 224 pp.

Herbert, M., 1973, *The snow people*, G. P. Putnam's Sons, New York.

Herbert, W., 1969, *Across the top of the world: The British Trans-Arctic expedition*, Longmans, London, 209 pp.

Herbert, W., 1971, *Across the top of the world: The last great journey on earth*, G. P. Putnam's Sons, New York, 347 pp.

Huntford, R., 1980, *Scott and Amundsen*, G. P. Putnam's Sons, New York, 665 pp.

Jackson, D. D., 1990, The quiet heroism of Lincoln Ellsworth, *Smithsonian*, 21, 7, 171–188.

Kirwan, L. P., 1959, *A history of polar exploration*, W. W. Norton and Company, New York, 374 pp.

Kuralt, C., 1968, *To the top of the world: The adventures and misadventures of the Plaisted polar expedition, March 28–May 4, 1967*, Holt, Rinehart and Winston, New York, 193 pp.

Levi, B. G., 1998, Search and discovery, *Physics Today*, 51, 11, 17–19.

Liljequist, G. H., Did the Josephine Ford reach the North Pole, *Interavia*, 15, 589–591.

Lopez, B., 1986, *Arctic dreams: Imagination and dreams in a northern landscape*, Charles Scribner's Sons, New York.

Maloney, E. S., 1978, *Dutton's navigation and piloting (thirteenth edition)*, Naval Institute Press, Annapolis, 910 pp.

McPhee, M. G., T. P. Stanton, J. H. Morison, and D. G. Martinson, 1998, Freshening of the upper ocean in the Arctic: Is perennial sea ice disappearing, *Geophysical Research Letters*, 25, 1729–1732.

Mill, H. R., 1951, *An autobiography*, Longman, Green and Company, London, 224 pp.

Momatiuk, Y., and J. Eastcott, 1999, Nanavut: Our land, *Native Peoples*, spring issue.

Montague, R., 1971, *Oceans, poles and airmen*, Random House, New York, 307 pp.

Paulson, C. A., and D. L. Bell, 1975, Meteorological observations during the AIDJEX main experiment, *AIDJEX Bulletin*, 28, 1–9.

Payne, B., 1995, The crunch to the Pole: Cruising to the North Pole on a nuclear-powered Russian icebreaker, *Conde Nast Traveler*, January, 86–93, 173–175.

Plaisted, R., 1968, How I reached the North Pole on a snowmobile, *Popular Science*, September, 55–59, 200, 204–206.

Roberts, D., 1982, *Great exploration hoaxes*, Sierra Books, San Francisco, 182 pp.

Ronne, F., 1979, *Antarctica, my destiny*, Hastings House, New York, 278 pp.

Schneider, D., 1995, Attached to the Pole, *Scientific American*, 273, 5, 14.

Smith, D. C., 1961, *By the seat of my pants*, Brown, Boston, 245 pp.

Steger, W., 1987, *North to the Pole*, Times Books, New York, 339 pp.

Thomas, L., 1961, *Sir Hubert Wilkins: His world of adventure*, McGraw-Hill, New York, 297 pp.

Thomson, K. S., 1988, Anatomy of the extinction debate, *American Scientist*, 76, 59–61.

Tierney, J., 1998, Explornography: The vicarious thrill of exploring when there's nothing left to explore, *The New York Times Magazine*, 26 July, 18–23, 33–34, 46–49.

Tucker, W., and D. Cate, 1996, *The 1994 Arctic Ocean Section: The first major scientific crossing of the Arctic Ocean*, U.S. Army Cold

Regions Research and Engineering Laboratory, Hanover, Special Report 96–23, 117 pp.

Victor, P.-E., 1963, *Man and the conquest of the Poles*, Simon and Schuster, New York, 320 pp.

Walker, G., 1998, On thin ice, *New Scientist*, 159, 2153, 33–37.

Wilkins, G. H., 1928, *Flying the Arctic*, G. P. Putnam's Sons, New York, 336 pp.

Wilkins, G. H., 1931, *Under the North Pole: The Wilkins-Ellsworth submarine expedition*, Brewer, Warren, and Putnam, New York, 347 pp.

Index